# TEACHING READING COMPREHENSION
# TO STUDENTS WITH LEARNING DIFFICULTIES

# The Guilford Series on Intensive Instruction
## Sharon Vaughn, Editor

This series presents innovative ways to improve learning outcomes for K–12 students with challenging academic and behavioral needs. Books in the series explain the principles of intensive intervention and provide evidence-based teaching practices for learners who require differentiated instruction. Grounded in current research, volumes include user-friendly features such as sample lessons, examples of daily schedules, case studies, classroom vignettes, and reproducible tools.

*Essentials of Intensive Intervention*
Rebecca Zumeta Edmonds, Allison Gruner Gandhi,
and Louis Danielson

*Intensive Reading Interventions for the Elementary Grades*
Jeanne Wanzek, Stephanie Al Otaiba, and Kristen L. McMaster

*Intensifying Mathematics Interventions for Struggling Students*
Edited by Diane Pedrotty Bryant

*Literacy Coaching in the Secondary Grades:*
*Helping Teachers Meet the Needs of All Students*
Jade Wexler, Elizabeth Swanson, and Alexandra Shelton

*Structured Literacy Interventions:*
*Teaching Students with Reading Difficulties, Grades K–6*
Edited by Louise Spear-Swerling

*The Structured Literacy Planner: Designing Interventions*
*for Common Reading Difficulties, Grades 1–9*
Louise Spear-Swerling

*Teaching Reading Comprehension to Students*
*with Learning Difficulties, Third Edition*
Sharon Vaughn, Alison Boardman, and Janette K. Klingner

# Teaching Reading Comprehension
## to Students with Learning Difficulties

**THIRD EDITION**

Sharon Vaughn
Alison Boardman
Janette K. Klingner

THE GUILFORD PRESS
New York    London

Copyright © 2024 The Guilford Press
A Division of Guilford Publications, Inc.
370 Seventh Avenue, Suite 1200, New York, NY 10001
www.guilford.com

Printed in the United States of America

This book is printed on acid-free paper.

Last digit is print number:   9   8   7   6   5   4   3   2   1

**Library of Congress Cataloging-in-Publication Data**

Names: Vaughn, Sharon, 1952– author. | Boardman, Alison, author. |
    Klingner, Janette K., author.
Title: Teaching reading comprehension to students with learning
    difficulties / Sharon Vaughn, Alison Boardman, Janette K. Klingner.
Description: Third edition. | New York : The Guilford Press, 2024. |
    Series: The Guilford series on intensive instruction | Revised edition
    of: Teaching reading comprehension to students with learning
    difficulties / Janette K. Klingner, Sharon Vaughn, Alison Boardman.
    Second edition. 2015. | Includes bibliographical references and index. |
Identifiers: LCCN 2024012203 | ISBN 9781462554805 (cloth) |
    ISBN 9781462554799 (paperback)
Subjects: LCSH: Reading comprehension—Study and teaching. |
    Reading—Remedial teaching. | BISAC: EDUCATION / Special Education /
    General | LANGUAGE ARTS & DISCIPLINES / Reading Skills
Classification: LCC LB1050.5 .K54 2024 | DDC 372.43—dc23/eng/20240418
LC record available at *https://lccn.loc.gov/2024012203*

*This book is dedicated to our coauthor, Dr. Janette K. Klingner.
Dr. Klingner was a dedicated educator and researcher who valued
conducting research in the context of real classrooms, schools,
and school districts. In addition to her well-known reading
comprehension strategies research, Janette was committed to studying
and explaining disproportionate representation of students of
color in special education. She made substantive contributions to
the research literatures on teacher learning, teacher collaboration,
and the sustainability and scale-up of effective interventions.
We could not have written this new edition without the longstanding
contributions of our amazing colleague and friend.*

*—S. V. and A. B.*

# About the Authors

**Sharon Vaughn, PhD,** holds the Manuel Justiz Chair in Education at the University of Texas at Austin and is Executive Director of the Meadows Center for Preventing Educational Risk. She has written numerous books and research articles that address the reading and social outcomes of students with learning difficulties, and is currently investigating effective interventions for students with reading difficulties and students who are English learners. Dr. Vaughn has served as Editor-in-Chief of the *Journal of Learning Disabilities* and coeditor of *Learning Disabilities Research and Practice*. She is a recipient of the Special Education Research Award from the Council for Exceptional Children, the Distinguished Researcher Award from the Special Education Research Special Interest Group of the American Educational Research Association (AERA), the Career Excellence Award from the University of Texas, and the Albert J. Harris Award from the International Literacy Association.

**Alison Boardman, PhD,** is Associate Professor in Equity, Bilingualism, and Biliteracy and Co-chair of Elementary Teacher Education in the School of Education at the University of Colorado Boulder. She works closely with educators to study and innovate literacy instruction across content areas in classrooms that include students with learning difficulties and multilingual learners. Current investigations focus on designing and studying the use of literacy-focused project-based learning with students with learning difficulties in inclusive classrooms. Dr. Boardman is a former elementary and middle school special education teacher.

**Janette K. Klingner, PhD,** until her death in 2014, was Professor of Bilingual Special Education at the University of Colorado Boulder. Her principal areas of research were reading comprehension strategy instruction in diverse, inclusive secondary science and social studies classes; professional development that enhances teacher quality in diverse, inclusive classrooms; response to intervention for English learners; and the disproportionate representation of students of color in special education. She authored or coauthored more than 130 articles, books, and book chapters. Dr. Klingner was past president of the Division of Learning Disabilities of the Council for Exceptional Children, Vice President of the International Academy for Research on Learning Disabilities, and Associate Editor of the *Journal of Learning Disabilities*. She was a recipient of the Early Career Award from AERA and the Distinguished Researcher Award from the Special Education Research Special Interest Group of AERA.

# Preface

When reading is effortless, which is likely the case for readers of this book, it is difficult to imagine what it might be like to be expected to read and yet not be able to understand or say much about it. Although we might occasionally not fully comprehend text that is unfamiliar or uninteresting, it is difficult for us to imagine what it would be like to experience these same challenges with *all* of the material that we read. Yet we have all taught students who find reading challenging, and we continue to struggle with ways to improve their reading and comprehension skills.

This book is for teachers of students who struggle with understanding and learning from text. We envision that teachers will use this book to help their students develop a love for the "world of imagination" as well as for the learning through text that can happen only when they truly comprehend what they read. From a very early age, children enjoy listening to books being read by others and discussing what they think might happen next or how a story connects to their own lives. In these early years, they acquire important strategies and develop competencies that will help them with reading comprehension later. Even in the primary grades, when students are learning how to identify words and are developing basic reading skills, teachers can promote reading comprehension through building vocabulary, listening comprehension, and background knowledge. As students acquire proficiency with basic reading skills, teachers shift their emphasis to helping them develop reading comprehension strategies and become more sophisticated readers of a variety of texts for a multitude of purposes.

The comprehension practices described in this book provide effective instruction to *all* students, including those who require additional support. Increasing demands for accountability and pressure to improve academic achievement for every student, including students with learning disabilities, require that teachers be even more knowledgeable and skillful in meeting the growing needs of a range of learners. And as the laws that govern special education increasingly call for instruction to take place in the general education setting, classrooms are becoming more heterogeneous. We view this further scrutiny of the success of typically underachieving students as an opportunity for teachers to exercise their best teaching practices, resulting in improved outcomes for all students.

In this book, we provide an updated version of the previous edition with current research, as well as two new chapters—one addressing issues related to selecting and using text features and another that identifies frequently asked questions about teaching reading comprehension. We focus on research-based methods for teaching reading comprehension to students with learning disabilities and reading difficulties. We provide descriptions of the knowledge base in each of the critical areas related to comprehension and also present specific strategies for teachers to implement with their students.

## ORGANIZATION OF THE BOOK

Chapter 1 provides an overview of reading comprehension as a domain of learning and serves as an organizing framework for the assessment and methods chapters that follow. We summarize current research on effective practices for improving reading comprehension for students with learning difficulties and disabilities, including how the science of reading influences reading comprehension. We describe how good and poor readers differ in their reading comprehension and the strategies good readers use to facilitate understanding. We also discuss the reasons that students with reading disabilities might struggle with reading comprehension, and we describe the cognitive processes involved in comprehension.

Chapter 2 reviews various reading comprehension assessment procedures that teachers can use either diagnostically or for progress monitoring purposes, including considerations for using assessments with English learners. We explain standardized tests, curriculum-based measurements, informal reading inventories, interviews and questionnaires, student observations, oral retelling, and think-aloud procedures. We emphasize that it is important for teachers administering different comprehension measures to be aware of exactly what each test assesses, what can and cannot be learned from assessments, and the limitations as well as the strengths of each one. We believe that a combination of different measures is the best way to assess reading comprehension.

Chapter 3 describes various ways to enhance vocabulary instruction and build background knowledge. Understanding words in all their complexity is an essential part of comprehending text. Many students with reading disabilities have underdeveloped vocabularies, often because their reading difficulties interfere with their learning new words through text. Numerous factors contribute to differential rates of vocabulary growth. Some students with reading disabilities demonstrate general language difficulties that affect their vocabulary learning, and others have problems with memory and/or recall. We describe numerous instructional methods designed to improve vocabulary learning that have helped students with reading disabilities as well as other struggling readers. Featured in this chapter is the importance of enhancing vocabulary as a mechanism for building background knowledge, which is essential to improving comprehension.

Chapter 4 details the specific instructional practices that promote reading comprehension. We organize these comprehension strategies according to whether they are typically used before, during, or after reading. Before reading, teachers should assist students in activating, building, and using their background knowledge to make connections with the text and predict what they will learn. During reading, students need to know how to monitor their understanding, use fix-up strategies to assist with comprehension, and consider linkages between what they are reading and previous knowledge and experiences. After reading, students should summarize the key ideas about what they have read and make connections.

Chapter 5 provides guidance on text selection and text structure. We present guiding principles for text selection, including when to use texts that are at students' independent reading levels, how to increase difficulty level and length over time, and matching the purpose for reading with a varied range of narrative and expository text. Teaching students to recognize and analyze common text structures can help them read more efficiently and monitor their comprehension.

Chapter 6 distinguishes between general content-area literacy skills and discipline-specific skills that are unique to reading in different content areas. We provide an outline of discipline-specific considerations. We also address the need for content teachers and specialists to collaborate to plan and deliver explicit instruction in both discipline-specific and general reading strategies to support students' reading development and content learning.

Chapter 7 specifies instructional practices for supporting English learners (ELs) by increasing their access to vocabulary, language, and background knowledge as a means of improving reading comprehension. Many of the instructional practices that improve reading comprehension for all students are also effective for ELs. However, this chapter details instructional practices necessary for engaging ELs effectively and improving outcomes in comprehension.

Chapter 8 describes intensive interventions for students with significant reading comprehension difficulties. Specifically, we identify the instructional practices that are necessary to ensure that students with the most intractable reading comprehension problems make progress. Using data-based decision making to inform selection and use of instructional practices are highlighted.

Chapter 9 presents multicomponent approaches to strategy instruction, including reciprocal teaching, collaborative strategic reading, and multistrategy inference intervention. With each approach, students learn to apply different strategies through modeling, explicit instruction, and guided practice, before, during, and after reading. Each approach includes discussions with peers as a central element. These methods have been found to be effective for improving the reading comprehension of students with learning disabilities as well as other students.

Chapter 10 identifies common questions that teachers have posed about reading comprehension and potential answers.

## FEATURES

This book is designed for teachers, including those in their preservice or graduate programs. The book includes many features that make it readily accessible to student teachers and educators. Each chapter has background information about the research supporting the aspect of reading comprehension under discussion. We also suggest how to carry out different instructional approaches and utilize numerous figures, graphs, and tables that illustrate our approaches. At the beginning of each chapter, we list three or four study-group questions that prompt reflection and dialogue about reading comprehension. Finally, the Appendix contains lesson plans that can be used as a springboard for applying the practices and strategies described throughout the book.

## USING THIS BOOK AS A STUDY GUIDE

We encourage you to use this book as a study guide in your school. It can serve as a valuable tool to guide your pedagogy, whether you are part of a formal study group or would like to start your own informal group. Much like the interactive comprehension practices associated with improved outcomes for students, we believe that educators who have opportunities to discuss and implement ideas from this book, along with feedback from their fellow teachers, are more likely to try the comprehension practices and continue to use them.

# Acknowledgments

We have many people to acknowledge but feel compelled to select just a few.

**Sharon Vaughn:** I would like to acknowledge the contributions of Isabel Beck and Jean Osborn. Isabel Beck is simply the most insightful and interesting person with whom I have talked about reading. She has shown enormous interest in my research, my thinking, and my analyses. She is also exceedingly generous with what she knows—and she knows a lot. She has not hesitated to "set me straight," and she has always been right. Jean Osborn and I have worked closely together on professional development materials since 1998. Jean is vigorous, dedicated, exacting, and sensitive. She wears me out with her precise rejuvenation of tired writing. She understands what teachers need to know and do to ensure that all students read well, often, and with enthusiasm. I simply have no words for how much I have learned from Jean about teaching, learning, and caring for others, and I am so thankful to count them as friends. Most of all I am grateful for the friendship and what I've learned from my coauthors, Alison Boardman and Janette Klingner.

**Alison Boardman:** We all know students who, despite their inquisitive minds, have a hard time learning to read. These students—and their teachers—have had a profound impact on my journey as an educator. I am also incredibly grateful for my coauthors, Sharon Vaughn and the late Janette Klingner, whose expertise and long-standing commitment to the field is nothing less than inspirational.

**Janette K. Klingner:** We know that Dr. Klingner would have recognized and expressed appreciation for the guidance of two experts in reading comprehension: Annemarie Palincsar and the late Michael Pressley. She first met Annemarie and

Michael in 1992 when, as a naive yet eager doctoral student, she approached each of them at an annual meeting of the National Reading Conference and asked if they would be willing to serve as consultants on a student-initiated research grant (for her dissertation). They both graciously agreed and, over the years, were very generous with their time, expertise, and wisdom. She learned much from them, not only about reading comprehension, but also about life. For this guidance she was very grateful.

# Contents

**CHAPTER ONE**

## Overview of Reading Comprehension                                           1

How Do the Reading Comprehension Skills of Good and Poor Readers Differ?   3
Word Reading, Fluency, and Vocabulary: Essential Features
    of Reading Comprehension   5
What Is Involved in Reading Comprehension?   10
Conclusion   14

**CHAPTER TWO**

## Assessing Reading Comprehension                                            15

Challenges of Measuring Reading Comprehension   16
Limitations of Traditional Comprehension Assessment Procedures   17
Reading Comprehension Measures   18
Measuring Metacognitive Reading Processes   31
Additional Considerations in Assessing Reading Comprehension   38
Conclusion   39
**APPENDIX 2.1.** Prompted Think-Aloud   41

**CHAPTER THREE**

## Vocabulary Instruction                                                     44

How Does Teaching Vocabulary Facilitate Reading Comprehension?   45
How Can We Assess and Monitor Vocabulary Learning?   46
Assessing Vocabulary Learning   47
What Are the Best Practices for Promoting Vocabulary Acquisition?   49
Conclusion   63
**APPENDIX 3.1.** Vocabulary Assessment within Social Studies Instruction   64

**CHAPTER FOUR**

### Instructional Practices That Promote Reading Comprehension          66

Instructional Practices in Reading Comprehension for Students with LD   67
Before Reading   68
During and After Reading   72
Strategies for Understanding Narrative Text   85
Reading and Writing Connections   87
Conclusion   91

**CHAPTER FIVE**

### Effectively Using Text to Promote Reading Comprehension          92

The Importance of Text in Reading Comprehension   92
Text Levels and Reading Comprehension Instruction   93
Selecting Appropriate Texts   96
Text Structure   98
Conclusion   104

**CHAPTER SIX**

### Promoting Content-Area Literacy          105

What Is Content-Area Literacy?   105
What Is Disciplinary Literacy?   106
Reading in the Content Areas   108
Conclusion   120

**CHAPTER SEVEN**

### Supporting English Learners with Learning Difficulties          122

Who Are ELs?   123
Factors That Influence Comprehension for ELs   125
Recommended Instructional Practices to Support ELs with Reading Difficulties   125
Conclusion   133

**CHAPTER EIGHT**

### Intensive Interventions for Students with Significant          135
### Reading Comprehension Difficulties

How to Accelerate the Progress of Students with Significant Reading
    Comprehension Difficulties   135
Implementing Strategies That Enhance Cognitive Processing   136
Intensifying Instructional Delivery   141
Conclusion   148

**CHAPTER NINE**

### Multicomponent Approaches to Strategy Instruction          150

Reciprocal Teaching   152
Collaborative Strategic Reading   157
Multistrategy Inference Intervention   164
Conclusion   168

**CHAPTER TEN**

## Questions Teachers Ask about Teaching Reading Comprehension                    169

The Role of Word Reading for Promoting Reading Comprehension   169
Secondary Content-Area Teachers and Reading Comprehension   171
Building Background Knowledge   171
Strategy Instruction and Reading Comprehension   172
Text Sources and Text Levels   173
Independent Reading, Reading Silently, and Reading Comprehension   174
Motivation and Reading Comprehension   177

**APPENDIX**

## Lesson Plans                                                                          179

Before-Reading Lesson Plans   180
   *Text Preview   180*
   *Vocabulary Maps   181*
   *Semantic Maps   183*
   *Systematic Morphology Instruction   184*
   *Essential Words Routine   185*
During-Reading Lesson Plans   187
   *Main Idea Sketch   187*
   *Get the Gist   188*
   *Identifying the Main Idea   190*
   *Does It Make Sense?   192*
   *Activating Background Knowledge While Reading   193*
   *Identifying Text-to-Self Connections   194*
   *Making and Checking Predictions in a Book   195*
   *Identifying Text-to-Text Connections   197*
   *Identifying Characters and Setting   198*
   *Identifying Sequence of Events in Story Structure   199*
   *Identifying Problem and Solution in Story Structure   200*
   *Identifying Cause and Effect   202*
   *Generating Questions   204*
   *Making Inference with Sentences   206*
   *Making Inferences in Science   209*
   *Click and Clunk   211*
After-Reading Lesson Plans   214
   *What Do You Know?   214*
   *Summarizing Information   215*
   *Key Word Review   217*

## Glossary                                                                              219

## References                                                                            223

## Index                                                                                 247

# Overview of Reading Comprehension

How is it that children learn to understand what they read? How do some students get lost in their reading and enter new worlds, build knowledge, and improve vocabulary, whereas others find reading a constant struggle that rarely nets comprehension? As teachers of students with reading difficulties and disabilities, we asked these questions anew each year with each incoming group of students. Few of the students we taught who had learning disabilities also read well and with comprehension. In this chapter, we present an overview of reading comprehension and related factors, particularly as they relate to students with significant reading and learning disabilities.

Understanding text, learning from it, and enjoying reading are the ultimate goals of learning to read. Although fundamental skills such as phonics and fluency are important building blocks of reading, reading comprehension is the "sine qua non of reading" (Beck & McKeown, 1998). Knowing how to read words has ultimately little value if the student is unable to construct meaning from text. Ultimately, reading comprehension is the process of constructing meaning by coordinating a number of complex processes that include word reading, word and world knowledge, and fluency (Cornoldi & Oakhill, 2013; McKeown et al., 2009; Rasinski et al., 2012; Wise et al., 2007).

The phonological awareness and decoding skills of students with reading disabilities have been identified as serious inhibitors to successful reading (Ball & Blachman, 1991; Bridges & Catts, 2011; Herrera et al., 2015; Wise et al., 2007). Although there is little question that difficulties in these foundational skills impede successful growth in reading for many students, it is also true that many students with learning disabilities have significant challenges understanding and learning from text even when they are able to decode adequately (Williams et al., 2016). Explicit and highly structured development of beginning reading skills is required, as is highly structured instruction in reading comprehension.

In a landmark reading study, Durkin (1978–1979) conducted a series of observations of reading comprehension instruction. She revealed that typical comprehension instruction wasn't very engaging or likely to improve reading comprehension. She summarized reading comprehension instruction as following a three-step procedure: mentioning, practicing, and assessing. That is, teachers would *mention* the skill that they wanted students to use, then they would give them opportunities to *practice* that skill through workbooks or skill sheets, and finally they would *assess* whether or not the students used the skill successfully. Instruction was noticeably missing. Perhaps of even greater concern than the quality of comprehension instruction was the dearth of reading instruction observed. Based on more than 4,000 minutes of reading instruction observed in fourth-grade classrooms, only 20 minutes of comprehension instruction was recorded. This study significantly influenced research in reading comprehension. However, subsequent observation studies revealed little influence on classroom practice (Klingner et al., 2010; McKenna et al., 2015; Swanson & Vaughn, 2010). The Common Core State Standards (CCSS) for English language arts were constructed, in part, to address the issue of opportunity to read text. The goal is that students spend adequate time reading and responding to highly challenging and engaging text.

In an attempt to improve reading comprehension instruction, several theories have been proposed that suggest ways to influence understanding of the teaching of reading comprehension: schema theory, reader response theory, direct instruction, and the simple view of reading. A brief description of each of these influential theories provides the background for interpreting the instructional practices related to teaching reading comprehension that are presented in more detail elsewhere in this book.

Schema theory suggests that what we know about a topic or construct influences how much we can or will learn by reading a passage that addresses that topic (Anderson & Pearson, 1984). Thus, our knowledge and experiences related to key ideas in a text influence what we learn and remember about what we read. World knowledge and word meaning influence our understanding of texts we read. The more we read and learn about the topic, the easier the next passage on that topic will be for us to understand.

From a reader response constructivist perspective (Beach, 1993), understanding what is read is related to the individual's experiences and interpretations of these experiences. This subjective component makes for a dynamic interaction between the reader and the text. Thus, what readers learn or how they respond to text is individualistic. Teachers and peers can facilitate and interact with other readers to enhance and extend learning.

Direct instruction approaches have been associated with improved outcomes in reading comprehension for students with learning disabilities, though outcomes are typically more robust for the foundation skills like phonics and word reading (Roman et al., 2009; Stockard et al., 2018). Direct instruction approaches provide for more explicit and systematic instruction related to the key ideas associated with improved reading comprehension. For example, because word meaning relates to understanding text, a direct instruction approach would ask teachers to identify key words in a passage and teach their meaning prior to reading.

The simple view of reading (SVR; Hoover & Gough, 1990) posits that reading comprehension is a product of decoding (accurate and efficient word reading) and linguistic comprehension (semantic and syntactic understanding often measured with listening comprehension). The proposition, which has been generally well supported through research, is that there is a multiplicative relationship between decoding and linguistic comprehension such that very low decoding even with high linguistic comprehension will yield low reading comprehension, and vice-versa. While research has largely supported the SVR model (Catts et al., 2006; Francis et al., 2018; Lonigan et al., 2018), there has been extensive work also arguing for additional components, such as active self-regulation, motivation, and engagement (Duke & Cartwright, 2021).

## HOW DO THE READING COMPREHENSION SKILLS OF GOOD AND POOR READERS DIFFER?

Many of the instructional practices suggested for poor readers were derived from observing, questioning, and asking good and poor readers to "think aloud" while they read (Dole, 1991; Jiménez et al., 1995, 1996). Reports of how good readers understand and learn from text suggest that they coordinate a set of highly complex and well-developed skills and strategies before, during, and after reading that assist them in understanding and remembering what they read (Paris et al., 1991). Good readers monitor their understand while they are reading and think about how what they are reading contributes to what they already know. The skills and strategies that good readers use include:

- Rapid and accurate word reading: Reading effortlessly allows these readers to think about what they are learning and make connections.
- Setting goals for reading: Whether it is to read for pleasure, read to learn, or read to take action—good readers read with a purpose.
- Noting the structure and organization of text: Whether inferentially or deliberately good readers look at how the text is organized and structured, and this information helps them better understand what they are reading.

- Monitoring their understanding while reading: Good readers consistently monitor their understanding, asking whether the text makes sense and rereading or repairing to improve understanding.
- Creating mental notes and summaries: Good readers write notes or mentally keep track of characters, events, or key ideas, which promotes comprehension.
- Making predictions: Good readers make predictions about what will happen, check them as they go along, and revise and evaluate them as needed.
- Capitalizing on what they know: Good readers capitalize on what they know about the topic and integrate that with new learning.
- Making inferences: Making inferences is a key skill, and good readers follow up their inferences by checking them.
- Using mental images: Visualization can assist good readers in remembering or understanding events or characters.

As you think about the reading comprehension of good and poor readers, consider whether you think of poor readers as homogeneous, with many shared reading difficulties. There is increasing evidence that fewer than 15% of readers have adequate and accurate word reading (above 90 standard score) but demonstrate poor comprehension (below 90 standard score). This subgroup of students likely demonstrates significant oral language difficulties, and preliminary evidence suggests that they benefit from a language-based reading intervention program (Kelso et al., 2022; Snowling & Hulme, 2011).

In contrast with the integrated and strategic approaches to understanding text applied by good readers, poor readers use few effective strategies for understanding and remembering what they read (Berkeley & Larsen, 2018; Edmonds et al., 2009). There may be many explanations for this. First, poor readers are less interested in reading, as the task is challenging for them. Second, they may view reading as a task to finish rather than understand. Third, they often have significant word-reading difficulties, which make processing text slow and laborious, and they have inadequate vocabulary and background knowledge with which to connect and link new ideas to previous learning. Furthermore, unlike good readers, poor readers lack the decoding, word-reading, and fluency skills to free up cognitive functioning so that their full attention can be focused on learning from reading.

Students with learning disabilities are often the poorest readers; they demonstrate multiple problems associated with low comprehension, including poor decoding, fluency, and comprehension (Berkeley & Larsen, 2018). These students also exhibit characteristics of inactive learners who do not monitor their learning or use strategies effectively. Yet, students with learning disabilities can improve their reading comprehension if teachers:

1. Teach strategies that have been documented as effective in promoting reading comprehension.
2. Design instruction that incorporates effective principles of direct instruction and strategy instruction.

3. Provide modeling, support, guided instruction, practice, attributional feedback, and opportunities to practice across text types.
4. Monitor students' progress and make adjustments accordingly.

Many of the reading comprehension strategies that have been associated with the highest effect sizes for students with learning disabilities are those that teach students by prompting them to monitor and reflect before, during, and after reading. These strategies ask students to (1) consider their background knowledge on the topic they are reading and use that background knowledge to integrate with text information, (2) summarize key ideas, and (3) self-question while they read (e.g., Gersten et al., 2001; Scammaca et al., 2016; Wanzek et al., 2010) (see Figure 1.1).

## WORD READING, FLUENCY, AND VOCABULARY: ESSENTIAL FEATURES OF READING COMPREHENSION

The majority of students with reading disabilities are likely to demonstrate difficulties with decoding, fluency (reading words quickly and accurately), and vocabulary; however, a small subgroup of students demonstrates only difficulties with reading

---

Explicit instruction, strategy instruction, or a combination of both are associated with the highest effect sizes in reading comprehension for students with reading disabilities. Both explicit instruction and strategy instruction have the following components in common:

1. Assessment and evaluation of learning objectives, including orienting students to what they will be learning
2. Daily reviews of learning objectives to assure mastery
3. Teacher presentation of new material, including giving examples and modeling expected student performance
4. Guided instruction, including asking questions to determine understanding
5. Feedback and correction
6. Independent practice and review
7. Monitoring student progress

The instructional components that contribute the most to improved effect sizes in reading comprehension include:

1. Teacher and students questioning
2. Interactive dialogue between teachers and students and between students and students
3. Controlling task difficulty and scaffolding instruction
4. Elaboration of steps or strategies and modeling by the teacher
5. Small-group instruction
6. Use of cues to help students remember to use and apply what they learn
7. Monitoring student progress and providing opportunities to chart progress
8. Reading a range of text types (e.g., narrative, biography, information) and across a range of reading levels

---

FIGURE 1.1. Key ideas in reading comprehension. Information in this figure is adapted from work conducted by Swanson and colleagues (Swanson, 1999, 2001; Swanson et al., 1999).

comprehension (Cirino et al., 2013). This subgroup has language-based reading comprehension difficulties, and initial evidence suggests that they may differentially benefit from instruction with a language focus (Snowling & Hulme, 2011). Students with significant difficulties in decoding, fluency, and vocabulary will demonstrate problems with reading comprehension. One reason for this interference is that readers have only so much short-term cognitive, or thinking, capacity for a task. If too much effort is allocated to decoding, little capacity is available for focusing on comprehension.

Myra, Laticia, and Jorge are sixth-grade students identified with learning disabilities who demonstrate significant problems understanding text. Myra has difficulty reading multisyllabic words and still confuses basic sight words such as *from*, *where*, and *laugh*. Although she has difficulty with decoding, Myra is interested in many topics related to social justice and is motivated to read and learn. Her difficulties decoding words slow down her reading and often require her to read slowly and to reread text in order to understand it. Myra's text reading improves when key words are reviewed and taught to her prior to reading. Laticia, though an accurate word reader, reads very slowly (about 60 correct words per minute). This slow reading negatively influences comprehension and also makes it difficult for her to read widely. Jorge reads quickly as long as he is very familiar with the words. Jorge's challenge is that he does not know the meanings of many words that appear in his expository text for science and social studies. Because he does not enjoy reading, he does not read often, and thus his knowledge of new words and ideas is limited. His limited vocabulary and world knowledge prevent him from fully understanding what he has read because he either lacks sufficient background knowledge or misses the meaning of so many words that comprehension on all but a superficial level is difficult.

Myra, Laticia, and Jorge provide examples of the difficulties that many students with learning disabilities have with reading comprehension and illustrate the value of teaching critical foundational skills such as word reading (decoding), fluency (accuracy and speed of reading), vocabulary (knowing what the words mean in context), and world knowledge (having sufficient background knowledge to benefit from reading text). Many students with learning disabilities have challenges in more than one area that influence their text comprehension. Teachers who are aware of the many elements that contribute to comprehension are more likely to consider these when assessing students' reading comprehension difficulties and implementing targeted instruction.

### *What Can Teachers Do If Older Students Have Poor Word Reading (Decoding)?*

Knowing how to read, or decode, words is not a small part of the reading process—it is a critical link whose absence inhibits understanding. The common belief is that word-reading and decoding problems only occur with students in the early grades (K–2), yet the vast majority of students with reading difficulties in grade 3 and above demonstrate difficulties reading words accurately. When students are beginning to read, they may have difficulty with such words as *saw*, *them*, and *their*. As students progress through reading, they may have difficulty reading such words as *challenge*, *fascinate*, and *immune*. The goal is to identify, prior to reading, the key words that students are likely to have challenges decoding and to teach these words so that students can read these words and use them in discussions and written expression. Achieving this goal with students with learning disabilities is no easy matter.

Teachers can provide support by teaching the decoding skills students need initially to read more basic words. After students can read basic words and have the fundamental phonics principles to decode words, then teachers need to provide instruction in the decoding of more complex and multisyllabic words. A few pointers to facilitate decoding in older students include the following:

- Practice decoding with very complicated, multisyllabic words. Break these words into syllables and then treat each syllable as a separate word type for decoding.

- Ask students to locate words that they cannot read. Keep these words in a word bank or on a word wall and use them for activities on teaching decoding.

- Teach students common rules for decoding and remind them to use these rules when reading multisyllabic words. Review rules using key words from the text. For example, in the word *reduction*, show students that there are three word parts: *re duc tion*. Use the rules students know and the words they currently can read to help them decode each word part and then read the entire word.

- Teach students common prefixes, suffixes, and affixes so that reading multisyllabic words is easier and more meaningful.

- Demonstrate that some words are "irregular" and do not conform with the typical rules of our language. Keep a word wall of irregular words that students need to practice.

- Indicate that proper nouns, such as the names of people, places, and things, are often difficult to read. Teaching what these names refer to in the chapter before students read and connect them, so that students know who the story is about, where it takes place, and other related issues, facilitates word reading and comprehension.

- Teach students to read complex high-frequency words that are phonetically irregular (e.g., *through*) and give them many opportunities to read these words in text correctly.

The What Works Clearinghouse (WWC) has released a guidance document on teaching reading comprehension to students in grades 4–9 with significant reading difficulties (Vaughn et al., 2022). They identify multisyllabic word reading as a useful technique to promote success. Students can learn to read and remember difficult words by selecting syllables from each of three columns to build multisyllabic words. For example, students can have a list of eight syllables in column 1, eight syllables in column 2, and eight syllables in column 3 and figure out how to select and combine them to make complex words. For example, the syllables *fre*, *quent*, and *ly* are combined to make *frequently*. The syllables *in*, *fec*, and *tion* are combined to make *infection*. Figure 1.2 provides a list of resources to assist with teaching decoding. Table 1.1 is a summary of practices identified in the WWC guidance document for teaching multisyllabic word reading (Vaughn et al., 2022).

> *Building Words: A Resource Manual for Teaching Word Analysis and Spelling Strategies* (2001) by T. G. Gunning. Boston: Allyn & Bacon.
>
> *Making Sense of Phonics: The Hows and Whys* (2nd ed.) (2013) by I. L. Beck & M. E. Beck. New York: Guilford Press.
>
> *Phonics From A to Z, 3rd Edition: A Practical Guide* (3rd ed.) (2017) by W. Blevins. New York: Scholastic Professional Books.
>
> *Phonics They Use: Words for Reading and Writing* (7th ed.) (2017) by P. Cunningham. Pearson.
>
> *Teaching Word Recognition: Effective Strategies for Students with Learning Difficulties* (2nd ed.) (2014) by R. E. O'Connor. New York: Guilford Press.
>
> *Word Journeys: Assessment-Guided Phonics, Spelling, and Vocabulary Instruction* (2nd ed.) (2013) by K. Ganske. New York: Guilford Press.
>
> *Words Their Way: Word Study for Phonics, Vocabulary, and Spelling Instruction* (6th ed.) (2020) by D. R. Bear, M. Invernizzi, S. R. Templeton, & F. Johnston. Pearson.

**FIGURE 1.2.** Resources for teaching decoding.

### What Can Teachers Do If Students Have Poor Fluency?

Reading words automatically and with accuracy allows students to "free up" their thinking so that they can concentrate on text meaning (Kuhn et al., 2010; Perfetti, 1985). Students who read by decoding too many words or with reduced accuracy also demonstrate difficulties keeping up with class expectations in reading and learning and have more difficulty remembering what they read. You can imagine how reading very slowly and laboriously might discourage students and reduce interest in reading and learning from print.

How fast should students read? Starting at fourth grade the correct words read per minute for 25th, 50th, and 75th percentile are 75, 94, and 125, respectively. The same data for fifth grade are 87, 121, and 153; and for sixth grade: 112, 132, and 169 (Hasbrouck & Tindal, 2017). To achieve this goal, students need to know how to read words automatically, without a lot of pauses to figure out the word.

Teachers can provide support by teaching fluency skills that students need in order to read for comprehension. A few pointers to facilitate fluency include the following:

- Monitor students' progress in reading by asking them to read informational passages at the grade level you are teaching. Calculate the correct words read per minute. Ask students to monitor their progress by graphing results.
- Model reading challenging passages while students follow along and then ask them to read them.
- Ask students to reread difficult passages.
- Ask students to work with peer partners to read and reread passages.
- Identify key words and proper nouns and preteach prior to asking students to read text.
- Have students listen to an audio version of the text prior to reading independently.

**TABLE 1.1.** WWC Recommendations on Building Skills for Multisyllabic Word Reading (Vaughn et al., 2022)

| # | Recommendation | Steps to implement |
|---|---|---|
| 1 | Build students' decoding skills so they can read complex multisyllabic words. | 1. Identify the level of students' word-reading skills and teach vowel and consonant letter sounds and combinations, as necessary.<br>2. Teach students a routine they can use to decode multisyllabic words.<br>3. Embed spelling instruction in the lesson.<br>4. Engage students in a wide array of activities that allow them to practice reading multisyllabic words accurately and with increasing automaticity. |
| 2 | Provide purposeful fluency-building activities to help students read effortlessly. | 1. Provide a purpose for each repeated reading.<br>2. Focus some instructional time on reading with prosody.<br>3. Regularly provide opportunities for students to read a wide range of texts. |
| 3 | Routinely use a set of comprehension-building practices to help students make sense of the text. | 1. Develop world knowledge that is relevant for making sense of the passage.<br>2. Teach the meaning of a few words that are essential for understanding the passage.<br>3. Teach students how to derive meanings of unknown words using context.<br>4. Teach prefixes and suffixes to help students derive meanings of words.<br>5. Teach the meaning of Latin and Greek roots. |
| 3B | Consistently provide students with opportunities to ask and answer questions to better understand the text they read. | 1. Explicitly teach students how to find and justify answers to different types of questions.<br>2. Provide ample opportunities for students to collaboratively answer questions.<br>3. Teach students to ask questions about the text while reading.<br>4. After students demonstrate comfort with reading stretch texts with the group, provide students with electronic supports to use when independently reading stretch text to assist with pronunciation of difficult words and word meanings. |
| 3C | Teach students a routine for determining the gist of a short section of text. | 1. Model how to use a routine to generate gist statements.<br>2. Teach students how to use text structures to generate gist statements.<br>3. Work collaboratively with students to generate gist statements. |
| 3D | Teach students to monitor their comprehension as they read. | 1. Help students determine when they do not understand the text.<br>2. Teach students to ask themselves questions as they read to check their understanding and figure out what the text is about.<br>3. Provide opportunities for students to reflect on what they have learned. |
| 4 | Provide students with opportunities to practice making sense of stretch text (i.e., challenging text) that will expose them to complex ideas and information. | 1. Prepare for the lesson by carefully selecting appropriate stretch texts, choosing points to stop for discussion and clarification, and identifying words to teach. |

- Give opportunities for students to showcase their reading by asking them to prepare a passage or dialogue to read aloud to the class. Advance preparation allows students time to read and reread material—an effective practice for improving fluency.
- Names of people, places, and things are often difficult to read; teach these names prior to reading.

Table 1.2 provides a list of resources to assist with teaching fluency.

## WHAT IS INVOLVED IN READING COMPREHENSION?

Reading comprehension involves much more than readers' responses to text. Reading comprehension is a multicomponent, highly complex process that involves many interactions between readers and what they bring to the text (previous knowledge, strategy use) as well as variables related to the text itself (interest in text, understanding of

**TABLE 1.2. Resources for Teaching Fluency**

For evidence-based curricula, check: What Works Clearinghouse
Website: *https://ies.ed.gov/ncee/wwc/FWW*

Peer-Assisted Learning Strategies—Reading (PALS) (Classwide Peer Tutoring)
Contact: PALS Outreach
Vanderbilt University
228 Peabody
110 Magnolia Circle, Suite 418
Nashville, TN 37203-5721
Website: *https://frg.vkcsites.org/what-is-pals*

Read Naturally
Contact: Read Naturally
1284 Corporate Center Drive, Suite 600
Saint Paul, MN 55121
651-452-4085
Website: *www.readnaturally.com*

Great Leaps
Contact: Great Leaps
P.O. Box 357580
Gainesville, FL 32635
Website: *www.greatleaps.com*

Corrective Reading
Contact: McGraw Hill
McGraw Hill
P.O. Box 182605
Columbus, OH 43218
Website: *www.mheducation.com/prek-12/program/ corrective-reading-2008/MKTSP-URA04M0.html*

Quick Reads: A Research-Based Fluency Program
Contact: Savvas Learning Company
Website: *www.savvas.com*

Wilson Reading System
Contact: Wilson Reading System
Wilson Language Training
47 Old Webster Rd.
Oxford, MA 01540
Website: *www.wilsonlanguage.com/ programs/wilson-reading-system*
Email: *eorders@wilsonlanguage.com*

Into Reading/Literature and Reading 180
Contact: HMH
Website: *www.hmhco.com*

Voyager Passport
Contact: Voyager Sopris
Cambium Learning Group
17855 Dallas Parkway, Suite 400
Dallas, TX 75287
800-547-6747
Website: *www.voyagersopris.com/literacy/ voyager-passport/overview*

text types). Effective reading comprehension also involves regulating thinking while reading as well as good working memory to hold the key ideas together.

## Cognitive Processes

What is actually happening when we comprehend what we are reading? Irwin (1991) describes five basic comprehension processes that work together simultaneously and complement one another: microprocesses, integrative processes, macroprocesses, elaborative processes, and metacognitive processes. We describe each of these next. While reading about these different cognitive processes, keep in mind that the reader uses these different strategies fluidly, going back and forth from focusing on specific chunks of text, as with microprocessing, to stepping back and reflecting about what has been read, as with metacognition.

### Microprocesses

*Microprocessing* refers to the reader's initial chunking of idea units within individual sentences. *Chunking* involves grouping words into phrases or clusters of words that carry meaning and requires an understanding of syntax as well as vocabulary. For example, consider the following sentence:

Michelle put the yellow roses in a vase.

The reader does not picture *yellow* and *roses* separately, but instead immediately visualizes roses that are the color yellow. The good reader processes *yellow roses* together.

Selective recall is another aspect of microprocessing. The reader must decide which chunks of text or which details are important to remember. When reading only one sentence, it is relatively easy to recall details, but remembering becomes more difficult after reading a long passage. For example, the reader may or may not remember later that the roses were yellow. To some extent, whether this detail is remembered will depend upon its significance in the passage. In other words, does it matter in the story that the roses were yellow, or is this just an unimportant detail?

### Integrative Processes

As the reader progresses through individual sentences, they are processing more than the individual meaning units within sentences. The reader is also actively making connections across sentences. This process of understanding and inferring the relationships among clauses is referred to as *integrative processing*. Subskills involved in integrative processing include being able to identify and understand pronoun referents and being able to infer causation or sequence. The following two sentences demonstrate how these subskills are applied:

Michael quickly locked the door and shut the windows.

He was afraid.

To whom does *he* apply? Good readers seem to automatically know that *he* in the second sentence refers to *Michael* in the first sentence. And good readers infer that Michael locked the door and shut the windows *because* he was afraid.

### Macroprocesses

Ideas are better understood and more easily remembered when the reader is able to organize them in a coherent way. The reader does this by summarizing the key ideas read. The reader may either automatically or deliberately (i.e., subconsciously or consciously) select the most important information to remember and delete relatively less important details. The skillful reader also uses a structure or organizational pattern to help them organize these important ideas. More proficient comprehenders know to use the same organizational pattern provided by the author to organize their ideas (e.g., a story map that includes characters and setting/problem/solution in a narrative or a compare-and-contrast text structure for an expository passage).

### Elaborative Processes

When we read, we tap into our prior knowledge and make inferences beyond points described explicitly in the text. We make inferences that may or may not correspond with those intended by the author. For instance, in the two sentences provided above about Michael, we do not know why he was afraid. But we can predict that perhaps he was worried that someone had followed him home, or maybe a storm was brewing and he was concerned about strong winds. When making these inferences, we may draw upon information provided earlier in the text or upon our own previous experiences (e.g., perhaps at some point the reader was followed home and hurried inside and quickly shut and locked the door). This process is called *elaborative processing.*

### Metacognitive Processes

Much has been made of the importance of *metacognition*, that is, thinking about thinking. Metacognition is the reader's conscious awareness or control of cognitive processes. The metacognitive processes the reader uses are those involved in monitoring understanding, selecting what to remember, and regulating the strategies used when reading. The metacognitive strategies the reader uses include rehearsing (i.e., repeating information to enhance recall), reviewing, underlining important words or sections of a passage, note taking, and checking understanding.

## The Science of Reading Comprehension

When people refer to the science of reading they are typically referring to phonics instruction and effective word reading (Shanahan, 2020). While many of the arguments in the so-called reading wars refer to the efficacy of phonics instruction, when we think about the science of reading it is beneficial to think beyond the foundation skills of reading and to consider that the ultimate goal is reading comprehension. In this book, we emphasize the findings from the science of reading as they relate directly to significantly improving reading outcomes for students.

## The CCSS and Reading Comprehension

How do the CCSS for English language arts relate to students with reading comprehension difficulties? The CCSS were developed by governors, state education agencies, local education agencies, and other professional groups working together to determine what knowledge and skills students needed to succeed in reading and language arts (as well as other content areas). The intention was to establish common standards across the United States so that whether students were attending school in Iowa, Georgia, Maine, or New Mexico, teachers and educational leaders would hold the same expectations for them. As of now, 35 states have full implementation of the Common Core standards, with Minnesota adopting only the English standards (Editorial Projects in Education, 2021). For the schools and districts in Common Core states the content of the CCSS will look very familiar. The foundation skills of phonemic awareness, phonics and word study, fluency, vocabulary, and comprehension are central to teaching students to read. Highlighted within the CCSS is an increased emphasis on more challenging and difficult texts and greater amounts of expository or informational text. What is the influence of the CCSS emphasis on challenging texts for students with learning and reading difficulties? For one thing, it means that all students, including students with reading problems, will be held to increasingly more challenging reading comprehension expectations. It also means that students are likely to be reading more "original texts" rather than texts that were rewritten at lower readability levels. It means that all students will be reading more informational texts. Furthermore, there is considerably less emphasis on teachers reading the text and increasingly more emphasis on students both reading and then rereading more challenging texts. While we learn more about what this means for all learners in the classroom as the CCSS are implemented, we can expect that students with reading comprehension problems will need the following:

- Opportunities to read text on a range of reading levels, including text on their level, text that is slightly too difficult for them, and grade-level text.
- Scaffolds and supports from highly knowledgeable teachers to appropriately access and learn from challenging texts.
- Opportunities to read text that is "required" but also text that is self-selected.
- Increased knowledge of academic vocabulary and key ideas to support access to understanding and learning from complex informational texts.

Several websites provide additional information about the CCSS for teachers. For teacher lessons with the Common Core, see *www.sharemylesson.com*. For information about the Common Core see *www.corestandards.org*.

## CONCLUSION

This book describes activities and assessments for reading comprehension that can be used to enhance reading comprehension outcomes for students with learning difficulties and disabilities. It is intended for general and special education teachers interested in assessing and intervening with students at risk for reading difficulties. We provide an up-to-date summary of what we have learned, as a field, from research on the reading comprehension of students with learning disabilities. We know that reading comprehension is a complex process of constructing meaning by coordinating a number of skills related to decoding, word reading, and fluency and the integration of background knowledge, vocabulary, and previous experiences. We know that improving reading comprehension is not about focusing on one thing (e.g., word reading), but about addressing the complex array of components that contribute to understanding reading—everything from word reading, to word meaning, to world knowledge. In this book, we address each of these components with the hope that they can be integrated into effective teaching.

# CHAPTER TWO

# Assessing Reading Comprehension

In this chapter we describe how to accurately assess the reading comprehension of students with learning disabilities (LD). Reading comprehension assessment has different purposes. One of these is to compare students' comprehension levels to those of students in a norming sample. Another is to find out if students have met preestablished criteria for their grade level. A third purpose is diagnostic, to determine a student's specific strengths and weaknesses. Assessments can be used to inform instruction by determining how students apply different reading comprehension skills and how efficiently they use comprehension strategies.

If the purpose is to determine why a student may be struggling, teachers must be adept at using assessment data to plan what, how, and when to teach (Haager & Klingner, 2005). The types of assessment materials and activities the teacher (or other examiner) uses should be determined by the purpose of the assessment. If we know what type of information we need, we can decide what process to follow.

A useful way to think of assessments is in terms of their purpose and use. Screening, diagnostic, formative, and summative are common categories for assessments. Screening assessments are typically given at the start of the school year to all students. Sometimes referred to as "universal screeners" these types of assessments are used to identify students who are at risk for reading difficulties. Diagnostic assessments are more in-depth than other types of assessments. When students are identified in screeners, or are not making sufficient progress, diagnostic assessments can be used to zero in on particular areas of strengths and weaknesses and to identify instructional needs.

Formative assessments are often informal and are used to monitor student learning and provide ongoing feedback that can be useful for instructional purposes. Such assessments generally are low stakes, meaning that they are not used for evaluative purposes. Students use formative assessment feedback to improve their understanding of what they need to work on to improve their comprehension. Examples include a concept map, a brief essay describing the main points in a reading, or a checklist to determine how students engage in a text-based discussion. When teachers observe their students and then adjust their instruction to provide additional support, they are engaging in formative assessment. Summative assessments are typically evaluative and used to determine grades or placement in subsequent classes. They may also be used to evaluate program, teacher, and school effectiveness. States' high-stakes tests are an example of summative assessments (such as the Regents Exam in New York). Sometimes classroom assessments are used for both purposes, to provide feedback to teachers and students, and for evaluation.

Next, we discuss the complexities associated with assessing reading comprehension. We then describe various traditional as well as innovative reading comprehension assessment measures, including standardized norm-referenced tests, criterion-referenced tests, informal reading inventories, curriculum-based assessment, curriculum-based measurement, interviews and questionnaires, observations, oral retelling, and think-aloud procedures (e.g., as illustrated by the study group prompts at the beginning of this chapter). For each technique we describe its purpose, how it is implemented, and its relative strengths and weaknesses. We also share considerations for English learners (ELs).

## CHALLENGES OF MEASURING READING COMPREHENSION

Perhaps the biggest challenge with assessing reading comprehension is that student performance can vary widely, depending on the assessment (Collins & Lindström, 2021; see Table 2.1). For instance, when students between the ages of 8 and 18 were given four different comprehension assessments, fewer than half were consistently identified with LD in reading on two or more assessments (Keenan & Meenan, 2014). Because of the complexities of reading comprehension, performance can vary based on a student's foundational skills, such as prior knowledge, vocabulary, decoding, working memory, and writing. The text used to measure comprehension also plays a key role. The genre of the text (e.g., narrative, expository), the length, and the reading level all contribute to students' ability to demonstrate their comprehension. Finally, assessment formats vary as well. Assessment might ask students to complete multiple-choice items, to fill in missing words or phrases using cloze procedures, or to respond to comprehension questions verbally or in writing. And to complicate matters further, some assessments are timed, while others allow students to work at their own pace. For students with LD, limits on time often result in many unanswered assessment questions. Would students have demonstrated their comprehension with more time? Or would the assessment have revealed additional difficulties?

Given these complexities, it can be difficult to determine how much students really know and what they are actually thinking. Educators need to be clear on what a comprehension assessment is measuring and how other factors contribute to student performance (see Table 2.1). Using multiple measures and comparing results across measures is the best way to accurately assess a student's instructional needs.

## LIMITATIONS OF TRADITIONAL COMPREHENSION ASSESSMENT PROCEDURES

Traditional measures of reading comprehension are limited in that they provide only a general indicator of how well a student understands text, and they are not based on experts' knowledge of what good readers do to comprehend text. It is commonly agreed that good readers connect new text with past experiences and interpret, evaluate, synthesize, and consider alternative interpretations of what they have read (Pressley & Afflerbach, 1995). Good readers are able to monitor their understanding and use all available information while attempting to make sense of the text (Baker, 2002; Flavell, 1979; Mokhtari & Reichard, 2002; Pressley, 2000a).

Despite views of reading as an interactive, reflective process, however, reading comprehension measures generally focus on recall as the primary indicator of students' understanding (Applegate et al., 2008). Comprehension is typically measured by requiring students to read a short passage and then answer multiple-choice or

**TABLE 2.1. Influences on Reading Comprehension Assessment Performance**

*Foundational skills*
- Attentive behavior
- Knowledge
- Listening comprehension
- Vocabulary
- Word reading
- Working memory
- Writing

*Text*
- Genre
- Length
- Level

*Assessment features*
- Response format
- Reading mode
- Time limit

*Note.* Based on Collins and Lindström (2021).

short-answer questions or by using a cloze task (i.e., asking students to fill in blanks where words have been omitted). These traditional measures of reading comprehension provide only a basic indication of how well a student understands text and offer little information about how the student uses cognitive and metacognitive processes (Kendeou et al., 2012). In short, they do not explain *why* a student may be struggling. Nor do they help us detect and diagnose specific comprehension problems. Keenan and Betjemann (2006) point out that multiple-choice tests can be problematic because it is possible to answer some questions without actually reading the passage. In fact, in an examination of the Gray Oral Reading Test (GORT; Wiederholt & Bryant, 1992, 2001, 2012), they noted that the best predictor of how well a child answered a question was not how well the child read the passage but rather how well the question could be answered without reading. Clearly, better standardized measures are needed, as well as innovative procedures that evaluate aspects of comprehension not assessed by standardized instruments. Teachers should have a repertoire of options at their fingertips. Assessment should reflect the dynamic, developmental nature of comprehension (Snow, 2002a). It should pick up individual differences in students who struggle with comprehension, identifying how, when, and why difficulties occur, and should reliably address social, cultural, and linguistic variation. In the next section we describe different assessment tools.

## READING COMPREHENSION MEASURES

A wide range of assessment instruments and procedures is available (see Table 2.2). When selecting a test or assessment procedure to use with students with LD, it is important to select the measure that most closely matches the users' needs or purpose. For example, comparing a student's scores with those of other same-age or same-grade students requires a norm-referenced assessment. Seeking information about how a student applies reading comprehension strategies while reading requires an individual assessment that includes thinking aloud. For more information about reading comprehension assessments, see Lipson and Wixson (2012) and Morsy et al. (2010).

Teachers should consider numerous factors when choosing a test or assessment procedure:

1. The purpose of the testing (screening, progress monitoring, assessing level of reading, research, or assessing students' competence in comparison to peers)
2. The specific information needed about the student's reading comprehension (e.g., inferencing, summarizing, strategy use)
3. The number of students being tested (i.e., an individual, a small group, or a whole class)
4. The length of the test (e.g., shorter tests can be easier to give and less stressful for the student but may not have enough questions or types of tasks to provide sufficient information about a student's performance)
5. The administration of the test, individually or as a group

**TABLE 2.2. An Overview of Different Types of Comprehension Assessments**

| Type | Description |
| --- | --- |
| Norm-referenced tests | Published tests are administered under standardized conditions (e.g., with computerized answer sheets, timed); students' scores are compared with those of a normative sample. |
| Criterion-referenced tests | Students' test scores are compared with predetermined criterion levels that indicate mastery of a skill or content; informal reading inventories are a type of criterion-referenced test. |
| Curriculum-based assessment | Tests are based on the actual curriculum used in the classroom, and students are assessed regularly and their progress is monitored. |
| Curriculum-based measurement | Students are assessed frequently with standard, brief tests; scores are monitored over time to assess progress. |
| Interviews and questionnaires | Students respond orally or in writing to a list of questions designed to assess their understanding of the reading process and their knowledge of reading strategies. |
| Observation | Examiners observe students' reading behaviors, using checklists, anecdotal records, or ethnographic note taking. |
| Retelling | Students are prompted to retell or reconstruct what they remember about what they have just finished reading. |
| Think-alouds | Students are prompted to voice their thoughts before, during, and after reading. |

6. The number of forms available with the test, particularly if multiple admin-istrations are needed (e.g., many norm-referenced tests come with two forms, making them useful for assessing progress over time—students are given one version of the test as a pretest and another as a posttest)
7. For norm-referenced tests, the extent to which the norming sample is similar to the students to whom the test will be administered
8. The examiner's qualifications (e.g., whether the tester has the skills to give highly specific tests)
9. The amount of training needed to administer a test, score it, and interpret results (e.g., norm-referenced tests typically require some training)

Reading comprehension measures should help teachers monitor the comprehension of their students over time and provide information that is useful in designing reading comprehension instruction and supports.

## Norm-Referenced Tests

Traditional norm-referenced tests—such as the Gates–MacGinitie Reading Tests, the GORT, the Iowa Test of Basic Skills, the Group Reading Assessment and Diagnostic Evaluation (GRADE), or the Stanford Achievement Test—provide an overall measure of reading comprehension and an indicator of how a student compares with age-level and grade-level peers (i.e., the normative sample). On these measures students typically read brief narrative and expository passages and respond to multiple-choice comprehension questions about each passage. Questions about narrative passages generally focus on the setting, characters, sequence, and plot of a story. Questions about expository text typically ask about the main idea and supporting details. Although some questions require inferential thinking, most rely on straight recall. The extent to which readers are able to identify this predetermined information establishes at what point they are placed on a continuum ranging from novice to expert reader. Most norm-referenced tests can be used with large groups and have the advantage of being relatively easy to administer and score (see Table 2.3).

Norm-referenced tests have been criticized for being too focused on lower-level comprehension processes and for not representing real-life reading tasks. Questions are typically presented in a multiple-choice format, and many are timed. Also referred to as standardized tests, these assessments do not adequately account for the effects of socioeconomic and cultural–linguistic differences on student performance (Papadopoulos et al., 2021; Snyder et al., 2005). Often a test has not been normed with a population that includes a sufficient number of ELs, for example, or students living in high-poverty areas. Further, standardized tests have been shown to negatively influence students' motivation and self-efficacy (International Literacy Association, 2017). Efforts in recent years have focused on trying to improve standardized tests. The National Assessment of Educational Progress (NAEP), the Stanford Achievement Tests–10 (SAT-10), and numerous statewide assessments have steadily shifted from objective multiple-choice questions to questions that require more open-ended responses. With the adoption of the CCSS by most states in the United States, the trend is toward more expository text and increasing text complexity. The intent is to better assess students' ability to *think* about a passage and to require them to explain their thinking with information from the passage. The new assessments are featuring more tasks focused on writing than previously.

To accurately determine what a reader comprehends, it is important to access the reader's thinking processes. These processes include forming perspectives, extending, analyzing, questioning, taking a stance, shifting interpretations, rethinking the role of the self as a reader, reflecting, and thinking critically (e.g., about disconnects and anomalies).

### Criterion-Referenced Tests

Criterion-referenced tests (CRTs) assess the extent to which students have mastered a skill based on a preestablished criterion. Unlike norm-referenced tests that compare a student's performance to that of other students, CRTs determine how well a student is making progress toward mastery of specific skills or subject matter. There are many available commercial CRTs that assess reading comprehension (see Table 2.4), or teachers can design their own. These assessment tools are constructed in relation to scope and sequence charts in a particular subject area, so that the skills they evaluate progress from the easiest to the most difficult. Because of this structure, CRTs are

**TABLE 2.3.** A Sample of Norm-Referenced Reading Tests

| Title | Ages/grades | Estimated testing time | Key elements of assessment | Validity and reliability | Administration |
|---|---|---|---|---|---|
| Aprenda: La Prueba de Logros en Español—3rd Edition (Pearson, 2004) | Grades K–12 | 60–80 minutes (for entire test, less for comprehension subtest only) | Riddles, modified cloze tests, and comprehension questions. Test also contains listening comprehension and English as a second language assessment sections. Modeled after the SAT-10. | Data not available | Individual |
| Batería III Woodcock–Muñoz: Pruebas de Aprovechamiento (Woodcock et al., 2005) | Grades PreK–12 | Varies | Passage comprehension (a cloze task) | *Reliability:* .80 or higher, based on cluster interpretation; no other reliability information specified. *Validity:* Publisher reports good validity based on a large and representative norming sample ($N = 8,818$) and co-norming of two batteries. | Individual |
| Diagnostic Assessment of Reading, 2nd Edition (DAR; Roswell et al., 2005) | Ages 5–adult | 40 minutes or less | Identifies students' strengths and weaknesses on a range of reading-related tasks, including overall comprehension of expository texts and oral reading fluency and accuracy. Each grade level has one passage with four comprehension questions. | *Reliability:* Split-half correlations corrected with Spearman–Brown (Reading Comprehension): .96. Predicting reading comprehension among ELs using oral reading fluency correlation between the Gates–MacGinitie and the DAR: comprehension ($r = .48$), total ($r = .47$). | Individual |
| Gates–MacGinitie Reading Tests, 4th Edition (MacGinitie et al., 2000) | Grades K–12 and adult reading | 55–75 minutes | Word meanings (levels 1 and 2); comprehension (levels 1 and 2: short passages of one to three sentences; levels 3 and up: paragraph reading). | *Reliability:* Internal consistency by subscale for each level for both fall and spring administrations range from upper .80s to .90s for grades 1–12. *Validity:* Data are provided largely by demonstrating the significant relationships between the Gates–MacGinitie and other measures of reading vocabulary and comprehension. | Group |

*(continued)*

**TABLE 2.3.** *(continued)*

| Title | Ages/grades | Estimated testing time | Key elements of assessment | Validity and reliability | Administration |
|---|---|---|---|---|---|
| Gray Oral Reading Test–5 (Wiederholt & Bryant, 2012) | Ages 6 years–23 years, 11 months | 15–45 minutes | Sixteen separate stories, each followed by five multiple-choice comprehension questions with an optional miscue analysis system. | *Reliability:* Internal coefficients are above .90; test–retest and alternative-form reliabilities are high (.85). *Validity:* Established by relating the Gray Oral Reading Test to other measures. | Individual |
| Gray Silent Reading Test (Wiederholt & Blalock, 2000) | Ages 7 years–25 years, 11 months | 15–30 minutes | Thirteen passages with five comprehension questions each. | *Reliability:* Coefficients are at or above .97; test–retest and alternative-form reliability are very high (above .85). *Validity:* Established by relating the Gray Silent Reading Test to other measures, including the Gray Oral Reading Test. | Individual, small group, or entire class |
| Group Reading Assessment and Diagnostic Evaluation (Williams, 2001) | Grades PreK and up | 45 minutes to 2 hours (depending on level and how many subtests used) | Sentence comprehension (a cloze task) and passage comprehension (student reads a passage and responds to multiple-choice comprehension questions). Also assesses listening comprehension. | *Reliability:* Coefficients for alternate form and test–retest in the .90 range. *Concurrent and predictive validity:* Assessed using a variety of other standardized reading assessments. | Individual or group |
| Iowa Test of Basic Skills (Hoover et al., 2001, 2003, 2007, depending on form used) | Grades K and up | 43 minutes for reading subtest | Reading comprehension is assessed with questions that evaluate literal understanding, inference/interpretation, and generalization. | *Reliability:* 84 coefficients (internal consistency) reported for the various subtests; six are in the .70s; others are in the .80s and .90s. The composite score reliabilities are all .98. *Validity:* Established through research studies; no other data reported. | Individual or group |
| Kaufman Test of Educational Achievement, 2nd Edition (Kaufman & Kaufman, 2004) | PreK–12+ | 30–60 minutes | Reading comprehension is assessed with passages of increasing length and complexity and responses to literal and inferential questions. | *Reliability:* Overall reliability coefficients ranged from .78 to .97 for all ages. *Validity:* Data that correlate performance on the Kaufman Test with other achievement tests are presented in the manual (e.g., WJ-III, WIAT-II, PIAT-R). | Individual or group |

| Test | Grade/Age | Time | Description | Reliability/Validity | Administration |
|---|---|---|---|---|---|
| Stanford 10 Reading Test (Harcourt Assessment, 2002) | Grades K–12 | 1 hour | Reading comprehension is assessed with narrative passages followed by open-ended questions focusing on three levels of comprehension (initial understanding, relationships in text and real life, and critical analysis) | *Reliability:* Assessed using internal consistency measures, alternate-form measures, and with repeated measurement. *Validity:* Determined using other standardized assessments (e.g., SAT-10, Otis-Lennon). Specific information is provided in the test manual. | Individual |
| Test of Early Reading Ability–3 (Reid et al., 2001) | Ages 3 years, 6 months–8 years, 6 months | 30 minutes | Comprehension of words, sentences, and paragraphs (also tests relational vocabulary, sentence construction, and paraphrasing). | *Reliability:* High across all three types of reliability studied. All but 2 of the 32 coefficients reported approach or exceed .90; coefficients were computed for subgroups of the normative sample (e.g., African Americans, Latinos) as well as for the entire normative sample. *Validity:* New validity studies have been conducted; special attention has been devoted to showing that the test is valid for a wide variety of subgroups as well as for a general population. | Individual |
| Test of Reading Comprehension, 4th Edition (Brown et al., 2008) | Ages 7 years–17 years, 11 months | 45 minutes or less | Test of silent-reading comprehension. Subtests assess relational vocabulary, sentence completion, paragraph construction, text comprehension, and contextual fluency. | *Reliability:* .90 range. *Validity:* Criterion validity measures assessed using a variety of measures across several examinations (summarized in the examiner's manual). | Individual, small group, or entire class |
| Test of Silent Contextual Reading Fluency (TOSCRF; Hammill et al., 2006) | Ages 7–18 years | 10 minutes | The TOSCRF measures how quickly students can determine individual words within a series of passages that increase in difficulty from a preprimer to adult level. | *Reliability:* Not provided. *Validity:* Large to very large relationships with other measures (e.g., WJ-III, GORT-4, SAT-9). | Individual, group, or entire class |
| Woodcock Reading Mastery Test, 3rd Edition (Woodcock, 2011) | PreK–12+ | 15–45 minutes | Listening comprehension; word comprehension (antonyms, synonyms, analogies); oral reading fluency; passage comprehension. | *Reliability:* .97. *Validity:* Correlations among WRMT-III tests and other commonly used reading tests (e.g., CTOPP; WIAT-III). | Individual |

**TABLE 2.4. A Sample of Criterion-Referenced Assessments**

| Title | Ages/grades | Estimated testing time | Key elements of comprehension assessment | Administration |
|---|---|---|---|---|
| Analytical Reading Inventory, 9th Edition (Woods & Moe, 2010) | Grades K and higher | Unknown | Student reads leveled narrative and expository passages (aloud and silently), retells passages, and answers specific comprehension questions. Listening comprehension can also be assessed. | Individual |
| Bader Reading and Language Inventory, 7th Edition (Bader & Pearce, 2012) | Grades PreK and higher | Varies depending on subtests given | Graded reading passages used to assess silent reading comprehension (also listening comprehension). | Individual |
| Basic Reading Inventory, 10th Edition (Johns, 2008) | Grades PreK and higher | Varies depending on subtests given | Oral and silent reading comprehension assessed through retelling and comprehension questions. | Individual |
| Developmental Reading Assessment, 2nd Edition (Beaver, 2005) | Grades K–3 | About 20 minutes | Comprehension is assessed through story retelling and comprehension questions with graded reading passages. | Individual |
| Flynt–Cooter Comprehensive Reading Inventory–2 (Cooter et al., 2013) | Grades 1 and higher | 15–30 minutes | Student reads a leveled passage of text silently and then retells what was read. Listening comprehension can also be assessed. Available in English and Spanish. | Individual |
| Qualitative Reading Inventory, 5th Edition (Leslie & Caldwell, 2010) | Emergent to high school | 30–40 minutes | Comprehension of oral and silent reading measured through story retelling and comprehension questions. Includes a prior-knowledge test. Listening comprehension can also be assessed. | Individual |
| Scholastic Reading Inventory (Scholastic, 2007) | Grades K–12 and higher | 40–60 minutes | Computerized. All questions assess main idea; sentences fill in are all summary statements. After each passage is a short statement with a missing word and students must select the word to fill in. | Group |
| Standardized Reading Inventory, 2nd Edition (Newcomer, 1999) | Ages 6 years–14 years, 6 months | 30–90 minutes | Assesses understanding of vocabulary in context and passage comprehension. | Individual |

ideally suited for the purposes of (1) determining the goals and objectives for students' individualized education plans (IEPs) and (2) evaluating students' progress toward achieving those goals. They are typically given as benchmarks to evaluate progress (e.g., once each grading period, but not more often than that). Other assessment approaches are more closely tied to the curriculum and thus are preferable for ongoing monitoring of progress and instructional decision making (e.g., curriculum-based assessment, observations, and think-alouds). Most CRTs are individually administered, though a few can also be group-administered. Informal reading inventories (IRIs) are a type of CRT.

### Informal Reading Inventories

IRIs are individually administered tests that yield information about a student's reading level as well as word analysis and comprehension skills. Some also assess background knowledge and interests. The test administrator keeps a running record while the student reads different passages aloud, and then the administrator asks comprehension questions. Although IRIs were originally developed by teachers, now many commercially produced IRIs are available. IRIs are time consuming to administer, but they provide in-depth information about a student's literacy skills. To save time, Snow, Morris, and Perney (2018) suggest limiting the number of passages used at each grade level and including a variety of oral instead of written questions, which are more time consuming and can interfere with students' ability to express their understanding of text.

One criticism of IRIs is that the comprehension questions often focus on literal recall or low-level inferences. Dewitz and Dewitz (2003) administered the Qualitative Reading Inventory (QRI) as a diagnostic tool for determining students' relative comprehension strengths and weaknesses. They did this by deviating from the guidelines provided by the QRI in order to take a closer look at students' responses to questions. Dewitz and Dewitz (2003) concluded that "we can improve our understanding of students' comprehension difficulties using available tools like the QRI or other informal reading inventories [by going deeper] into the thinking, or lack thereof, underlying the difficulties that students have in reading comprehension" (p. 434). They recommended that teachers use IRIs in this way to gather information they can then use to tailor instruction to meet students' needs. One way to do this would be to combine IRIs with think-alouds (described below in "Think-Aloud Procedure").

## Curriculum-Based Assessment

The primary purpose of curriculum-based assessment (CBA) is to systematically assess students' progress toward instructional goals and objectives. Overton (2011) described CBA as the best measure of how much a student has mastered in the curriculum. CBA procedures are based on three fundamental principles: Test items are taken from the curriculum; evaluations are repeated frequently over time; and results are used to develop instructional plans.

CBA procedures provide a way to monitor the effectiveness of reading comprehension instructional interventions and to identify learning problems. Through the use of actually reading passages from the curriculum, with accompanying comprehension questions, students' ability to answer questions correctly can be assessed at regular intervals. This assessment information should be recorded on graphs, providing students and teachers with a visual representation of students' progress. By looking at these graphs, teachers can quickly see which students are not improving. Whereas the trend lines of most students slant upward, the lines of students who are struggling remain relatively flat. Klingner and Vaughn (1996) successfully used this procedure to assess the effectiveness of their reading comprehension strategy intervention with ELs with LD. Similarly, CBA can be used as a way to assess the performance of students who are ELs, in both English and their native language, and determine if they may have an LD (Ortiz & Wilkinson, 1991; Shin & McMaster, 2019; for more information on assessment and ELs, including CBA, see Rivera & McKeithan, 2022). Various forms of CBA have evolved over the years. One of these is curriculum-based measurement (CBM).

### Curriculum-Based Measurement

CBM is a type of CBA that includes a set of standard, simple, short-duration fluency measures of basic skills in reading as well as in other subject areas. It was developed in the 1980s and 1990s (Deno, 1992; Fuchs & Deno, 1992; Marston & Magnusson, 1985). To implement CBM, assessments of equivalent difficulty are repeated at regular intervals (e.g., weekly or monthly) over a long period of time. In general, assessments are somewhat broad in scope, touching on the variety of skills that are needed to attain curriculum goals (Fuchs & Fuchs, 1999). However, the assessments should also be sensitive enough to pick up change over relatively short periods of time. Student progress is plotted on equal-interval graphs (i.e., a linear graph in which the distance between lines is the same), either manually or with a computerized version of CBM, and displayed in individual and class profiles. This visual representation of the data is easy to interpret and facilitates communication among teachers, parents, students, and others (Deno, 1992).

A commonly used CBM assesses oral reading fluency (ORF). Numerous studies have examined the associations between ORF and reading comprehension and determined that ORF is an effective and quick predictor of reading comprehension proficiency (e.g., Denton, 2012; Fuchs & Vaughn, 2005; Shin & McMaster, 2019). For example, in a study with urban first graders, Riedel (2007) found that ORF was a better predictor of comprehension than other subtests on the Dynamic Indicators of Basic Early Literacy Skills (DIBELS; Good & Kaminski, 2002), including a retell task designed to measure comprehension. Vocabulary was an important factor in the relation between ORF scores and comprehension. Students with satisfactory ORF scores but poor comprehension had lower vocabulary scores than students with satisfactory ORF scores and satisfactory comprehension. ELs were not included in these analyses.

Results for ELs using ORF to predict reading comprehension are mixed. Crosson and Lesaux (2010) demonstrated that connections between text-reading fluency and reading comprehension are strongly influenced by English oral language proficiency. In other words, ELs can be very good word callers who do not understand what they read. They may actually slow down when they are focusing on understanding text as they try to figure out the meanings of unknown words. Crosson and Lesaux's study supports Riedel's (2007) finding that text-reading fluency is not as reliably predictive of comprehension for ELs as it is for native English speakers. For ELs in upper elementary grades, language comprehension difficulties are a greater predictor of reading comprehension than challenges with decoding (e.g., Cho et al., 2019; Kieffer & Lesaux, 2012). Taken together, these studies show that for students who are developing their English language skills, results from ORF CBMs should be interpreted cautiously.

In summary, although CBA and CBM procedures provide a quick indication of students' reading comprehension levels and are useful for monitoring their progress, they do not provide an in-depth picture of students' underlying strategic processing. They tell us only what students comprehend at a basic level, not why they make errors. In an investigation of oral reading fluency as a predictor of comprehension, Valencia et al. (2010) found that students can have the very same reading fluency as measured by words read correctly per minute but demonstrate quite different instructional needs. Some students may need to focus on word identification, for example, and other students require help with vocabulary. Like other traditional measures of comprehension assessments, CBA and CBM have been criticized for providing only a narrow portrayal of students' comprehension. Yet, when implemented in combination with other procedures, they can be a valuable tool (e.g., Hale et al., 2011; Marcotte & Hintze, 2009; Shapiro et al., 2008).

## HOW TO USE CBM

The following is an example of how you might use CBM to track students' progress in reading fluency and comprehension using a maze fluency measure (Fuchs & Fuchs, 2003). Students complete a maze reading activity (i.e., multiple-choice cloze task), and the scorer keeps track of the number of correct word choices.

> Maze task example: When her mother called,
> Briana jumped down from the [tree, mousetrap, cereal] and . . .

- First, obtain or create the maze fluency passages that represent alternate forms of the difficulty level expected at the end of the year. To generate a maze task, delete every seventh word in a passage and replace it with three multiple-choice responses. Do this for several passages of the same difficulty level.

- Once each week (or month), present each student with a maze passage for 2.5 minutes and record the number of correct responses.

• Record each student's scores over time on a graph. To see how students are progressing, set up a graph with the correct response items on the $y$ axis and the weeks/months of instruction or evaluation dates on the $x$ axis. Determine a performance goal. The information used to set a goal might come from a CBM assessment, be based on an individual goal, or be based on grade-level expectations. To monitor progress using this information, create a goal line by drawing a line between the first score, or baseline score, and the predicted outcome score. Figure 2.1 presents a maze fluency CBM graph for "Tanya" for one school year. Evaluate each student's scores to monitor the student's progress and make instructional adjustments. If scores fall below the goal line, the student is not progressing as expected. If scores fall on or above the goal line, a student is making adequate progress. Share this information with students so that they can see their progress and generate goals for themselves.

• Use the results of the CBM to make instructional decisions based on student progress.

• Many CBM measures provide estimates of typical progress (slopes) so teachers can judge if students are on track for meeting end-of-year goals. If a student's slope is increasing, the student is making progress toward the annual goal; if the slope decreases or is flat, the student is not benefiting from instruction. In this case, the teacher should make changes or provide additional instruction. For example, if a student has three points that lie above the goal line, you can raise the end-of-year goal and move the goal line upward (a steeper line indicates faster progress). If a student has two to three points in a row that are below the goal line, progress is less than expected and instruction should be adjusted to increase learning (Nocedal & Wright, 2006). Teachers can also learn about instruction by comparing progress among students in a class or grade. If most of the students in the class fail to make progress, the instructional program may need to be enhanced. If only a few students make little or

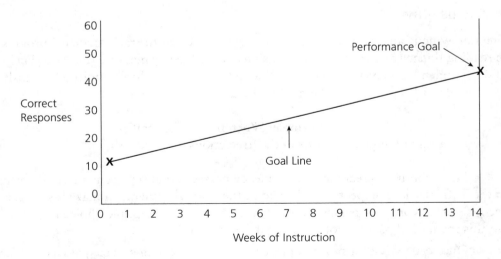

**FIGURE 2.1.** Maze fluency CBM graph for Tanya.

no progress, an effective instructional response would be to intensify and specialize instruction for those students.

## Retelling

Oral retelling is a useful technique for monitoring students' reading comprehension. After reading a passage, students are asked to tell in their own words either the main ideas or everything they can recall from what they just read. Because retelling requires the integration of many skills that are part of the comprehension process, asking students to retell something they have read provides a valuable alternative to traditional questioning techniques for evaluating their reading comprehension. Retelling a story entails understanding, remembering, and sequencing the events and major concepts presented in text. Students must remember factual details and be able to relate them in some organized, meaningful pattern. Additionally, they need to come up with inferences to compensate for information they are not able to recall clearly so that they can reconstruct a coherent retelling.

An advantage to retelling is that the teacher can learn a great deal about what the student understands and where the student may have gaps. This information is helpful when determining which comprehension skills the student still needs to learn. An interesting research finding is that ELs have been able to retell more in their native language than in English, even when reading English-language text. This finding is noteworthy if the examiner's goal is to determine how much a student understands when reading English text, because the student may provide a more accurate portrayal of comprehension when encouraged to share this information in the student's native language.

A disadvantage to retelling is that it must be conducted individually and is time consuming to administer and score. Results may also vary depending on whether students read a passage orally or silently. Another limitation is that students who have difficulties with expressive language may not be able to convey what they understand. And, as already noted, ELs may have difficulty articulating their understanding in English. It is important to provide ELs with alternative ways to express what they know. Recent research has suggested that to get a complete picture of a student's comprehension, retelling should be used as one measure of comprehension and in conjunction with other measures that tap into higher-order thinking skills (Cao & Kim, 2021; Reed & Vaughn, 2012).

### How to Use Retelling

Retelling is a relatively easy assessment to implement. The procedures are as follows:

1. Select an appropriate text for the student to read. The passage should be at the student's instructional or readability level and can be narrative or expository.
2. Ask the student to read the passage silently, orally, or both silently and orally (a recommended technique with students who are struggling readers).

3. After the student has finished reading, ask the student to retell the passage. The specific directions for this vary depending upon what type of passage has been read:
   a. With a narrative retelling (Lipson et al., 1999), say:
      i. Pretend I have never heard this story and tell me everything that happened, or
      ii. *Start at the beginning and tell me the story.*
   b. With informational text (Gunning, 2013), direct the student to
      i. *Tell me as much information as you can remember from the passage you just read*, or
      ii. *Tell me what you learned from the passage.*
4. If the student provides incomplete information, probe or prompt the student by asking,
   a. *Can you tell me anything more?* or
   b. *Anything else?*

Students with sufficient writing skills can be asked to write their retellings rather than state them orally. Although this is not a suitable option for students who resist writing or lack these skills (e.g., some students with LD), it can work well with confident writers. An advantage of written retellings is that many students can be asked to retell a story at the same time, thus saving time.

### How to Score Retells

Evaluating a student's performance on a retell varies depending on whether the student has been asked to retell a narrative passage or an informational text. With a narrative passage, the student should be able to relay the story's plot and describe its characters and setting. With expository text, the student should be able to convey an understanding of the most important information learned and supporting details. With both types of retellings, sequence is important.

While a student is retelling a passage, note the quality and organization of the retelling, whether all essential information is present, and whether there any inaccuracies that indicate faulty or partial comprehension. Also, observe the student's actions before and during reading for clues about the student's affect and signs that they seem to be applying comprehension strategies. The following questions can serve as a guide.

1. Does the student accurately depict the main ideas of the passage?
2. Are most or all of the key points included?
3. Does the student accurately recount supporting details?
4. Does the student use the same vocabulary as in the original, or simplify or embellish it? In the case of a narrative retelling:
   a. Does the student provide the beginning, middle, and end of the story, and in the correct order?
   b. Does the student describe the characters and setting in the story?
5. Does the student relate information in the text to personal knowledge?

6. Does the student note interrelationships among ideas?
7. Does the student do anything with the text prior to reading (e.g., seem to read the title and subheadings and look at any pictures) or start reading immediately?
8. While reading, does the student look at a glossary or illustrations or seem to reread portions of text?
9. Does the student seem anxious or withdrawn? Or does the student seem confident and comfortable with the task?

Rubrics can be used as a way to tally the quantity and quality of students' responses. The quality of a response might simply be marked as "low," "moderate," or "high." Or a scale of 0–4 or even 0–5 can be used. For example:

0  No response given.
1  Response is inaccurate and incomplete.
2  Some information is accurate and some is inaccurate; the response is sketchy.
3  Information is generally accurate and complete, but not well developed.
4  Response is complete and accurate.
5  Response is complete and accurate, plus the student points out interrelationships between elements or makes connections to personal knowledge.

Recording sheets can also be used. For a sample recording sheet for an informational text retelling, see Figure 2.2.

### Retelling with Younger Students or Struggling Readers

Paris and Paris (2003) created a version of the retelling procedure for primary-grade students, called the Narrative Comprehension of Picture Books task. Students retell wordless picture books rather than printed text. This procedure has multiple advantages. First, it is useful to determine if young students or struggling readers can decode print. Second, it can be used flexibly and adapted to many different narrative picture books. Third, it correlates well with the QRI retelling, suggesting that eliciting retellings from picture narratives is an effective approach. Paris and Paris emphasized the importance of narrative comprehension in beginning reading and contended that narrative competence may be a general feature of children's thinking that is essential for early literacy success as well as cognitive development. They provided convincing evidence that children's understanding of narrative stories is an important foundational skill when learning to read.

## MEASURING METACOGNITIVE READING PROCESSES

TEACHER: When I give you this to read, what is the first thing you do?

STUDENT 1: I guess what it is going to be about. I predict. I read the title and then I start reading. Sometimes I look at the pictures to help predict, and the title

Student's Name _____ Date _____

Text _____

Selected by: Student _____ Teacher _____

| | Unprompted | Prompted |
|---|---|---|
| **Main Ideas:**<br>2 points: Identifies all main ideas.<br>1 point: States most of the main ideas.<br>0 points: Cannot recount any main ideas.<br>Comments: | | |
| **Relevant Supporting Details:**<br>2 points: Identifies some details to support each main idea.<br>1 point: States some details to support some main ideas.<br>0 points: Does not identify any supporting details.<br>Comments: | | |
| **Sequence (states main ideas in order of presentation):**<br>2 points: Correct<br>1 point: Partial<br>0 points: Does not indicate recognition of text order.<br>Comments: | | |
| **Conclusion**<br>2 points: States conclusion.<br>1 point: Partially states conclusion.<br>0 points: Does not state conclusion.<br>Comments: | | |
| **Total Score**<br>(8 points possible)<br>**Additional Comments** | | |

**FIGURE 2.2.** Sample recording sheet for an informational text retelling. Adapted by permission from Saskatchewan Learning (2002). Copyright © 2002 Saskatchewan Learning.

and the map and things to help. (*reading*) "About 25 years ago, logging companies began cutting rainforest trees on Borneo. The loggers call the trees 'green gold' because the trees are worth so much money. They cut the trees to make paper, chopsticks, and other products."

TEACHER: What are you thinking?

STUDENT 1: That the people that are cutting them are so selfish because they think that once they cut down the trees they are going to get a lot of money and they are going to cut those trees for wood, paper, chopsticks, and "firewoods" and things that kill the trees.

TEACHER: Anything else?

STUDENT 1: And the people don't care; they are ruining the rainforest and all they want is the money and they don't care about the people who live there—they want to get trees. (*reading*) "The people are the Penan. They live in an ancient rainforest on Borneo, an island near Asia. They live by gathering fruits, nuts, and roots, and by hunting. The Penan way of life, along with the rainforest, is being destroyed. 'I just want to cry when I hear the bulldozers and saws,' says Juwin Lihan, a Penan leader."

TEACHER: What are you thinking?

STUDENT 2: That they are saying that they don't like the sound of bulldozers, saws, or anything that cuts trees—and they told them to stop and that it is happening and that they don't. Most of the rainforest is going to be destroyed. They are going to kill all the animals that live there and leave their habitat, and maybe they will kill thousands and hundreds of baby animals that are extinct like the gray wolves—I don't know if they are extinct—and rhinoceros and other animals.

TEACHER: What do you do when you do not understand a word or an idea the first time you read it?

STUDENT 2: I use the clunk strategies we have in CSR [collaborative strategic reading]. First, we read the sentence without the word and second, we read the sentence before and after the clunk looking for clues . . . We find the prefix and suffix. Finally, we would break the word apart into smaller parts to help us know what the meaning of the word is. . . .

(Excerpts from the responses of two fourth-grade students with learning disabilities to the prompted think-aloud [from Klingner et al., 2004]. See Chapter 9 for more on CSR and "clunk strategies.")

As shown in the excerpt above, the teacher prompts students to share what they are thinking as students are talking through the meaning of a text passage. Assessing students' decision making and application of reading strategies provides important information about how students approach the reading process. In the following set of assessment procedures, we explore several methods that reveal students' thinking as they read.

## Interviews and Questionnaires

Interviews and questionnaires are informal assessment measures designed to elicit students' understanding of the reading process and their knowledge of reading strategies. These assessment tools provide useful information for the teacher and can also promote students' self-awareness of the underlying processes involved in reading. Oral interviews are conducted individually or in small groups, whereas written questionnaires can be group-administered. Unlike the prompted think-aloud procedure (described in a subsequent section), interviews and questionnaires usually are not linked with a specific reading passage.

### Interviews

Interviews can be informal or more structured. Gunning (2013) suggested that questions should not be asked all in one sitting but rather used flexibly and interspersed in pre- and postreading discussions. Broader questions, such as what do students consider before, during, and after they finish reading a passage, can be followed up by more specific probes. For example, do they look at headings before they start reading, or do they think first about what they already might know about the topic? Gunning also suggested asking students what they do when there are words they don't understand or when the text is confusing and whether they can picture the characters and places they are reading about. These are all good examples of interview questions that serve to immerse students more fully in their reading and allow them to build on what they know.

### Questionnaires

Questionnaires provide a similar means of learning about students' strategic processing. Because responses are written, the test can be group-administered. Thus, they potentially provide a time-saving way to collect data. Mokhtari and Reichard (2002) developed the Metacognitive Awareness of Reading Strategies Inventory (MARSI), a self-report instrument, to assess adolescent and adult readers' metacognitive awareness and their perceptions about their use of strategies while reading academic texts. It is intended to supplement other comprehension measures rather than serve as a comprehensive or stand-alone tool. The questionnaire includes 30 different strategies that students may use when reading, for example whether they read more slowly and carefully when the text becomes difficult or whether they use context to help them understand what they read.

Questionnaires such as this provide teachers with a feasible way to monitor the type and number of reading strategies students implement. In addition, they can help students become more aware of the reading strategies they use. However, as with other self-report measures, it can be difficult to know for certain if students are actually engaging in the strategies they report using, and alternatively, because strategies are often used unconsciously, students may not report all strategies they use.

## *Observations*

Observations are an integral part of the assessment process and provide evidence of what children actually do rather than just what they *say* they do (Baker, 2002). Observing students while they are engaged in peer tutoring or cooperative learning activities that involve the application of reading comprehension strategies can be particularly illuminating. Listening to how a tutor describes strategy implementation to another student, for example, can provide useful information regarding what the student knows and can do (Klingner & Vaughn, 1996). It is also useful to observe students during independent reading time.

### *How to Conduct Observations*

There are multiple ways of conducting and recording observations. One approach is to use an observation checklist that includes various reading behaviors. The teacher or other observer simply notes which reading-related activities are observed and which are not. Figure 2.3 is an example of a checklist that is used to examine students' understanding of narrative text.

Another method is to keep anecdotal records (Gunning, 2013). The observer should record the time, date, setting, and names of those involved, in addition to information about a student's reading behaviors. For example:

> "11:20, 9/20/23: John seems to be doing better at monitoring his understanding and using contextual clues to figure out word meanings. He just asked me for the definition of a key term in his social studies textbook and was able to figure out the word's meaning when I prompted him to reread the sentence looking for clues."

Anecdotal records can be quite brief. We suggest that teachers keep a notepad handy for recording comments about students. Some teachers maintain a spiral notebook and use dividers to create a separate section for each student. Other teachers give students their own journals to keep with them during reading activities. With this method the teachers' comments are available to students, and students can add their own reflections. Anecdotal records should be reviewed periodically as a way to keep track of their areas of need as well as their improvements over time.

Ethnographic note taking is similar to anecdotal record keeping except that notes are more elaborate. Ethnographic note taking is useful when the goal is to focus attention on a specific student. This process involves taking repeated and detailed notes for an extended period of time—or, as Irwin described it, writing "as much as possible as often as possible" (1991, p. 196). Klingner, Sturges, and Harry (2003) provided a detailed explanation of how to use ethnographic observation and note-taking techniques to learn about students' reading practices.

A limitation of observations is that it can be difficult to know for certain what comprehension strategies a student is using or why the student may be behaving in a particular way. We cannot actually observe thought processes; we can only observe

| Never (0)<br>Sometimes (x)<br>Usually (✓)<br>Always (+) | Student _____ | Date _____<br><br>Notes |
|---|---|---|
| **Story Structure** | | |
| | Identifies the time and place a story occurs | |
| | Names main characters | |
| | Describes main characters | |
| | Identifies goals/challenges of main characters | |
| | Explains problem/solution | |
| | Describes beginning, middle, and end of story | |
| | Summarizes story after reading | |
| **Monitoring Understanding** | | |
| | Rereads to clarify | |
| | Asks questions to clarify | |
| | Uses pictures to clarify | |
| | Uses context to figure out unknown words | |
| | Uses decoding to figure out unknown words | |
| | Makes predictions | |
| | Makes personal connections | |
| | Make connections to other texts | |
| | Interprets or infers from plot/characters | |

**FIGURE 2.3.** Narrative understanding log.

the outcomes of these processes (e.g., what the child does or says). Therefore, it is important to be cautious when interpreting observation notes and to recognize that there can be alternative explanations for a child's actions. For example, a child who does not volunteer to answer comprehension questions and who seems to remember little might simply be shy or intimidated when speaking in front of others. A child who has difficulty answering questions may have a limited vocabulary or be in the process of acquiring English as a second language (Klingner, 2004). Another limitation of observation methods is that they can be time consuming. However, by combining observations with other assessment methods, the teacher is likely to obtain a more comprehensive picture of students' skills.

### Think-Aloud Procedure

With the think-aloud procedure the student is asked to voice their thoughts while reading. Asking students to "think aloud" can provide useful insights into their metacognitive and cognitive processing strategies (Duke & Pearson, 2002; Jiménez, 1997; Kucan & Beck, 1997), as well as their word-learning strategies (Harmon, 2000) and working memory (Whitney & Budd, 1996). It also conveys information about the text features students find interesting or important (Wade et al., 1999). These are all processes that have been difficult to evaluate with other assessment procedures. An additional advantage to the think-aloud procedure is that students become more aware of the mental processes they use while reading and can thereby improve their reading comprehension (Oster, 2001). In a recent study, after modeling from the examiner, children read two narrative and two expository passages. Each sentence was printed on a separate page and children were prompted to report what they were thinking after each sentence (Karlsson et al., 2018). Three reader profiles were identified: *literal readers* stayed close to the text with few inferences, *paraphrasing readers* tended to paraphrase what they read with some inferences, and *elaborating readers* were able to enrich their mental model of what they read with background knowledge and inferences. Similarly, Klingner and colleagues combined a prompted think-aloud procedure with follow-up interview questions in an investigation of reading comprehension strategy instruction with students with LD. The purpose of the measure was to capture whether and how students applied the comprehension strategies they had learned on a transfer task (see Appendix 2.1 at the end of this chapter for a version of this measure). Understanding the ways that individuals process texts can guide educators to focus reading comprehension instruction on specific aspects of the reading process.

### How to Use the Think-Aloud Procedure

Think-alouds must be administered individually. As with other approaches to comprehension assessment, begin by selecting a passage that is at a student's instructional level. The passage should be readable but not too easy for the student, because some cognitive and metacognitive processes are only activated when a text includes challenging components. Then ask the student questions that help them think aloud before, during, and after reading, such as the following (adapted from Gunning, 2013):

- *Before reading* (the entire selection): What do you think this passage might be about? Why do you think this?
- *During reading* (after reading each marked-off segment or chunk of text): What were you thinking while you read this section? Were there any parts that were hard to understand? What did you do when you came to parts that were hard to understand? Were there any words that were hard to understand? What did you do when you came across hard words?
- *After reading* (the entire selection): Tell me what the passage was about.

While the student thinks aloud, record the student's responses word for word as closely as possible. Keep in mind that thinking aloud is initially difficult for many students. Therefore, it is important to model this process first and allow students time to practice. Note that the "after reading" prompt is much like that used when asking to students to retell what they have read.

After the student has finished the think-aloud process, analyze their responses and note which strategies they used, such as:

- Making predictions prior to reading
- Revising predictions while reading, based on new information
- Considering (thinking about) information read previously
- Making inferences
- Drawing conclusions
- Making judgments
- Visualizing or creating mental images
- Paraphrasing
- Summarizing
- Generating questions
- Reasoning about what was read
- Monitoring understanding
- Using context to figure out difficult words
- Rereading challenging sections
- Looking at illustrations to aid comprehension

Finally, draw conclusions about the extent to which the student appears to use strategies effectively and efficiently for monitoring understanding. Use this information to come up with recommendations for instruction.

Baker (2002) identified several possible limitations to the think-aloud procedure. It may disrupt the process of reading itself. Like other measures that ask students to explain their thinking, students may have trouble articulating or be unaware of what they are thinking. Personal characteristics such as age, motivation, anxiety level, and verbal ability can affect responses. Students might be cued to provide certain responses by the instructions, probes, or questions asked. Students may only reveal the use of cognitive and metacognitive strategies when the text is sufficiently difficult, yet passages that are too difficult will be too hard for students to read. And, like other individually administered assessments we described, think-aloud protocols can be time-consuming and difficult to score. To some extent these limitations can be overcome. For instance, practice with thinking aloud helps students become more aware of, and able to articulate, the mental processes they are using. Despite its weaknesses, the think-aloud procedure is a valuable assessment technique. As with other assessment tools we have described, it is best used in combination with other approaches.

## ADDITIONAL CONSIDERATIONS IN ASSESSING READING COMPREHENSION

### Assessing the Components of Reading Comprehension

Given the complexity of reading comprehension processes, teachers need to use multiple measures of reading comprehension as well as measures that assess a range of linguistic and cognitive processes to adequately understanding students' strengths and needs in reading comprehension instruction. Areas such as (but not limited to) decoding, fluency, vocabulary, background knowledge, working memory, and even motivation contribute to a more complete picture of how a student will approach and understand what they read. Further, finding ways to assess reading comprehension that match evolving reading processes and genres is also important. One promising practice involves scenario-based assessments (SBA; Sabatini et al., 2020). The Global Integrated Scenario-Based Assessment (GISA) is a computer-administered assessment that includes a variety of response formats, including paraphrasing, summarizing, and short answer, that can be taken in a relatively short amount of time (about 45–50 minutes) and scored using automated processes. Using a unique structure to assessment, students are given a purpose for reading a set of related texts and are asked to engage in such tasks as evaluating sources, solving problems, and making decisions, based on what they read. Additional factors such as background knowledge are also included in the assessment. As described by the authors, "SBA designs model and reflect the way an individual might interact and use literacy source materials when learning from text or making decisions in or outside of school settings; in contrast to the discrete passage paradigm of traditional reading comprehension tests" (Sabatini et al., 2020, p. 10). Initial results of SBAs are promising and expand what can be learned from reading comprehension assessments, though more research is needed to determine the feasibility and use with student with LD.

### Assessing Classroom Comprehension Instruction

The final assessment method we discuss in this chapter is not designed to tap students' comprehension processes, but rather to help teachers assess their own instruction, including whether students have been taught key comprehension skills, and whether teachers have provided explicit instruction, modeled strategies, and provided both guided and independent practice. Duke and Pearson (2002) provided a list of self-assessment questions for classroom teachers (in general or special education) in order to identify the strengths and areas in need of improvement in their comprehension instruction.

## CONCLUSION

Perhaps the most important "take-home" message about comprehension assessment is that no one test or procedure should be used alone. It is important for those administering different comprehension measures to be aware of just what each test assesses, what can and cannot be learned, and what the limitations as well as strengths are of each (Klingner, 2004). The best way to assess reading comprehension is with a combination of different measures. Standardized tests, informal reading inventories, interviews and questionnaires, observations, retelling, and think-aloud procedures all have a slightly different purpose and can contribute a unique perspective on students' strengths and areas of need. Through a combination of approaches, we can learn much more than whether a student can read a passage and answer comprehension questions correctly or how the student's comprehension compares with that of others. We can explore the student's underlying thinking processes and uncover information about the strategies the student uses well, overuses, misuses, or does not use. We can find out how students approach a reading task, how they tap into background knowledge, what information they draw upon to answer questions, whether they answer questions from memory or look back into the text, whether and how they come up with inferences, how they go about trying to determine the meaning of unknown words, and what they do to help themselves remember what they have read. All of this information is helpful when planning instruction.

Comprehension should be assessed frequently as a way to track students' growth and provide useful information that can guide instructional and diagnostic decision making (Klingner, 2004). The assessment tools we have described, when used effectively, can provide psychologists, teachers, and reading specialists with a thorough understanding of the comprehension skills of their students with LD. In addition, they can help struggling readers become more aware of the comprehension processes they are using. We are optimistic that through this increased awareness, students will become more active, strategic, responsive, and thoughtful readers.

# APPENDIX 2.1.  PROMPTED THINK-ALOUD

Directions:

(Say:) I am going to ask you to read a page from a magazine. While you are reading I'm going to ask you to tell me what you are thinking. You can tell me what you're thinking in either Spanish or English. (Do:) **Ask the student to say what they are thinking whenever you come across an asterisk in the text below or whenever the student pauses for 2 seconds or more. You may help the student read words, but do not explain what they mean. Also, after each response, probe for more information by asking, "Anything else?"** Note: The student reads from the actual text, while you use the following:

- When I give you this to read, what is the first thing you *do*?

- Anything else?

- What are you thinking about that? (Note: Here you probe for more information in response to the first question; e.g., if a student says, "I look at the picture," you say, "What are you thinking about when you look at the picture?")

- Anything else?

### THE PENAN
### *An Endangered People Living in a Dying Rain Forest*

*The sun rises, waking the people who live in one of the world's oldest rainforests. Then the people hear the first sounds of the morning. But they don't wake to chirping birds and other natural sounds. They wake to the roar of chainsaws and the thud of falling trees.*

- What are you thinking?

- Anything else?

*The people are the Penan. They live in an ancient rainforest on Borneo, an island near Asia. They live by gathering fruits, nuts, and roots and by hunting. The Penan way of life, along with the rainforest, is being destroyed. "I just want to cry when I hear the bulldozers and saws," says Juwin Lihan, a Penan leader.*

- What are you thinking?

- Anything else?

*A Green Gold Rush*

*About 25 years ago, logging companies began cutting rainforest trees on Borneo. The loggers call the trees "green gold" because the trees are worth so much money. They cut the trees to make paper, chopsticks, and other products.*

- What are you thinking?

- Anything else?

*As a result of the logging, the land and rivers have become* polluted.

- **What are you thinking about that word?**

- **Anything else?**

*"Clear rivers have turned into the color of tea with milk," says environment expert Mary Asunta. Government officials, however, say that logging has been good for the area. They point to the more than 100,000 new jobs created in the area by logging companies. The companies have constructed new roads and buildings.*

- **What are you thinking?**

- **Anything else?**

*Bring Back the Forest*

*Many of the Penan people don't want the jobs and roads. They want their forest back. "Before the forest was destroyed, life was easy," says Liman Abon, a Penan leader. "If we wanted food, there were wild animals. If we wanted money, we'd make baskets. If we were sick, we would pick medicinal plants." Now, he says, that's all gone.*

- **What are you thinking?**

- **Anything else?**

- **You may stop reading now. What do you do to help yourself remember what you have read?**

- **Anything else?**

- **What do you do to make sure you understand everything you have read?**

- **Anything else?**

- **What do you do when you do not understand a word or an idea the first time you read it?** (Note: You only need to ask this question if the student does not spontaneously talk about words in response to the previous question.)

- **Anything else?**

### Scoring Procedures

The grading of the prompted think-aloud relies on a rubric. Students can earn a total of 6 points on the prereading questions. The areas in which students can earn points include brainstorming what they already know and predicting what they think they will learn. Students also earn points if they mention any strategy from the four following areas: looking at headings or subheadings; looking at words that are italicized, bolded, or underlined; looking at pictures, tables, or graphs; and describing a strategy but not employing it.

For the "during-reading" questions, students can earn 2 points for a good "gist" or main idea statement and 1 point for a retelling. Responses to the question asking students to define a word are scored with the following points: no points if the student gives a tangential answer (i.e., answer had nothing to do with the story or the word); 1 point if the student defines the word without making reference to the story; 2 points if the student defines the word while making reference to the story; 1 point if the student's response is a reaction to the word without making reference to the story; and 2 points if the student's response is a reaction to the word while making reference to the story.

Postreading responses are scored on a different scale. Students can earn a maximum of 2 points for each postreading question. They receive 2 points if they mention any one of the following strategies: testing, summarizing, questioning, understanding, or making an outline. They earn only 1 point for the following responses: asking a parent, looking in a dictionary, asking a classmate, or reading it again. All points are added to obtain a single score for each student with the maximum being 26 points.

# CHAPTER THREE

# Vocabulary Instruction

1. Before reading this chapter, ask members of your study group how they are currently teaching vocabulary. Make a list of current practices. After reading this chapter, review the list and determine how you would modify current practices.

2. Select a common passage or book that you ask your students to read. Identify the key words that you would teach. Discuss why you would select the words you did. After reading the chapter, consider the words you chose and whether you would make changes.

3. Consider how you might integrate vocabulary instruction throughout the day. After reading the chapter, determine if there are practices you would use to assure that vocabulary instruction is a more highly featured aspect of your program.

4. Becoming "word conscious" is a valuable way to build vocabulary. Becoming word conscious occurs throughout the day by listening for words you don't know, recognizing words you don't know the meaning of when you read, and searching for words to express ideas. Think of ways you can organize homework assignments to encourage students to look for words that they don't know the meaning of and "capture" the words to bring to your classroom.

Vocabulary instruction has recently received considerable attention as a critical element of successful reading. Quite simply, it is impossible to understand text if we do not know much about a significant number of the words in the text.

Some examples for adults help us understand just how important knowing what words mean is to understanding text. Examine the following passages.

**PASSAGE 1**

We are acquainted with space–time domains which behave (approximately) in a "Galileian" fashion under suitable choice of reference–body, i.e., domains in which gravitational fields are absent. (Einstein, 1961, p. 77)

**PASSAGE 2**

Degenerate stars may also be the cause of the so-called planetary nebulae. When these heavy discs of light were first seen in the early telescopes, they were mistaken for planets. But they didn't move and had to be outside the solar system. They are gas spheres and the star at the center is blowing off material. The degenerate core is slimming down to the white dwarf stage. Calculations show there is a process of convective dredging going on. (Hawkins, 1983, p. 236)

Chances are that you may not have understood the text in either of the two passages. Why? Terms such as *convective dredging* and *degenerate core* may not be part of your vocabulary. Furthermore, these terms are technical and have specific meanings that are related to physics and astronomy and depend on concept and construct knowledge in those fields. For example, most of us would not know what a "white dwarf stage" was, though we would probably conjure up some pretty interesting and inaccurate images. Furthermore, we wouldn't know whether there were stages that preceded and followed the "white dwarf stage" and how those stages were related. Overall, vocabulary knowledge and construct knowledge are the essence of comprehension in all text.

## HOW DOES TEACHING VOCABULARY FACILITATE READING COMPREHENSION?

Regardless of what you teach—math, science, history, biology, or government—one of your major responsibilities is to teach key vocabulary and concepts so that students can comprehend what they read and understand the academic language of the discipline (this is particularly important after second grade and with expository text). For example, in mathematics, the words *minus, divided,* and *area* have specific meanings that allow students to comprehend math problems. Even if students understand what the words mean generally, they will also need to learn the specific academic meaning of the words. Vocabulary instruction is a necessary part of comprehension instruction because understanding text is significantly influenced by vocabulary development.

One of the most essential ways of promoting reading comprehension is *building students' world and word knowledge* (Vaughn et al., 2022). The Institute for Education Sciences Practice Guide on promoting reading comprehension for students with reading difficulties (Vaughn et al., 2022) recognizes the importance of building world knowledge so that students can better understand what they are reading and hearing. Several suggestions for doing this include:

- Provide a 3- to 5-minute introduction to build background knowledge either by reading a passage that is easier and related, watching a brief video (2–5 minutes), or looking at pictures that help students visualize what they will be learning.
- Teach students a few key words that build links to what they are learning.
- Provide questions to consider before reading and ask students to record their questions while reading.

## HOW CAN WE ASSESS AND MONITOR VOCABULARY LEARNING?

How do we know that when we work very hard to expose, integrate, teach, and review vocabulary words, students are actually learning them? How do we determine which words students know and understand and which ones slip away? There is probably no area in reading that is more difficult to assess than vocabulary knowledge. Not only is it difficult to measure but typical practices for assessing vocabulary (e.g., write the definition of the word) are often not liked by teachers or students—and actually tell us very little about how well the student knows the word. This is because what we know about a word varies considerably based on how many meanings the word has and how many of those meaning we know. For example, the word *equal* means something different in mathematics than it does in social studies.

Dale (1965) described the stages of knowing the meaning of a word. It may be helpful to consider these stages as we think about assessing how well students know word meanings.

- Stage 1: The student knows nothing about the word—never saw or heard it before.
- Stage 2: The student has heard of the word but has no idea what it means.
- Stage 3: The student knows something about the word when the student hears or reads it in context.
- Stage 4: The student knows the word well.

Beck and colleagues (Beck et al., 1987) have extended this "word knowing" along a continuum:

- No knowledge of the word
- General sense of the word
- Narrow idea of the word bound by context
- Knowledge of the word but may not be able to recall and use readily
- Rich understanding of the word's meaning and its connection to other words

Teachers may want to consider the following types of questions and instructions as ways of "tapping" students' knowledge about words:

- What does *nomenclature* mean?
- Use *obsequious* in a sentence.

- What is the opposite of *homogeneous?*
- What means the same as *gauche?*
- Give an example of how someone would behave who was *frivolous* with their money.

For many students with reading difficulties, these words are either so difficult that they have no idea what they mean, or they have heard of the words but have only a broad idea of their meaning. Simmons and Kame'enui (1998) found that 10- and 12-year-old students with LD had less extensive vocabularies than peers without disabilities. What are the implications of this finding? Students who read a lot and read well have better developed vocabularies. Thus, in addition to increasing the amount and range of reading, vocabulary instruction is a beneficial practice.

There are literally hundreds of thousands of words students need to learn. Also, not all students know the meanings of the same words. How can we determine what words students know, what words students are learning, and what words students need to learn? If we are interested in determining whether students are learning the words we are teaching in language arts, social studies, and science, how do we assess them?

## ASSESSING VOCABULARY LEARNING

Whereas assessment and progress monitoring of vocabulary in typically achieving students are challenging, the problems are even greater for assessing and monitoring students with LD. For many students with reading difficulties, writing and spelling difficulties co-occur, so whenever tests require tapping their knowledge through writing, poor performance may be a result of not knowing the meaning of the word or not being able to write about it. Thus, when constructing progress monitoring measures and using more formal measures, we have to consider what knowledge and skills the measures are tapping.

When oral language is assessed broadly, usually five components are tapped (Rathvon, 2004):

- Phonology—discriminating between and producing speech sounds
- Semantics—understanding word meaning
- Morphology—using and understanding word formation patterns that include roots, prefixes, suffixes, and inflected endings
- Syntax—using correct phrasing and sentence organization
- Pragmatics—using language to communicate effectively

For the purpose of teaching vocabulary, we are most interested in determining whether students have knowledge of semantics and morphology. So, what are some ways teachers can determine the progress students are making in acquiring word meaning (semantics) and using word formation patterns (morphology)? Formal assessments of vocabulary typically ask students to point to pictures that best represent the words provided. Sentence completion measures, in which sentences are read aloud and students select or provide appropriate missing words, are also used. One way to assess students' knowledge of words and their meaning is through curriculum-based measures of vocabulary.

## Using CBM to Assess Vocabulary

Some teachers have begun to measure vocabulary and content learning simultaneously by using CBM. What is a CBM? CBM uses sample items from what is taught (i.e., key words taught) to monitor students' progress by providing regular assessments in a curricular area and tracking students' progress over time (Deno, 1985; see Chapter 2 for more information on CBM and reading comprehension). Espin et al. (2005) used a CBM vocabulary measure to track middle school students' learning in social studies. Weekly assessments took about 5 minutes and included 22 words and definitions generated randomly from a master list of 146 vocabulary terms. Students were asked to match each term with its definition. The authors found that knowledge of social studies content could be adequately measured by monitoring progress on the vocabulary matching assessment. The use of CBM in this study measured both vocabulary acquisition and social studies content learning, providing further support for the link between vocabulary knowledge and content learning. A similar method for measuring word knowledge was used by Vaughn and colleagues (2009, 2013), who determined students' knowledge acquisition in social studies by asking students to do vocabulary matching as well as multiple-choice items related to reading-related social studies texts. A sample of the questions used are provided in Appendix 3.1 at the end of this chapter.

Perhaps the first step in assessing vocabulary is to determine what students already know about the essential words in a unit or story. Consider the following steps to determine what students know about words:

1.  Review the unit or story. Select the key words that students need to know to understand the story. If there are relatively few key words (two to three), also select difficult words that may not be essential to understanding the story but would enhance students' vocabulary.
2.  Consider if there are ways in which the words could be grouped together. Grouping can be based on several types of linkages the words have in common. For example, if the unit is on manufacturing, all of the key words that relate to the production of goods can be grouped together. If the reading is a narrative story, all of the words that describe the characters in the story can be grouped together.
3.  Read the words aloud to students and show them the word groupings. Ask them to tell you why the words go together in a group. Support students' responses by extending and linking their ideas with the word meanings and their connection to text.
4.  Now ask students to work with a partner and to brainstorm key words or associations that describe or inform the vocabulary words selected.
5.  Ask students to share their words and associations. Be sure to clarify if students are providing information that is not related to the word or is misleading.

Most teachers are interested in determining whether students are learning many of the key words they teach. There are many occasions, though, when educators need to know more information about students' vocabularies, and they need to better understand whether students' vocabulary problems are small or large. The best way to understand the relative performance of a student's vocabulary is to know how it compares to same-age or same-grade students on a standardized measure of vocabulary.

Are there standardized vocabulary measures? Yes, teachers can administer standardized tests of vocabulary that provide information on the relative standing of a student compared to classmates. These measures are often individually administered; however, there are several group-administered vocabulary measures as well.

## WHAT ARE THE BEST PRACTICES
## FOR PROMOTING VOCABULARY ACQUISITION?

Whereas teachers may include some sort of vocabulary instruction across subject areas, the challenge is to provide meaningful learning opportunities so that students can go further than only recalling word meanings for a weekly test, to develop a deep understanding of words that enables them to apply their understanding across contexts. Just to keep up with their peers, *students need to learn between 2,000 and 4,000 new words per year* (Graves, 2004)—that is, approximately 40–50 new words each week! And it takes about 12 encounters with a word to know it well enough to improve reading comprehension. Further, research shows this number can have large amounts of variation depending on the individual and factors regarding the exposure (McKeown et al., 1985; Uchihara et al., 2019). "Vocabulary knowledge seems to grow gradually, moving from the first meaningful exposure to a word to a full and flexible knowledge" (Stahl, 2003, p. 19). With this teaching challenge in mind, teachers need to provide a range of experiences with new vocabulary so that students can learn new words in meaningful ways. Ten key practices for promoting vocabulary learning for students are described in Figure 3.1.

Should vocabulary instruction be different for students with disabilities, or are all strategies equally effective? Although many strategies are effective for students with varying abilities, a review of the small body of literature on teaching vocabulary to students with disabilities highlights several strategies (Solis et al., 2012; Wright & Cervetti, 2017). Strategies that yielded positive results include:

- Mnemonic or key word strategies that provide phonetic or imagery links to target words.
- Direct instruction of word meanings (e.g., providing definitions, giving synonyms) with ongoing practice.
- Concept enhancement procedures that assist students in making cognitive connections (e.g., semantic or concept mapping).

In general, regular instruction (several times weekly) was provided for short periods of time, indicating that teachers do not need to devote large portions of

- Teachers provide a language-rich classroom environment by intentionally and regularly using academic vocabulary and supporting students' use of academic vocabulary.
- Teachers identify academic vocabulary to teach and use in their daily instruction.
- Teachers introduce academic words in context by giving brief student-friendly definitions and clear examples.
- Students are given multiple opportunities to encounter and use academic vocabulary in natural contexts through listening, reading, speaking, and writing.
- Teachers help students to understand associations between words.
- Students learn a variety of word-learning strategies to independently identify the meaning of new words.
- When learning new words, students are made aware of both orthographic and phonological characteristics.
- Teachers create a classroom environment that supports word consciousness.
- Teachers regularly assess students' targeted vocabulary knowledge.
- Students engage in regular and wide reading across a variety of topics and genres.

**FIGURE 3.1.** Ten key practices for promoting vocabulary learning. From Meadows Center for Preventing Educational Risk (2020).

instructional time to teaching vocabulary to students with LD. In addition, the most effective strategies included some sort of manipulation of the vocabulary words that encouraged students to actively engage with words and word meanings and provided structured time to practice. Therefore, vocabulary instruction for students with LD should not be limited to one strategy but should combine methods (e.g., direct instruction and mnemonic devices) to maximize word learning. Furthermore, as with any instruction, the type of vocabulary strategy should reflect teaching goals (Jitendra et al., 2004). For example, direct instruction methods are most appropriate for introducing new vocabulary, whereas comprehension and generalization are promoted during concept enhancement activities.

Research on vocabulary instruction for students with a range of abilities supports the following components of instruction to promote the acquisition of new words (Graves, 2009). These are described in the following section, with strategies that have been studied with LD populations highlighted throughout.

- Selecting key words to teach
- Providing definitions that assist in word learning
- Using mnemonic or key word strategies
- Making the most of sentence writing
- Teaching students to monitor their understanding of difficult words
- Teaching words related to a theme or concept

### Selecting Key Words to Teach

With so many words to learn, one of the first questions teachers ask is how to select which words to teach. Perhaps the most frequent question teachers ask is how to determine what words are important? There are many sources of key vocabulary words, two of the most commonly used being the Cambridge English Vocabulary list and the Coxhead list.

The Cambridge English Vocabulary list provides a resource for teachers and parents of high-priority words students should know the meaning of (*www.cambridgeenglish.org/images/84669-pet-vocabulary-list.pdf*). Averil Coxhead developed a list of the most impactful academic words that permit students to access a range of content learning (Coxhead, 2000). The words were selected with inclusionary and exclusionary criteria, which limits the list to words that are used with frequency, across domains, and with uniformity of use. Words are excluded if they are assumed to be known (General Service list), if they have narrow usage, if they are proper nouns, or if they are Latin forms (Victoria University of Wellington, n.d.; *www.eapfoundation. com/vocab/academic/awllists*).

Consider an adult with a fully developed vocabulary. Beck et al. (2013) grouped a person's vocabulary into three tiers. Tier One consists of commonly used and understood words such as *person, talk,* and *begin.* These are words that students encounter frequently, so there is usually no need to "teach" them at school. However, even Tier One words will be unknown to some students (e.g., students with disabilities or ELs). Teachers cannot assume that all students are familiar with Tier One words and should use assessment procedures to verify how to select the types of words that need to be taught directly.

Tier Two consists of words that are integral to a mature adult vocabulary because they are used with some frequency across contexts. Stahl and Stahl (2004) refer to these as "Goldilocks" words because they are not too difficult or too easy, but just right. However, these words are used more in written text than in spoken language and are thus likely to be unfamiliar to students. Examples of Tier Two words are *prominent, conscientious, beguile,* and *belligerent.* Tier Two words often need to be addressed through instruction. Tier Three contains words that are domain-specific with a low frequency in terms of general use. It usually makes sense to learn these words only when they need to be applied in specific contexts. For example, although scientists require a deep and varied understanding of the word *genotype,* for most people it would be appropriate to learn what a genotype is during a science unit on genetics, and the application in that domain would be sufficient.

Another way to consider the important words to teach is to consider those words that might be identified as "academic vocabulary." Academic vocabulary refers to words that are relatively common and important in specific fields (e.g., engineering) but are less common in other kinds of texts (Hyland & Tse, 2007). For example, a word like *analyze* has specific meaning and importance in both math and science but would not otherwise be considered a high-frequency word. There are many words, like *function* and *design,* that have very specific meanings in certain content areas and these meanings are important to learn. It might be useful to consider the key words in social studies (e.g., *justice*), science (e.g., *method*), and math (e.g., *variable*) and decide in which grade these key words will be taught. The academic word list developed by Coxhead (2000) provides a list of the most important and useful academic words.

Once you have selected the key words that students need to know from literature or content-area curriculum, there are many ways to teach them. However, although it may be practical to teach the same words to all students, a review of vocabulary instruction techniques suggests that word lists should be personalized. Teachers often create a core list of key words to teach and then individualize the list to meet individual student needs by adding words or emphasizing fewer words. Some of the practices that have been supported by research are discussed below.

### Providing Definitions That Assist in Learning Word Meanings

Learning the meaning of new words creates interest—and occasionally excitement. We enjoy learning new big words and using them. The breakfast was *scrumptious* is so much more fun to say than the breakfast was *good*. Finding ways to make learning new words fun throughout the day is a valuable way to increase vocabulary knowledge and to engage students in the lifelong adventure of learning and using new words.

You can provide meaningful explanations of new words with multiple examples that are scaffolded, as noted in the following sequence:

1. Present the word in the context of the text source from which the word was selected.
2. Provide a *student-friendly explanation* of the word by (a) describing it in everyday language that is understandable to your students; (b) using connected language to describe the word in different situations, not single words or short phrases (that lack context and are difficult to remember); and (c) including references to "you," "something," and "someone" to help students make a connection with the new word and their own lives.
3. Ask students to connect the new word with their own examples. For example, when teaching the word *eager,* ask students to "tell about something you would be *eager* to do." You may have to ask further questions to guide students to come up with an example that is different from the context in the text or that given by you.
4. Students are asked to say, read, and write the word in multiple contexts. Students are more likely to remember the word's meaning if they use the word in other contexts.

Really knowing and understanding a new word requires frequent and continued exposure by hearing others use it, seeing it in print, and using it yourself. Most students will require ongoing exposure to and use of new words to assure that they understand and retain the meaning and use of the words.

Other suggestions that have had positive results include presenting or creating synonyms or antonyms for the key word that are familiar to students. Similarly, providing examples and nonexamples can help enrich understanding, as students try to hone in on a word's meaning in different contexts. One technique is to give students two similar sentences that describe a key word, one that is an example of its definition and one that is not (Beck et al., 2013). In the following illustration, students are presented with an example and a nonexample of the meaning of the word *encourage.*

EXAMPLE

Before going up to bat, Joey's teammates tell him he's a great player and that he'll get a hit.

NONEXAMPLE

Joey's teammates tell him to get a hit this time or else they will lose the game.

If students are using dictionaries or other sources that provide a definition (e.g., sidebars in science or social studies textbooks often provide definitions of key terms), rewriting definitions in their own words can also be helpful. Once they have a working definition of the word, students can then provide examples of it with prompts such as "Tell about a time when you *encouraged* someone" or "What are some things that you could say to *encourage* someone who is feeling frustrated?" The initial activities in which students engage when learning new words are important because they have the potential to peak a student's interest (or not) and lay the groundwork for learning the sometimes complex and varied meanings of words.

## Using Mnemonic or Key Word Strategies

Mnemonic or key word strategies assist students in remembering the meaning of new words. Students benefit from connections created by linking a familiar key word or image with a novel word (Bryant et al., 2003; Jitendra et al., 2004; Kame'enui & Baumann, 2012). Although mnemonics can be used for a variety of memory tasks, we highlight a mnemonic practice described by Mastropieri and Scruggs (1998) that specifically promotes vocabulary acquisition. In this strategy an association is created between a new word (e.g., *trespass*) and a familiar but unrelated word (e.g., *tiger*). In this case, the teacher created an image of a tiger entering a schoolyard and showed it to the class.

TEACHER: What is the key word for *trespass*?

STUDENT: *Tiger.*

TEACHER: Yes, *tiger* is the key word for *trespass*, and *trespass* means entering a place you are not supposed to enter. Here is a picture of a *tiger trespassing* in a schoolyard. A *tiger* is not supposed to enter a schoolyard. So when you think of the word *trespass*, think of a *tiger* and remember the picture of the *tiger trespassing* in the schoolyard.

It is important to note that both teacher-created and student-created mnemonic images are effective for learning the definitions of new words. However, when students create the images, it takes more time and requires careful monitoring and feedback (Scruggs et al., 2010).

## Making the Most of Sentence Writing

Teachers frequently ask students to write a sentence using a newly learned word.

• Engage students actively in writing these sentences, encouraging them to manipulate new words to increase their understanding and retention.

● Discuss the sentences students create using key vocabulary words by comparing the meaning in different sentences and the types of sentences that are the most useful for word learning. Students can then select which sentence helps them remember the word and record that example sentence in their notes. Take the word *ripe*, for example. As you can see from the list of sentences below, sentences 1, 2, and 3 include varying meanings of *ripe*, whereas the fourth sentence is not acceptable because it does not contain enough information to glean the meaning of the word.

1. If you pick the banana from the tree before it is ripe, it will be green and taste terrible.
2. The old woman lived to the ripe age of 95.
3. After studying all week, the students were ripe to take the math test.
4. The peach is ripe.

● Have students use more than one new word in a sentence. In this way, students can connect new words with each other and challenge themselves to use them accurately in a similar context. Students also enjoy creating stories around a group of key words and then sharing how the same words can result in such different stories.

● Have students create fill-in-the-blank activities with new words. Students can create five sentences with five new words and then have peers "do" their activity. If definitions are not clear, students can work together to create sentences that provide a better explanation. Giving feedback about correct usage and acceptable sentences that facilitate understanding is part of the process during any sentence- or story-writing activity.

### Teaching Students to Monitor Their Understanding of Difficult Words

Some of your students may be so accustomed to reading words that they do not know, they gloss over them, not pausing or wondering what the word means. They may fail to recognize that they do not understand words or concepts as they read. Students can learn to identify difficult words, sometimes called "clunks," as they read and then use "fix-up" strategies to repair their understanding (Klingner, Vaughn, et al., 2012). Fix-up strategies cue students to use word-level skills (e.g., break the word apart and look for smaller words you know) or context clues (e.g., read the sentence without the clunk and see what word makes sense) to assist them in figuring out the meanings of words during reading. Students use fix-up strategies to gain enough information to repair understanding while reading. However, to assist students in gaining a deeper knowledge of important words, teachers must provide additional instruction and practice opportunities. To learn more about using fix-up strategies, the section on collaborative strategic reading (CSR) in Chapter 9 and see the lesson plans in the Appendix.

In addition to reading, students can learn to monitor their understanding of words or concepts as they listen. For example, announcers or characters on television may use words that students don't understand. Teachers can encourage students to keep track of these words to develop their "word consciousness," and to bring the unknown words to class to discuss. Furthermore, teachers can introduce new words into their oral vocabulary that students then acquire. Rather than saying "use a quiet voice," the teacher can say, "suppress your voices." Introducing new words each day and week will increase everyone's vocabulary.

## Teaching New Words around a Theme or Concept

Creating concept representations of word meanings assists students in making connections between new words, their existing knowledge, and the concepts being taught in school. For students with LD, these concept enhancement strategies are more effective for learning new words and remembering them in the future than direct instruction alone or other more traditional strategies such as finding dictionary definitions (Jitendra et al., 2004). Among the many instructional practices used to develop conceptual representations of new words, we discuss clarifying tables, semantic maps, concept maps, and Venn diagrams.

- Clarifying tables (Ellis & Farmer, 2005) help students organize information about important vocabulary and keep track of the words they have learned (e.g., in a notebook of important words). Teachers may present a word that students will encounter in their reading or content learning and then complete the clarifying table with students after the word has been encountered. In the following example, the word *mockery* was integral to understanding the character of Mrs. May in *The Borrowers Afloat* by Mary Norton, a book selected by students in a classroom book club. Figure 3.2 is an example of the clarifying table created by the fourth-grade students and their teacher to help them learn and remember the meaning of *mockery*.

- Semantic maps are used to help students learn important words and to make connections with related key words or ideas. Semantic maps are often created as webs with linkages designated by connecting lines. The teacher may lead a semantic mapping activity prior to reading to introduce key terms, activate prior knowledge, and as a preassessment. Alternatively, semantic maps may also be used after reading to summarize and review key terms and ideas and to informally assess student understanding. Figure 3.3 shows a semantic map created after reading a chapter on Egypt. Semantic maps represent many key terms and ideas and allow students to see how the ideas are related to one another.

- If the instructional goal is to define or clarify the meaning of a key concept, teachers may elect to use a concept map. Similar to clarifying tables or semantic maps, concept maps are visual representations of the relationship between the terms

| Term: Mockery | | |
|---|---|---|
| **Definition:** imitation or joking to insult or be mean (noun) | | |
| **Text example:**<br>Mr. Beguid was always a bit worried that Mrs. May would make a mockery of something he said. | **Clarifiers:**<br>• Caricature<br>• Farce<br>• Mean joking<br>• Making fun of | **Real-life examples:**<br>• *Saturday Night Live* skits about the president<br>• Imitating someone's gestures<br>• Making fun of the style of a famous musician<br>• Dressing up like a "washed-up" movie star for Halloween |
| **Don't confuse it with:**<br>Tribute—paying respect to or honoring another person | | |
| **Example sentence:** The new teacher was insulted by the students' mockery of her Southern accent. | | |

**FIGURE 3.2.** Clarifying table.

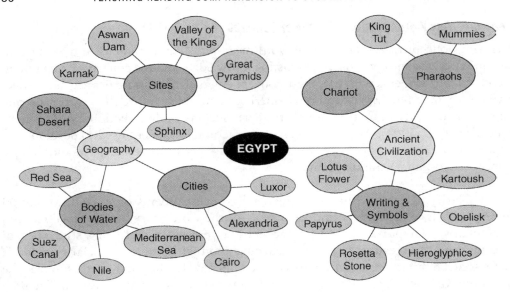

**FIGURE 3.3.** Example of a semantic map.

associated with a particular concept (e.g., body parts, oceans, migration). Through group discussion, concepts that encourage students to share individual expertise are developed. For example, in developing the concept of *seasons,* one student may have knowledge of the seasons (fall, winter, spring, summer), whereas another student may understand a bit about the earth's rotation around the sun. The process of establishing associations between related vocabulary terms is particularly useful for students with a limited vocabulary or understanding of the concept; these students need assistance to make connections and deepen their understanding. There are many ways to create concept maps. In one study, a teacher and her students created a concept map around the concept of racism (Scott & Nagy, 2004). The group discussed racism and the ways to visually represent it. The teacher also added key terms related to understanding the concept of racism. Students then created their own posters that represented their ideas about racism, using the vocabulary terms identified in the original mapping activity.

In general, the steps for concept mapping are as follows:

1. Select a key concept.
2. Display the key concept and ask students to brainstorm words that relate to the concept.
3. Generate categories around words and create the map.
4. Continue to use the concept map by leading discussions that identify varied meanings and uses of key words, expand themes, and draw conclusions. Students can also extend the use of concept maps by completing projects such as the racism posters discussed above, using them as a study guide for tests or as a reference when learning new concepts.

For younger children, it is often helpful to provide headings to guide the development of categories in a concept map. For example, heading guides for the concept *weather* might include *precipitation, measurement,* and *patterns.* Older students may be more adept at brainstorming terms and then classifying them into categories with the help of the teacher. Figure 3.4 gives an example of a concept map created for the term *arachnid.*

• Methods for comparing and contrasting provide another way to extend understanding of key vocabulary around a theme or concept. Students can create Venn diagrams that compare and contrast two or more concepts. See Figure 3.5 for an example of a Venn diagram using the terms *cruelty* and *oppression.*

Concept maps, Venn diagrams, and other concept representations are widely used in classrooms to frame student understanding of a variety of curricular objectives. However, in terms of vocabulary instruction the focus is on developing an understanding of the key words associated with these important concepts. For example, a Venn diagram might be used to compare and contrast two novels that students have read on colonial America. A different Venn diagram or other concept representation (or possibly the same one) might be created to highlight and discuss specific terms associated with colonial America and the study of history, in general, that are essential to student understanding.

### Teaching Strategies for Independent Word Learning

Most of the new word meanings we learn are acquired independently—reading and listening. We can model independent word-learning practices for our students, using such techniques as: (1) efficient use of dictionaries, thesauri, and online word

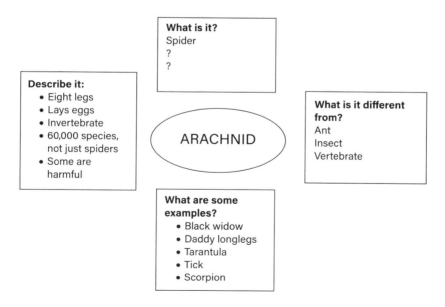

**FIGURE 3.4.** Partially completed concept map. Students originally thought that an *arachnid* was a spider. After they completed an introductory reading, the map was expanded to include other species (e.g., tick, daddy longlegs, scorpion) with more detailed information on each. From there, the class divided into groups and each selected a species to research further.

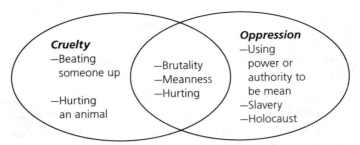

**FIGURE 3.5.** Venn diagram: *cruelty* versus *oppression*.

resources; (2) analyzing word parts (prefixes, suffixes, roots, and compounds); and (3) using context clues to identify the meaning of unknown words. Each of these word-learning strategies is discussed separately.

### Efficient Use of Resources

The critical word in using resources to support word meaning is *efficient*. We know that looking up a new vocabulary word in the dictionary and then writing its meaning is a common, but often misused, classroom practice. The dictionary is of no use if it does not assist a student in understanding what a word means. Teaching students how to understand the abbreviations, italics, and common format of dictionary definitions, having a variety of dictionaries on hand at different levels, and allowing students to create their own dictionaries of new words with definitions, parts of speech, and sample sentences may help them learn to use this valuable tool. Likewise, using a thesaurus to find words that are synonyms and antonyms of vocabulary words, or even using internet resources, can be valuable activities when students are provided with instruction on how to find and use information specific to the source.

### Word Analysis Skills

There is growing support for the use of morphemic or word analysis skills in word learning. For example, in one study fifth graders at varying skill levels were taught word analysis skills that increased their word learning in social studies (Baumann et al., 2003). However, the authors of this study caution that because this skill only transfers to novel words that contain the specific affixes that have been taught, it should be used as one of several strategies that students are taught to use when they come upon a word they do not know. Instruction involves teaching word-part meanings and skills for breaking apart words and putting the pieces together to come up with meanings of unknown words.

Of the various components of words to analyze, prefixes are perhaps the most worthwhile to teach because although they are present in a large number of words, there are relatively few to teach and learn, their spelling is fairly consistent, and they are always found at the beginning of a word. In fact, 20 prefixes account for 97% of words with prefixes in English (White et al., 1989). For example, the prefix *dis-* means "apart" or "not"; *dis*respect means "not respected." There are a few drawbacks to prefixes as well. First, some words begin with prefix spellings that are not used as prefixes. For example, *pre* means *before* in the word *predetermined* but not in the word *present*. Or, *re* means *again* in *repeat*, but not in *resent*. Also, some word roots have a different meaning without the prefix, so having knowledge of the prefix still does not assist the reader in understanding the unknown word. This is the case in the word *invert* in which the Latin root *vert,* meaning to turn, is of little help unless you are familiar with Latin. Though not the only part of word analysis skills, prefixes are a logical place to start. See Figure 3.6 for a list of commonly used prefixes.

### Context Clues

How often have you said to your students, "reread the sentence and see if you can figure out what the word means"? When you provide that guidance, you are asking your students to use context clues to figure out the meaning of a word by relating it to the text that surrounds it. The clues can be examples, contrasts, definitions, or restatements that provide some information about a word's meaning. Teaching students to successfully use context clues is a process that requires careful modeling, scaffolding, and a great deal of practice, especially for struggling readers. Effective use of context clues involves making connections between the known meaning of the text and the unknown word. For example, in CSR (described in more detail in Chapter 9) students are taught to employ such techniques as rereading the sentence and looking for clues or rereading the sentence before and after the unknown word, again looking for clues (Klingner, Vaughn, et al., 2012).

While context clues can be useful, particularly when you know something about the word, the understanding gained from a context clue is likely to be low on the "word

| Prefix | Definition | Example |
|---|---|---|
| *dis-* | not, opposite of | *disable, disrespectful* |
| *en-, em-* | cause to | *entrust, embody* |
| *in-, im-, ir-, ill-* | not | *incomplete, imperfect, irresistible, illegal* |
| *inter-* | between | *interstate, international* |
| *mid-* | middle | *midsection* |
| *mis-* | wrongly | *misrepresent, misguide* |
| *over-* | too much | *overuse, overspend* |
| *pre-* | before | *premature, prehistoric* |
| *re-* | again | *return, reinvent* |
| *semi-* | half | *semifinal, semicolon* |
| *sub-* | under | *subway, submarine* |
| *trans-* | across | *transatlantic, transportation* |
| *un-* | not, opposite of | *unwind, uncommon* |

**FIGURE 3.6.** Common prefixes.

knowing" continuum discussed earlier and will require additional and varied experiences to gain a deeper understanding of the new word. Here is another strategy that has improved students' ability to use context clues to find the meaning of unknown words (Beck et al., 2013). Over time, students go from teacher-led discussions to internalizing this strategy when they come across unknown words in their reading. Consider the following passage containing the unknown word *unsatisfactory*.

> First, Maggie missed the school bus and then she ripped a hole in her new tights when she fell off the swing at recess. Later, as she went to line up for lunch, she realized she had left her lunchbox on the kitchen table. It was not even noon, but already Maggie considered the day **unsatisfactory** in every respect.

Now apply the following steps to enact this word-learning strategy:

1. *Read and paraphrase.* The teacher or student reads the passage with the unknown word (target passage) and then restates the passage. Initially, the teacher paraphrases the passage, but students should take over this step as they become more familiar with the strategy.

2. *Establish the context.* Students are taught to ask and answer questions such as "What is going on?" or "What is this passage about?" Again, when students are first learning this step, the teacher guides the questioning and probes responses until the student is able to correctly describe the context.

3. *Initial identification and support.* The student is asked to state what the word could mean and to provide support from the context for their choice. "What do you think *unsatisfactory* might mean?" The teacher asks probing questions such as "Why do you think that?" You may have to restate the context and then ask again for possible word meanings.

4. *Other options.* In this step, the student is asked to generate other plausible word meanings and to defend their choices. Students are encouraged to consider several options because there isn't always one correct word meaning. Students are asked, "What else might *unsatisfactory* mean?" and then, "Can you think of any other meanings?"

5. *Summarize.* In the final step, the student is asked to put all of the information together. In this way, the student learns to reflect on the contextual information that might be used to find the meaning of an unknown word. Consider the following summary conversation.

TEACHER: So what might *unsatisfactory* mean?

STUDENT: Maggie had a bad day.

TEACHER: *Unsatisfactory* means bad day?

STUDENT: She thought it was bad or terrible—at least, not like how things are supposed to be because she got hurt and missed her bus and stuff.

TEACHER: So *unsatisfactory* might mean bad or terrible or not like how things are supposed to be. You're right. *Unsatisfactory* means not acceptable or "not like how things are supposed to be." Maggie felt that her day was unsatisfactory or unacceptable because of all of the bad things that happened to her.

In the final step, the student is also encouraged to recognize when contextual information does not provide clues to word meanings and to try another strategy when that is the case. For example, the following passage does not provide useful information about the meaning of the word *conspicuous*.

> It was late afternoon. There was no reason to think that she was conspicuous as she walked along the sidewalk. She took a key from her pocket and unlocked the door.

The independent use of strategies such as using a dictionary, word parts, or context clues requires *both* recognizing that a word is unknown *and* the knowledge of specific practices that could be used to help find its meaning. To make the most of these practices, helping students monitor their reading and listening for words and concepts they don't understand is an important first step. After students' proficiency in monitoring understanding is improved, then teaching them tools for acquiring understanding of these words and concepts is useful. Even with these necessary practices, the most important way vocabulary is acquired is through multiple exposures. Exposure to a word and its meaning in one setting is rarely adequate to acquire understanding and use. Thus, effective vocabulary instruction involves continued use and review of target words.

### Giving Students the Opportunity to Read a Variety of Texts

Although the number of words that students need to learn may seem daunting, promoting student engagement with text is a pleasurable and important way to increase word learning, and more important, leads to increased comprehension of what students read. Put simply, the amount that students read is related to the number of words they know and, in turn, allows them to read and understand increasingly complex text. For young children, teachers can read to students from texts that are selected based on their interest level, concepts, and vocabulary. Read-alouds are followed by engaging students in discussion that fosters understanding of the content of what was read, helps students make connections to background knowledge, supports the development or expansion of target concepts, and increases the acquisition of new vocabulary words. Remember that students enjoy and learn from read-alouds on various topics; teachers need not overrely on fiction (Hirsch, 2003) when reading to students. Magazine or newspaper articles, technical books, and other nonfiction resources are especially valuable in promoting vocabulary development, especially when several different resources are read on one theme or concept. Storybook reading (Giroir et al., 2015; Hickman et al., 2004 ; Wright, 2019) is a technique that uses read-alouds specifically to build vocabulary. Storybook reading can also be used with older students who are unable to read the selected books or passages independently. Additionally, storybook reading has been shown to help develop skills in topics across domains separate from literacy, such as mathematical concepts (McGuire et al., 2020). In applying this strategy, consider the following steps:

1. Choose a high-interest book that contains key vocabulary or concepts. You may want to select a short passage or read just a few pages each day, depending on the length of the book.
2. Before reading, select a few difficult words and give simple definitions using familiar language. Write down the words and definitions (e.g., *flee: to run away*).
3. During reading, tell students to listen for the vocabulary words (or to look for the key vocabulary if they are reading) and encourage them to use clues in the story to find out what the words mean.
4. After reading, engage students in a discussion about the story and the key words. Ask questions to help students *explain* and *describe* what has been read. Encourage students to describe how the key words were used and how they fit into core ideas of the text. You may also ask students to use the new vocabulary to summarize or retell the story or passage.

Parents may be interested in how to engage their children in interactive read-alouds using similar practices to those used in the classroom. The Meadows Center for Preventing Educational Risk provides a read-aloud practice in English and Spanish that parents can readily use to engage their children in vocabulary building (*https://meadowscenter.org/library/resource/la-lectura-interactiva-en-el-hogar*).

Providing rich and varied reading experiences around key concepts increases the acquisition of new vocabulary words as well as the "world knowledge" that is needed to connect the words with the text in order to improve reading comprehension. Consider the following resource from the Meadows Center for building vocabulary in upper elementary students through book reading: *https://meadowscenter.org/files/resources/TextTalks-Flipbook_WEB.pdf*.

### Increasing Students' Knowledge of, and Interest in, Words

Throughout this chapter we have provided examples of activities that allow students to actively engage in word learning—to play with words, to think about words, and to become interested in words and their many and varied uses. This notion of developing *word consciousness* is supported by research (e.g., Anderson & Nagy, 1992; Beck & McKeown, 1983; Scott & Nagy, 2004; Cox et al., 2015) and occurs through meaningful vocabulary activities.

Language play is another way to increase students' interest in words and to facilitate the production and understanding of language. Teachers and students can create all sorts of games, including memory games, crossword puzzles, codes, word scrambles, guessing games, bingo, charades, tongue twisters, alliteration, letter games, and categories that challenge students to play with, discover, and remember words and to develop an appreciation for how they are used. The following list divides word play into seven categories that provide a springboard for a multitude of word games (adapted from Johnson et al., 2004):

- *Onomastics* is the study of names. Students are encouraged to think about names, their origins, why certain names are given (*Maple Street*, a dog named *Woof,* a cat named *Princess*), and to look at the meaning of, and play on, words that are common in names (*Comeback Inn, Four Eyes*).
- *Expressions* include idioms (*hang on*), proverbs (*Don't count your chickens before they've hatched*), slang (*decked out*), catchphrases (*24/7*), and slogans.
- *Figures of speech* are words that are not used literally but suggest another meaning. Examples include similes (*as big as a whale*), metaphors (*the rainbow is beauty*), hyperbole (*I cried a thousand tears*), euphemisms ("temporarily displaced"—*stolen*), and oxymorons (*cruel kindness*).
- *Word associations* are recognized ways to connect words to each other, such as synonyms (*ugly, unattractive*), antonyms (*huge, tiny*), homographs (*desert, desert*), and homophones (*plane, plain*).
- *Word formations* include acronyms (*USDA*), compounds (*backyard*), and affixes (*neo-, -ing*).
- *Word manipulations* play with letters and include anagrams, or rearranging the letters in a word to make a new word (*mane, name*), palindromes, or words or phrases that read the same backward and forward (*bird rib*), and rebuses, or using pictures to represent parts or words of phrases (I ⌒ U).
- *Ambiguities* are words, phrases, or sentences that are open to more than one interpretation (*Robber gets 6 months in violin case*).

Idioms are used prevalently in English and can be challenging to understand, particularly when acquiring English as an additional language. Idioms are complicated because they represent a set of words that convey meaning that is different from the literal meaning of the words. When we say it is "raining cats and dogs," we do not mean that anyone should expect to look up and see a cat or dog falling from the sky. Instead we mean that it is raining very hard. Likewise "blowing hot and cold" does not refer to the wind or to someone actually blowing but instead to someone behaving inconsistently at different times. Consider identifying common idioms, using them, and checking your students' understanding.

## CONCLUSION

Understanding words in all their complexity is an essential part of comprehending text. As students encounter more challenging words and concepts, assisting them in understanding and learning from text requires effective practices for teaching vocabulary. Students who are "word conscious"—that is, they pay attention to words they don't know and strive to learn more about those words—are likely to reap the benefits of improved word and concept knowledge. Perhaps the most important outcome of improved vocabulary is improved comprehension.

## APPENDIX 3.1. VOCABULARY ASSESSMENT WITHIN SOCIAL STUDIES INSTRUCTION

**DIRECTIONS: Read each question and circle the best answer.**

1  Which colonial region was characterized as having a plantation system, low population density, and long growing seasons?
   A  Southern region
   B  Middle region
   C  New England region
   D  Western region

2  A colony can best be described as—
   A  an isolated settlement
   B  a group of people living in the New World
   C  land controlled by a distant or foreign nation
   D  land that is independently controlled by its settlers

3  Another word for tolerance is—
   A  acceptance
   B  prejudice
   C  bias
   D  kindness

4  One who disagrees with established beliefs or majority opinion is a—
   A  dissenter
   B  loyalist
   C  conformist
   D  traitor

5  A representative government is a government that—
   A  includes all of its citizens as representatives of their interests and concerns
   B  uses representatives to vote for its citizens
   C  represents its interests and concerns to its citizens
   D  is chosen by citizens and promises to represent citizens' interests and concerns

6  Money that the government collects in the form of taxes, fines, or fees is called—
   A  profits
   B  revenue
   C  proceeds
   D  debts

7  An army composed of ordinary citizens rather than professional soldiers is called—
   A  a fleet
   B  a militia

From *Promoting Adolescent Comprehension of Text* (PACT; *www.meadowscenter.org*). Developed with funding from the Institute of Education Sciences to Sharon Vaughn (Principal Investigator), Reading for Understanding.

C   an army

D   a military

8   Another word for treason is—

A   betrayal

B   loyalty

C   honor

D   opposition

9   A boycott occurs when—

A   people make a contract to buy goods from some person or organization

B   people work in exchange for goods for some person or organization

C   people refuse to buy goods from some person or organization

D   someone buys goods for some other person or organization

10   In colonial America, the idea that the people would rule instead of a king was known as—

A   democracy

B   pacifism

C   independence

D   republicanism

11   Which of the following is the definition of a mercenary?

A   A soldier who serves in the army

B   A soldier from another country who serves in the army

C   A paid soldier who serves in the army

D   A captured soldier from another army

12   Guerrilla warfare can be described as—

A   an ancient technique used in fighting war

B   a hit-and-run technique used in fighting war

C   an open-field battle technique used in fighting war

D   a siege technique used in fighting war

13   Patriots can be best described as American colonists who—

A   were determined to fight the British for American independence

B   joined the British army

C   were captured by the British army

D   served in the First Continental Congress

14   People who believed in British rule over the American colonies and were against the war for independence were called—

A   colonists

B   loyalists

C   royalists

D   red coats

# CHAPTER FOUR

# Instructional Practices That Promote Reading Comprehension

STUDY GROUP PROMPTS

1. Before reading this chapter, discuss the ways you support students to understand what they read before, during, and after reading. Are there strategies that have been especially beneficial for students who struggle to understand and remember what they read? Are there strategies that are not as effective as you would like them to be?

2. As you read the chapter, make note of strategies that you might like to implement. Consider when you would use these strategies and with what types of texts.

3. After reading, select one new strategy that you and another colleague will implement. Create a plan that includes how you will (a) integrate the strategy into your reading program, (b) introduce it to your students, and (c) monitor student progress. Be sure to schedule times to check in and share ideas.

You might have participated in discussions about how best to improve reading comprehension. Should teachers focus on word reading or on building word and world knowledge, or should the focus be on teaching reading comprehension strategies? Does instruction in reading comprehension strategies take time away from content learning or knowledge building, particularly as students get older? Do teachers tend to overemphasize isolated reading strategies as the goal rather than using strategies to support text comprehension and content learning? Duke et al. (2021) reminded us that teaching reading comprehension strategies is supported by years of research and can be effectively embedded in rich content learning activities. Further, teaching reading strategies doesn't mean teachers don't also emphasize other components of reading, such as teaching decoding and building fluency. This chapter focuses on effective ways to teach students to use comprehension strategies before, during, and after reading to assist them in understanding and remembering what they read.

Most of the time, mature readers monitor comprehension unconsciously, or at least so seamlessly that they are not always aware that they are using self-thinking, questioning, and monitoring, which are often referred to as metacognitive strategies. A good way for very experienced readers to check their comprehension strategies is by reading unfamiliar text. Consider the strategies you use while reading the following passage.

> In addition to reducing the concentration of bacteria and suspended particles in the treatment process, protozoa are also biotic indicators. The presence of protozoa reflects an improvement in effluent quality and is essential for the production of good quality effluent. (Lee et al., 2004, p. 371)

When we encounter difficult text, even good readers make explicit use of strategies. How did you approach this passage? Did you find yourself rereading elements of the text? Did you wonder about the meaning of some of the vocabulary words, such as *effluent* and *biotic?* Our guess is that most of us without a science background would have found it useful to link our understanding of similar topics to information in this passage. If this topic were unfamiliar, it might help to know that the key idea of this paragraph, and those that follow, is that microorganisms present in wastewater treatment plants are responsible for water quality. Also, we often talk about how important it is to have a "purpose" for reading. Would you have benefited from a purpose for reading this text? Reading unfamiliar text with unknown words or ideas is facilitated when the reader is equipped with effective reading strategies as well as opportunities to ask questions and interact with others. In this chapter we review what we know about reading comprehension instruction and what teachers can do to successfully improve the reading comprehension of their students with LD and other students who struggle to make sense of what they read. We do not provide a listing of every reading strategy, but rather, we focus on several exemplary practices whose effectiveness was supported by research.

## INSTRUCTIONAL PRACTICES IN READING COMPREHENSION FOR STUDENTS WITH LD

Students with LD and other reading difficulties are less able to attend to important information when reading text than their peers who are stronger readers are (Cerdán et al., 2011). As a result, students with LD often feel frustrated and unsuccessful, and tend to disengage or rush through the reading process (e.g., Fogarty et al., 2017; Kim et al., 2017; Wanzek et al., 2017). What instructional practices can teachers use to improve the reading comprehension of struggling readers? First consider the skills identified in Chapter 1 that are associated with improved reading comprehension: word study, fluency, vocabulary, and world knowledge. Reading comprehension is supported by integrating a variety of instructional practices into your teaching routines, including the reading comprehension strategies and skills presented in this chapter.

There are several valuable sources of information on effective instruction in reading comprehension. One source is a recent practice guide for educators focused on providing reading interventions for students in grades 4–9 (Vaughn et al., 2022). An expert panel of reading researchers reviewed contemporary research and shared evidence-based reading interventions that have been found to be effective for students with LD and reading difficulties (Vaughn et al., 2022). They concluded that the most powerful practices for improving text comprehension include:

1. Building world and word knowledge to support sense making (see Chapter 3)
2. Providing students with opportunities to ask and answer questions to facilitate understanding
3. Teaching students to monitor their understanding as they read
4. Teaching a routine for generating a main idea, or gist, of a short section of text

Within the guidelines above, Stevens and Austin (2022) highlight the importance of selecting a few strategies and using them over time with lots of opportunities to practice and receive feedback. It is also productive to incorporate two or three strategies into one lesson. Multicomponent strategies that integrate several skills are described in Chapter 9. Reading comprehension strategies are not isolated skills that can be confined to worksheets and isolated tasks. Rather, comprehension improves with "practices that support text processing, meaning the practices are implemented while students read and engage with text" (Stevens & Austin, 2022, p. 163). This authentic engagement can incorporate text-based discussions that support students to apply strategies and to work together to make sense of what they read.

The following suggestions are provided for introducing, practicing, and applying reading strategies:

1. Teachers provide explicit instruction, including demonstrating how to use the strategy and explaining what the strategy is, why it is important and when to use it.
2. Over time, as students build competence, the focus of instructional time shifts to students applying strategies on their own. Teachers focus on monitoring, providing feedback, and supporting students who require additional instruction.
3. Teachers can also transition relatively quickly to a more student-led collaborative process where students apply strategies in pairs or small groups (Vaughn et al., 2022).

Next we describe practices that can help students with LD and students with other reading difficulties to learn strategies, skills, and routines that have demonstrated effectiveness in improving reading comprehension.

## BEFORE READING

What can teachers do before reading text to enhance reading comprehension for students with significant reading comprehension difficulties? As you read about in

Chapter 3, teachers who spend even a few minutes linking students' background knowledge to the text they are about to read improve their students' understanding of that text (Cromley & Azevedo, 2007; Pressley, 2000b). For students who are familiar with the content of a passage, linking related background knowledge to text is relatively easy. On the other hand, students with learning difficulties may lack relevant prior knowledge, or they may fail to make connections between what they know and what they are learning. Connecting or building world knowledge is especially important for ELs, who may be less familiar with the instructional content (e.g., Goldenberg, 2011). It is important for teachers to create a context for students that facilitates comprehension by previewing the text and preteaching key concepts, ideas, and words, especially when reading expository text (Readence et al., 2012; Vaughn et al., 2013). This brief introduction to the text (usually 5 minutes or less) provides enough background for many students to prepare them for reading and learning from what they read. See Chapter 3 to learn about practices for connecting to what students already know, building world knowledge, and incorporating explicit vocabulary instruction into a prereading routine.

### Setting a Purpose

Reading is an activity that has a purpose. When you want to know how to change a flat tire on your bicycle, you might type into your internet search engine, "How to fix a flat bicycle tire" and then read a variety of sources to learn what you need to know. If you are researching the history of the computer, you might select an article or book that outlines the progression of computer use and its influence on society over time. If you are interested in adventure travels, you might read through a website about a person who toured the world in a hot-air balloon. Whether you are reading for enjoyment, to gain factual or procedural knowledge, or to learn skills, being aware of the purpose for reading is an essential first step.

But sorting out the purpose for engaging with a particular text can be a challenge. Blanton and colleagues (1990) suggest that for struggling readers, it is best to set one purpose for reading, as opposed to multiple purposes. Furthermore, the purpose should be broad enough to apply to an entire reading selection. Schunk (2003) also suggests providing students with a goal for reading, or a guide to the task that they will be asked to engage in after reading. In most cases, setting the purpose for reading involves simply stating *why* students are reading the selection. For example, before using a microscope for the first time, a teacher might want students to build background knowledge of what a microscope is and how it is used. A teacher might say:

> "Today we will be using a microscope for the first time. To introduce you to why microscopes are used, we will read about how scientists came to use microscopes to learn about things that are too small to see with just your eyes."

This short introduction to the reading guides students to read efficiently. They will be asked not to memorize or critique the text, but to acquire background knowledge that will prepare them for the activity of using a microscope to analyze scientific specimens. Achieving the goals set by the purpose for reading can help students build self-efficacy.

## Text Preview

Text preview is a technique that motivates students to read for understanding by providing a structure with which they can integrate prior knowledge with the ideas from a new text (Burns et al., 2011; Graves et al., 2001; Vaughn & Edmonds, 2006). Following are a few practices for text previewing that we found especially useful.

### Teacher-Presented Text Preview

This previewing method is prepared and presented by the teacher, who provides an organizational framework that assists students in bridging their experiences to the reading by (1) cuing them to the new reading, often by discussing an interesting or important part of the text, (2) providing the theme or organization of the text, and (3) presenting questions to guide the reading. Next we illustrate the three steps involved in a text preview with examples that relate to an expository reading from *The New York Times*, "How Many Ants Are There on Earth?" (Dzombak, 2022), that is part of a student science exploration around what sustains and harms ecosystems:

1. Read a short selection from the text or provide interesting information about the reading that piques students' interest. For example, "Did you know that there are 20 quadrillion ants on Earth?"
2. Give a brief description of the theme or story organization. For example, "This article explains why there are so many ants on Earth and how knowing about ants helps us understand how ecosystems work."
3. Ask questions to guide reading. For example, "What are some of the ways that ants help us learn about ecosystems?"

### Interactive Text Preview

Another format for previewing text is interactive. The teacher still leads the preview, but this form also involves discussion and input from students. One strategy is to create a K-W-L (what I already *know*, what I *want* to learn, what I *learned*) chart (Ogle, 1986, 1989). A K-W-L chart can be done as a whole group, in a small group, in partners, or as an individual activity. There are several versions of this activity; we provide a popular format below:

1. Give each student a copy of the reading material and the K-W-L chart.
2. Before reading, teach students to preview the passage by looking at such text features as headings and subheadings, pictures and captions, and words in bold or highlighted print.

3. Students then use a chart (either individually or as a whole class) to record "What I already know" about this topic in the first column of the chart and "What I want to learn" in the second column.

4. During reading, students write in the third column of the K-W-L chart, "What I learned," what they learned in the text related to what they already knew or wanted to learn.

5. After reading, revisit the chart as a wrap-up to reading. Lead students in a discussion in which they review what they already knew, how it was addressed in the reading, what they learned that was new, and what they still need to confirm or learn more about.

A confirmation guide is a variation on the traditional K-W-L chart (Texas Education Agency, 2001; see Figure 4.1). The purpose of the confirmation guide is to assist students in making explicit connections between prior knowledge and what they read. Similar to the K-W-L chart, students first preview the text and then write what they already know about the topic. The purpose of previewing the text prior to writing what they know about a topic is to assist students in grounding their prior knowledge in the specific text they will be reading. For example, during a general brainstorming session on whales, students are likely to provide a wide array of relevant and irrelevant information. However, after previewing a reading on endangered humpback whales, teachers can guide students to connect what they already know *as it relates to* endangered species and humpback whales. During reading, students provide information that confirms or rejects their prior knowledge statements. They provide evidence or "proof" of this information by including the page number where they read the information. Again, after reading, teachers lead a discussion of what was learned in the reading, how it connects to prior knowledge, and how the new information adds to, or changes, previous understandings about the topic.

| Name(s): | | |
|---|---|---|
| Topic: | | |
| Confirmation Guide | | |
| What I already know | What I learned | Pages |
| | | |
| | | |
| | | |
| | | |
| | | |

**FIGURE 4.1.** Confirmation guide. Adapted from Texas Education Agency (2001) and University of Texas Center for Reading and Language Arts (2001). Copyright © 2001 Texas Education Agency. Adapted by permission.

*Concept or Semantic Maps*

These visual representations are used to present key ideas and vocabulary and to make connections to previously learned material. One such strategy includes the following steps:

1. Tell students the theme or big idea of the text and identify key concepts or vocabulary. Write the big idea in the middle circle on an overhead or chalkboard.
2. Ask students to connect the big idea to what they already know about the topic. Organize big idea and prior knowledge statements given by students and draw connecting lines between them.
3. Use the concept map to identify and briefly address misconceptions; clarify ideas and connections.
4. Ask students to make predictions about what they will learn by looking at the title, headings, and pictures of the reading.

Although previewing activities are common among teachers, it may be helpful to consider the following guidelines:

- Prepare and lead previewing. In most cases, even when students collaborate in discussions, it is appropriate for teachers to direct the previewing activities. The teacher (1) provides links or facilitates student-provided connections that activate background knowledge, (2) intersperses "hooks" that motivate students, and (3) identifies key ideas and vocabulary.
- Keep it short; 5–10 minutes is usually sufficient. It is not necessary or recommended to teach the entire text before reading. Revisit the previewing activity after reading to assist in reviewing, summarizing, and making connections.

A few well-planned minutes of providing a purpose for reading, previewing, and building background knowledge will yield dividends in students' comprehension (Schunk, 2003).

## DURING AND AFTER READING

It can be difficult to separate reading strategies since, more often than not, the actions students take to make sense of what they read overlap. Below we discuss three interconnected types of strategies that can be utilized during and after reading. As recommended in the reading intervention guide (Vaughn et al., 2022), these include (1) teaching students to monitor their comprehension, (2) providing students with opportunities to ask and answer questions, and (3) teaching students to synthesize their understanding by stating the main idea and summarizing their understanding.

### Teach Students to Monitor Comprehension

The most important strategies for students to engage in while they are reading are those that assist them in monitoring their understanding (Joseph & Eveleigh, 2011). All of us can remember times when we were turning the pages, but we were not monitoring what we were reading. All of a sudden, we looked down and noticed that we were several pages past when we last remembered what we were reading. In other instances, as in the example of expository text at the beginning of this chapter, the text is very dense and difficult, and we do not readily comprehend as we read. What do we do? Most of us go back and reread quickly and try to repair what we missed. Sometimes we seek assistance by getting more background information or finding the meaning of unfamiliar words or concepts. Other times we look forward in the reading to find explanatory information. There are two key components that support readers' actions. Metacognition, often described as "thinking about thinking," helps readers monitor understanding and know when and how to use strategies that support comprehension. A reader might think, "I have no idea what I just read. Let me consider what I can do to figure it out." Self-regulation refers to the ability to consider one's actions, to stop an impulse, and to think ahead. Self-regulated learners can stay with the task, even when it becomes challenging. Mason et al. (2013) noted that students who struggle with learning may not have developed the metacognition needed to support the multiple processes required to understand what they read. Together, metacognition and self-regulation involve tuning in while reading, recognizing when you don't understand something, and being able to take action that helps you make sense of what you are reading.

What can teachers do to assure that students monitor their own comprehension? Most students with LD need to learn the same strategies that mature readers use to identify when understanding breaks down and know how to repair what they missed. Teachers can assist students in monitoring comprehension by:

- Helping students determine when the text does not make sense, including making note of difficult words, concepts, or ideas
- Teaching students to ask themselves questions as they read to monitor their understanding and to figure out what is going on in the text
- Supporting students to reflect on what they are learning

### Help Students Determine When the Text Does Not Make Sense

Knowing in the moment if something makes sense or not is not intuitive for all readers; therefore, activities that increase awareness of how well a student is understanding what they read are critical to increasing metacognition. One way to make the process more visible to students is to provide a series of sentences, some of which are nonsensical. Students read through each sentence and make a decision about whether or not it makes sense. If a sentence doesn't make sense, students learn to note the words or phrases that are confusing. Teachers then engage students in a discussion about the difficult sentences and support students to consider what they can do if they don't know a word or phrase when they are reading. Once students have practice with sentences, they are ready to move on to longer sections of text, and teachers can use readings that are relevant to content learning whenever possible.

### Teach Students to Ask Questions to Monitor Understanding

Asking questions is a way to check understanding (Fogarty et al., 2017; Vaughn et al., 2016). For instance, Crabtree et al. (2010) studied the effects of self-monitoring of narrative story elements on the reading comprehension of high school seniors with LD and significant attention problems. They found that their self-monitoring intervention helped to improve students' comprehension. Questions included:

- Who are the main characters?
- What is the setting?
- What is the story about?
- What are the problems and conflicts?
- How did the story end?

Students read stories and stopped reading at three predetermined places in the text and recorded answers to prompts on a recording sheet. This process of responding to self-monitoring prompts improved their understanding and recall of the passage.

Teachers can model the way that asking questions during reading can help the reader take action. For instance, the teacher can read a short section of text and then stop to ask: "Are there any words I cannot read or that I don't know? What strategies can I use when I don't understand a word?" Students are then prompted to consider strategies they have learned when they don't understand a word, such as rereading the sentence or using morphemic analysis strategies to determine the meaning of an unknown word (see Chapter 3). A teacher can also model self-questions around main ideas. Again, after reading a short section of text, the teacher could say: "I am going to ask myself, what was this section about? If I don't know, I will first reread the section slowly to see if that helps." When it is time for students to practice, they can begin by working with a partner or a small group and can use a guide to prompt them to stop at the end of short sections of text. This guide helps students identify which questions to ask, and what to try if something doesn't make sense.

### Support Students to Reflect on What They Are Learning

Opportunities to reflect on what they are learning helps students become more aware of what they have read and how they engaged with the text. After reading, students can be asked to share (in writing or verbally) what they learned from the reading and what was confusing or hard for them. Reflecting on the content of reading can support students to remember what they read and what they need to attend to as they continue with a text. Students can respond to questions such as:

- Today I learned . . .
- A question I have about what I read today is . . .
- One part I was confused about is . . .
- I want to find out more about . . .

Students can also reflect on their own engagement with reading by recording what they did well in terms of strategy use, and what they can work on next time. Questions related to monitoring comprehension might include:

- Today I stopped after each section of text to check if I understood. [always, mostly, sometimes, not really]
- I used strategies to figure out unknown words or ideas while I was reading. [always, mostly, sometimes, not really]
- One strategy that helped me today was . . .
- A goal for reading next time is . . .

Reflecting on comprehension monitoring focuses students on content and on processes. In the next section we expand on questioning strategies, an important component of reading comprehension for both teachers and students that incorporates self-reflection.

## Asking and Answering Questions

One of the teacher's more challenging jobs is to ask questions that engage students in thinking about what they've read. Teachers view questions as a means of determining whether students truly understand and make connections with text. Questioning is an essential feature of assessing reading comprehension and a tool for extending understanding of what was read. On the other hand, many questions teachers ask can limit responses and critical thinking. Asking good questions that engage and involve students to promote understanding is a skill. Although questioning occurs before, during, and after reading, some of the most important questioning occurs after reading. Students with LD benefit from instruction that teaches them about the varied purposes of asking and answering questions throughout the reading process. Without such knowledge, many students assume that most questions require literal, factual, test-like answers (Hollenbeck, 2011). Next, we offer strategies for making the most of teacher and student questions.

### Teacher-Initiated Questions

In a classic study of teacher questioning, Susskind (1979) observed that teachers in grades 3–6 asked an average of about 50 questions in a 30-minute period. In that same time, students asked fewer than two questions. Furthermore, teachers typically wait less than 2 seconds for a student response and even less time for students who are perceived to be low achieving (Stahl, 1994). Students benefit when you give them just a little bit more "wait time" before moving on to another student or answering your own question! When you increase silent wait time to just 3 seconds, the following benefits are likely to occur (Rowe, 1986; Stahl, 1994):

- Students' responses are longer and more accurate.
- The number of "I don't know" and no-answer responses decreases.
- Correct responses by a larger proportion of the class increase.
- The number of teacher-initiated questions decreases, but the quality and variety of question types increase.

There are many factors that go into asking effective questions. The types of questions asked should relate to the content and skills that are being taught. Whereas some questions promote short, factual answers, others encourage discussion and evaluation of the material. Teachers who identify *why* they are asking questions and what outcomes they are expecting from students, ask questions that yield better responses. For example, teachers might be looking for students to provide a factual answer supported by specific information from the text. Or they might want students to consider the text in terms of how it relates to their own lives. This kind of question would require a more in-depth response. Teachers also need to be aware of their own wording of questions to ensure that the questions are focused and clear and easily understood by students.

Often, teachers overlook the skills it takes for students to answer their questions. In general education classrooms, low-achieving students and students with LD not only are asked fewer questions than their typically achieving peers, they also answer far fewer questions (Klingner et al., 2010; McIntosh et al., 1993). Teaching students how to answer teacher-initiated questions can increase comprehension (e.g., Barth & Elleman, 2017). The Common Core standards also emphasize asking and answering a range of questions to support comprehension of key ideas and details (Haager & Vaughn, 2013).

Teaching the following procedure assists students in organizing the process of answering teacher-initiated questions (Walsh & Sattes, 2005). Teachers can give students a question cue card to guide them in answering questions. For example, for a student who tends to blurt out answers without thinking first, the teacher can cue the student to respond more thoughtfully by referring to the following steps listed on a question cue card:

1. Listen to the question.
2. Figure out what you are being asked.
3. Answer to yourself.
4. Answer out loud.
5. If needed, rethink and try again.

In another strategy that assists students who struggle to answer teacher-generated or end-of-chapter-type questions, the teacher imparts explicit instruction in identifying and differentiating between various question types (Blachowicz & Ogle, 2001; Bos & Vaughn, 2002; Raphael, 1986). Raphael (1986) came up with question–answer relationships (QARs) to teach students strategies with which to answer different question types. Students learn to categorize questions by the type of information that is used to answer them. In the technique described next, specific QARs are taught and practiced by students. Students can use the following QAR question types to analyze and answer teacher-initiated questions or to create their own questions:

1. *Right There:* Answers to these literal questions can be found in one sentence in the text. For example: "When was George Washington born?"
2. *Think and Search:* To find the answer to this type of question, students must draw conclusions, which requires that they integrate information from more than one place in the reading. Because these questions are more complex, they often require a sentence or more to answer. For example: "What factors might influence global warming?"
3. *The Author and You:* These questions require students to connect information from the text to what they have already learned and may require students to consider their own experiences and opinions or to extend ideas from the text. For this question type, students are told that some of the information needed to answer the question comes from the text, but other information comes from things they already know or from inferences they can make from the text. For example: "What would you have done if you were in Simone's position? How are the Comanche similar to other Native American tribes we have studied?"

Several studies have also included specific attention to inferencing type questions. For instance, Barth and Elleman (2017) taught students to answer inference questions as part of a multicomponent intervention to improve inferencing with middle school students identified for reading intervention. They found that students were able to learn to use the strategy to answer different kinds of inferential questions, resulting in improved scores on a proximal measure of content knowledge and a standardized reading comprehension assessment. In another study, students used strategies that cued them to be aware of their prior knowledge, to attend to the type of inference they were being asked to make, to note the key words in the questions that would help them search for clues in the text, to search for those clues, and to problem solve once they had gathered the clues to make inferences about the information in the passage (Fritschman et al., 2007, p. 248).

Common to these questioning practices, students first interact with the text to identify important information, then they analyze individual questions (e.g., in-text inference, elaborative inference, vocabulary, main idea), and finally they use strategies to formulate answers based on the question type.

### Student-Generated Questions

Up to this point we have focused on questions that are provided in textbooks or those that are teacher initiated. Teacher-generated questions that require students to draw conclusions, apply what they have learned, analyze what they have read, and synthesize and evaluate text advance student understanding and knowledge of reading. However, regardless of how interesting the question is, students are limited to answering a question posed by someone else—a relatively passive activity (Kamil, 2004). Therefore, it is important for teachers not only to ask good questions, but also to teach and provide time for *students* to ask and answer their own questions (National Institute of Child Health and Human Development, 2000; Rosenshine et al., 1996). Generating questions helps students engage with the text, monitor their understanding, remember what they've read, and connect what they are learning to what they already know. One technique that is very effective is teaching students to use the QAR question types described earlier to generate questions after reading. For example, after reading, students can create one question of each QAR type about what they read. To reinforce what they learned while reading, students can then ask each other their questions.

An essential component of student questioning is the provision of direct instruction, support, and feedback to students as they learn how to ask and answer questions. Students who are familiar with QARs still need to learn how to generate questions, and teachers can adjust modeling and practice based on their experience. If students are not familiar with the question types, teachers can provide instruction on them and on how to generate questions at the same time. To do this, teach the question type by describing what the question is and thinking aloud about how to create and answer the question. For example, when introducing Right There questions, the teacher might say something such as:

> "Today we are going to learn about the first type of question. We call this a Right There question because the information needed to answer a Right There question can be found in one place in the reading selection. Look at the passage we just read about the Paleolithic Era, which took place 2.5 million years ago. I can see here that it says, 'The key human development of the Paleolithic Era was the creation of stone and bone tools such as axes and arrows.' That looks like a Right There answer because it's a fact and it's all in one sentence. My question is 'What was the key human development of the Paleolithic Era?' The answer is right there in the sentence."

Then allow students to practice, as you monitor and provide feedback. When students have a clear understanding of what a Right There question is, it prepares them to write their own questions.

For factually dense material such as some social studies and science texts, teaching students to ask themselves "why" questions as they read can be especially effective. As students read, they are taught to continually ask themselves why the facts make sense. In a study of fourth- to eighth-grade science classrooms, students asked themselves "why" (e.g., Why do skunks eat corn? Why do owls prey on skunks?) and then attempted to answer using information from the text and prior knowledge (Pressley, El-Dinary, et al., 1992; Wood et al., 1990). Students who learned to ask "why" questions remembered what they had read better than students who read the text without asking questions. This procedure is effective because it helps students connect relevant prior knowledge to what they are reading, and it makes the facts they are reading about more memorable.

Question asking can be scaffolded for students with disabilities in several ways. For example, a student who is still struggling with basic understanding might be asked to focus for a lesson on just one question type, whereas other students might be asked to generate and answer one question of each type. Or a student may be working on higher-level questioning but with a shorter section of text or by using question starters such as the following:

- Who was _____ and what did they do?
- What were some of the reasons for _____?
- How are _____ and _____ similar/different?
- What is the author's viewpoint on _____?
- What caused the problem of _____?
- Why do you think _____ happened?

Further, students who have difficulty generating questions can work at their own level but still answer a variety of questions created by other students. Students need not be limited by their reading level when asking and answering questions.

Discussions that involve students with disabilities conversing with their peers about complex text benefit everyone (Barth & Elleman, 2017; Hollenbeck, 2011). Students can generate their own questions and then ask and answer questions with their peers in small groups. During discussions, as part of answering questions have students practice justifying their responses by providing evidence from the text, such as pointing to the place or places in the text where they found the answer. In questions that go beyond the text, such as inference questions, teach students to explain their reasoning by making connections within and across texts or to previous learning. Students can work in pairs or small groups to ask and answer questions using the following procedures:

1. Students read the selected passage as determined by the teacher (e.g., choral reading, taking turns, one partner reads while the other follows along).
2. Each group member generates at least three questions from the reading.
3. Each student asks their questions to the partner or small-group members.
4. Students respond, providing evidence from the text and their reasoning for their answers.
5. The student who asked the question gives feedback.

### Combining Teacher and Student Questions

An effective way for teachers to guide students in asking and answering worthwhile questions about what they read is a questioning-the-author technique (Beck et al., 1996, 2020). The idea of this technique is that students benefit when they think about why the author made the decisions they did and what questions or comments they would have for the author if they could meet the author. For example, after reading

*The Lorax* by Dr. Seuss (Geisel, 1971), a student asked, "Why didn't Dr. Seuss draw a picture of the Onceler?" This question spurred a lively discussion among students and the teacher about why the author would choose to leave one of the main characters hidden from our view, and how this choice influences how we understand and interpret the story. Other suggestions include exploring the author's message by questioning what is actually said in the text as well as the meaning behind it. Beck et al. encouraged helping students link information—how does one event connect with other aspects of the text—and also suggest asking whether authors have successfully conveyed their ideas and what questions students may ask themselves or the author in order to make the text more clear. According to McKeown and Beck (2004), "the development of meaning in this technique focuses on readers' interactions with text as it is being read, situates reader–text interactions in whole-class discussion, and encourages explanatory, evidence-based responses to questions about text" (p. 393). Through their study of many classrooms, McKeown and Beck found that as teachers and students adopted this new stance to reading and questioning, patterns of discussion went from students giving pat answers to test-like questions to collaborative discussions that involved both teacher and students in questioning the creation and elaboration of new ideas.

For more ideas about how to integrate effective questioning into reading comprehension instruction, see Chapter 9.

### Formulating Main Ideas and Summarizing

Really understanding what we read can probably best be determined by how well and accurately we state a main idea and summarize our understanding. Although the terminology varies, there are generally two ways to think about these important skills. First, readers need to identify the central message or "gist" of small portions of text. We refer to this skill as finding the main idea. Second, readers must know how to synthesize larger amounts of text (e.g., several paragraphs, a page-long section, a chapter) into a summary that contains only the most important information.

Whether students are reading small or larger amounts of text, they often erroneously do one or more of the following when asked to summarize what they have read:

- Write about everything.
- Write a headline or overly general statement (e.g., This section is about clouds).
- Write about selected details.
- Copy word for word.
- Don't write anything.

In contrast, when we teach students strategies to summarize after reading, they learn to do the following:

- Distinguish between important information and details.
- Use key vocabulary or concepts.
- Synthesize information.

- Use their own words.
- Write only what is needed to present the main idea(s).

Although we separate these strategies into main ideas and summarization portions, you will see that many of the main idea skills can be extended to longer portions of text, and many of the summary strategies can also be pared down for paragraphs or short sections. In general, if students cannot determine the key ideas of what they have read once you have taught (and students have learned) a main idea or summarization strategy, then choose texts that are less difficult and shorten the length of text.

### Main Idea

Sometimes the main idea is stated explicitly (as in the topic sentence) and other times it is implicit and must be inferred. Knowing how to construct the main idea about what is read is essential because it helps students identify what is important to know and remember and helps students with other aspects of reading, such as answering comprehension questions (e.g., Stevens et al., 2019). Learning how to state or write a main idea may be even more important for students with LD because they rarely use comprehension strategies even when the difficulty level of the reading passage increases (Simmons et al., 1988). Fortunately, when students are offered explicit and systematic instruction in how to identify the main idea, the result is improved outcomes in reading comprehension (Jitendra et al., 1998, 2000; Miller et al., 2010). Also, direct instruction plus strategy instruction appears to be the best combination for implementing powerful interventions for students with LD (Swanson, 1999, 2001); thus, main idea instruction that includes both direct instruction and a strategy component is likely to yield the highest outcomes. Despite research on the importance of teaching main idea strategies to students, many reading programs do not emphasize the process for teaching and practicing these strategies to the extent that is required to learn this skill, particularly for students with LD (Jitendra et al., 2001).

Jitendra et al. (2000) combined strategy and direct instruction to improve main idea use for students with LD. Students who learned this strategy significantly outperformed students who received reading instruction as usual, and their gains were maintained over time. In this study, middle school students were taught to use a main idea strategy in eight 30-minute lessons. The length of instruction is important to note because teaching reading comprehension strategies (or any learning strategies, for that matter) takes time. It is often the case that when students fail to apply a particular strategy it is because they have not learned it well initially (Bransford et al., 1999). A routine for generating a main idea statement includes the following:

1. Present the main idea strategy.
2. Model the application of the strategy with a reading passage.
3. Demonstrate the use of a self-monitoring cue card that describes the steps of the strategy.
4. Provide opportunities for guided and then independent practice using the

main idea strategy with the self-monitoring cue card. During this phase the teacher monitors performance and provides corrective feedback.

## GENERATING A MAIN IDEA

The following routine provides straightforward steps students can use to get the main idea while reading (e.g., Barth & Elleman, 2017; Ritchey et al., 2017; Vaughn et al., 2019). When students are learning this strategy, it is helpful for them to be able to annotate directly on the text to keep track of their ideas by marking or highlighting key information.

1. Identify and note the most important who (person) or what (place or thing) in a section of text.
2. List the most important information about the most important who or what.
3. Synthesize the information into a gist statement.
4. Write the gist statement in your own words in a complete sentence.
5. Check that the gist statements makes sense.

## PARAPHRASING

Paraphrasing can be a useful technique with students across the grade levels. With third-grade low comprehenders, Hagaman et al. (2012) investigated the effects of the RAP paraphrasing strategy taught using the self-regulated strategy development model. RAP is a three-step strategy:

1. Read a paragraph.
2. Ask myself, "What are the main idea and two details of this paragraph?"
   - If I am not sure, complete the following:
     - This paragraph is about _____.
     - It tells me about _____.
   - If I need more information:
     - Look in the first sentence of the paragraph.
     - Look for information that is repeated with the same word or words in more than one place.
     - Identify what the details describe or explain.
3. Put the main idea and details into my own words.
   - Must be a complete sentence (subject and verb).
   - Must be accurate.
   - Must contain new information.
   - Must be in your own words.
   - Must contain only one general statement per paragraph.

Hagaman and Reid (2008) conducted a similar study, also using RAP, but this time with middle school low comprehenders. In both studies, they found that the RAP strategy improved comprehension. RAP was originally developed by Schumaker et al. (1984). Students first practice using the steps with a variety of informational sources, such as textbooks, articles, and even teacher lectures. As students become more familiar with this strategy, they learn not only why and how to apply it, but when it is the most useful (Berry et al., 2004).

## Summarizing

Summarization requires students to generate multiple main ideas from across a reading and then to combine them to form a summary. In addition, students must be able to generalize from specific examples and be able to identify when information is repeated (National Institute of Child Health and Human Development, 2000). Learning to summarize is an effective strategy for improving comprehension for students with LD (Gajria & Salvia, 1992; Gajria et al., 2007; Nelson et al., 1992). Many summarization strategies include rules that students learn to use to write summaries. Through modeling, feedback, and many opportunities to practice, students are taught to use the following rules (National Institute of Child Health and Human Development, 2000):

1. Delete trivial information.
2. Delete redundant information.
3. Use one word to replace a list of related items.
4. Select a topic sentence.
5. Invent a topic sentence if one is not explicitly stated.

Students are first taught to use the rules to write main idea statements for every paragraph. They are then taught to use the same rules to combine the information from their main idea statements to form a summary of main ideas. In other words, summarization is a hierarchical skill whereby readers gain experience first by finding the main idea of single paragraphs, then, once they have mastered the main idea skill, they learn to combine main ideas to form summary statements. In another application of summarization, Jenkins and colleagues (Jenkins et al., 1987) improved performance on the retelling and recall of passages by students with LD by systematically teaching them to answer questions about what they read: (1) Who is it about? and (2) What's happening? Similarly, Malone and Mastropieri (1992) taught students to self-question while reading by asking (1) Who or what is the passage about? and (2) What is happening? Students with LD who participated in the training outperformed control students on recall of passage content.

Some students benefit from strategies that involve ways to cue recall of information visually. One way to do this is to use visual representations of the main ideas and supporting details for a reading selection (McCormick, 1999). Baumann (1984) combined instruction in summarization with this sort of visual representation with sixth-grade students. Results indicated that the strategy improved students' ability to conduct well-organized summaries. To use this strategy, students first generate main ideas of paragraphs or short sections as they read. After reading, the teacher leads a discussion using a picture to guide students' thinking. Each main idea statement is written onto the summary image. For example, in a text about ants, students are given a picture of an ant in which the body represents the topic statement and the legs represent the main ideas and supporting details. Once students are familiar with the strategy, they are given their own figure (or can create their own) and work together with a partner to complete representations of the main ideas and supporting details. When introducing the strategy or using it with younger students, visual representations can also be used to find the main idea of a paragraph. For example, students might first write details on the branches of a tree and then use the details to generate a main idea statement. Note that visual representations are more effective when used in combination with other summarization strategies, such as using the rules described above to combine main ideas.

Other strategies assist students in summarizing what they have learned by teaching procedures for retelling. Idol-Maestas (1985) developed an approach called TELLS for guiding students' probing while reading a story. TELLS is an acronym that prompts students to follow a series of steps:

- T: Study story Titles.
- E: Examine and skim pages for clues.
- L: Look for important words.
- L: Look for difficult words.
- S: Think about the story Settings.

TELLS can be posted on a wall in the classroom and/or provided individually to students. The teacher helps students learn how to apply each of the steps, one at a time, and then use them all when reading a story. Idol-Maestas (1985) suggested that it is important to continue prompting students to use this and other comprehension strategies even after they appear to have become proficient in strategy implementation. Explicit instruction using transfer activities to help students internalize strategies and generalize their usage to other tasks is important, especially for students with LD.

Ridge and Skinner (2011) used the TELLS retelling procedure to enhance comprehension levels and reading rates among three ninth-grade students with reading skills deficits. Results suggest that the TELLS procedure enhanced both comprehension levels and reading rates across all three students. Using a similar model, Lapp et al. (2010) investigated what they refer to as "Text Mapping Plus" to improve comprehension through supported retellings. They taught students a routine that supports reading and remembering the salient features of text. Students added words and graphics to their maps to support their retells of both fiction and nonnarrative text.

Formulating main ideas and summarizations involves synthesizing a lot of information to come up with what a paragraph, section, or passage is mostly about. Summarization skills demonstrate a student's ability to articulate an understanding of what is read. Summarization is also the area with which students who struggle with reading comprehension have the most difficulty. The main idea and summarization strategies presented in this section are examples of effective techniques that teachers can use to improve these essential skills.

## STRATEGIES FOR UNDERSTANDING NARRATIVE TEXT

The next section of this chapter focuses on strategies that are especially (although not exclusively) useful with narrative text.

### Story Maps

Visual representations such as story maps can be beneficial for all students and are especially helpful for students with LD (Baker et al., 2003; Boon et al., 2015). Story maps take numerous forms, but all are visual representations of the key information in a narrative text. They can be used after reading to summarize or during reading to keep track of key events and information. One variation we like is the organization sheet developed by Englert (1990, 1992) to help students plan for writing; the topic or title of the story is written in a circle in the middle of the page and the subtopics or components of the plot are written in the surrounding circles. MacArthur and colleagues (1995) added the C-SPACE mnemonic device for helping students remember the elements of a story (C—characters, S—setting, P—problem, A—action, C—conclusion, E—emotion).

Isikdogan and Kargin (2010) investigated the effectiveness of story mapping on reading comprehension skills among students with mild intellectual disabilities. Findings showed that the story-mapping method positively affected the reading comprehension skills of the students in the experimental group. Wade et al. (2010) explored the efficacy of story mapping with the integration of Kidspiration software to enhance reading comprehension skills in relation to story grammar components for elementary-age students with LD. They investigated the effect of a computer-based story-mapping procedure on the acquisition of nine specific story grammar components and found a dramatic increase in students' comprehension levels.

Story mapping has typically been applied to narrative texts. However, with the increased emphasis in schools on reading nonfiction, these strategies have been successfully applied to expository texts as well. For example, Stagliano and Boon (2009) examined the effects of using story mapping to improve and enhance the reading comprehension skills of fourth-grade students with LD. Their study was conducted in pull-out special education resource classrooms in which the participants regularly received reading instruction. The participants were each instructed on common elements of a story and taught to complete a story map while reading expository text passages. After completing the story map, the participants answered five comprehension questions about the selection. The use of the story-mapping procedure improved participants' percentage of correct comprehension questions on expository text passages. As always, the teacher should consider the purpose for reading and then determine which strategy can be applied to support understanding.

### Story Retelling

Story retelling is a strategy that involves recounting what has just been read in sequential order. Story retelling can be an effective practice for determining and assuring reading comprehension of narrative text (Bos, 1987) and has also been shown to increase the quality of students' writing (e.g., Traga Philippakos et al., 2018). Retelling a story demonstrates a student's ability to identify the story's important events and also provides a purpose for continued reading.

Teachers can first model the retelling strategy by identifying the key components of a story: character, setting, and problem and resolution. For students who struggle with these components, teaching them separately and then combining them can be an effective tool. For example:

*Simple Retelling*
- Identify and retell the beginning, middle, and end of the story.
- Describe the setting.
- Identify the problem and resolution.

*More Complete Retelling*
- Identify and retell events and facts in a sequence.
- Make inferences to fill in missing information.
- Identify and retell causes of actions or events and their effects.

*Most Complete Retelling*
- Identify and retell a sequence of actions or events.
- Make inferences to account for events or actions.
- Offer an evaluation of the story.

## Identifying Themes

Students with LD can learn to identify themes from stories and determine the extent to which those themes apply to their own lives (Williams, 1998). Identifying themes helps students feel personally connected to what they are reading and renders the information more relevant and thus more memorable. Text that contains a suitable theme (e.g., cooperation, responsibility, or respect for others) is identified and used as the source for the following lesson parts:

1. *Conduct a prereading discussion about lesson purpose and story topic.* The teacher identifies the theme and facilitates understanding initially, then scaffolds the use of this strategy with the goal of having students identify the story theme independently.

2. *Read the story.* The teacher now reads the story and stops to ask questions to ascertain whether students are connecting what they are reading to the story theme.

3. *Discuss important story information using organizing (schema) questions.* The following three questions are used to assist students in organizing the story information:

> Who is the main character?
> What did the main character do?
> What happened?

After students understand the organization of the story, they are asked the following questions to assist them in integrating the story information with the theme:

> Was this good or bad?
> Why was this good or bad?

4. *Identify the theme in a standard format.* Students learn to state the theme in a standard format by identifying what the character should or should not have done and then what they (the students) should or should not do.

5. *Apply the theme to real-life experiences.* In this section, the students are encouraged to consider to whom the theme applies and under what conditions.

### Story Planner

Teaching students to write stories can improve their understanding of story grammar and facilitate their comprehension when they read stories. Students can be given a template or graphic organizer (see Figure 4.2) to help them construct stories by having them complete each section prior to writing, or it can be completed after students read a story as an exercise for analyzing story structure. We present an original story, "Randy Raindrop" (Figure 4.3), and then illustrate how we used the story planner to examine the structure of the story (Figure 4.4).

### Scrambled Stories

For this approach, the teacher breaks a story into categories (chunks) and then mixes them up (Whaley, 1981). Next, the teacher has students put the pieces of the story back together in the right order. The teacher and students discuss which way makes the most sense and why. A variation of this technique is to use it with the language experience approach and stories students themselves wrote (Haager & Klingner, 2005). Prepackaged blank sentence strips can be useful for this process.

## READING AND WRITING CONNECTIONS

The connections between reading and writing are strong, though they have often been underemphasized as integral components of reading models (Hebert et al., 2013; Philippakos & Graham, 2023; Traga Philippakos & MacArthur, 2022). Writing plays a supportive role in improving reading comprehension and has also been linked to increased content learning (Graham & Perin, 2007). Writing activities that support reading comprehension include summary writing, generating and answering questions, note taking, and longer writing activities such as essay writing and journaling (Graham & Hebert, 2011). Hebert et al. (2013) outlined several reasons why writing may influence reading comprehension:

```
┌─────────────────────────────────────────────────────────┐
│ CHARACTERS                                                │
│                                                           │
│                                                           │
│      Describe your main character:                        │
│                                                           │
│                                                           │
│                                                           │
│ SETTING(S)                                                │
│                                                           │
│                                                           │
│      Describe your main settings:                         │
│                                                           │
│                                                           │
│                                                           │
│ STORY OUTLINE/PLOT                                        │
│      How does the story begin?                            │
│                                                           │
│                                                           │
│      What happens next?                                   │
│                                                           │
│                                                           │
│      Climax:                                              │
│                                                           │
│                                                           │
│      Describe how your character feels:                   │
│                                                           │
│                                                           │
│                                                           │
│ RESOLUTION                                                │
│      Ending:                                              │
│                                                           │
│                                                           │
│      What was learned?                                    │
│                                                           │
└─────────────────────────────────────────────────────────┘
```

**FIGURE 4.2.** Story recipe. From *Teaching Reading Comprehension to Students with Learning Difficulties, Third Edition,* by Sharon Vaughn, Alison Boardman, and Janette K. Klingner. Copyright © 2024 The Guilford Press. Permission to photocopy this material, or to download and print additional versions (*www.guilford.com/vaughn3-forms*), is granted to purchasers of this book for personal use or use with students; see copyright page for details.

- The act of converting thoughts into writing necessarily involves choices about what is important, how best to explain ideas, and what vocabulary to use to express understanding. This process helps structure thinking.
- The written product can be revised, compared, and reviewed, which may solidify or even extend understanding.
- Some writing tasks require comparisons, synthesis of understanding, and identifying relationships.
- Awareness of an audience for writing can encourage students to figure out the information a text is conveying.
- Students may employ metacognitive strategies throughout the writing process as they plan, organize, and revise their writing. This active engagement supports comprehension.

For ELs, writing expands the temporal space in which reading occurs, allowing for a closer examination of ideas that isn't possible during the quick pace of oral discussions (Baker et al., 2014; Pearson, 2002). The use of writing during reading also supports individual accountability and allows teachers to monitor student understanding.

Many of the reading strategies throughout this book incorporate writing components that support comprehension. Teachers are encouraged to consider the ways in which a particular writing task might influence what a student learns and remembers from text. For example, summary writing encourages the synthesis of big ideas in a text while asking factual questions encourages remembering specific key ideas. Varying and combining writing activities that occur before, during, and after reading allow students to apply a broader range of skills that can link to comprehension.

---

Randy Raindrop

Once upon a time there was a little raindrop named Randy. Randy lived in a big, white, fluffy cloud with his parents, Raymond and Rita. He loved to play with other little raindrops. But sometimes he and his friends wandered far away from their parents. Their parents warned them to stay close by. One day when Randy was playing hide and go seek with his friends, he went too far. Then the big cloud got dark. There was a loud BOOM and a flash of light, and the cloud shook. Randy tried to hurry back to his parents, but he was too far away. He stumbled and fell out of his cloud. Down, down he fell, until he landed with a splash on the ground. He got up and looked around. He didn't know where he was, and he didn't know any of the other raindrops he saw. He was scared and sad. He missed his parents! He thought, "I should have listened to them and stayed closer!" More and more raindrops fell to the ground around Randy. Then Randy started moving, faster and faster, with the other raindrops around him. They rolled down a hill and into a river. The river was flowing quickly, rushing and gushing. Randy thought he would never stop, but finally the river slowed down and Randy was able to look around him. And who did he see? His parents! They had also fallen out of the cloud, and had been looking for him. Randy and his parents were so happy to be together again! They gave Randy a big hug, and Randy promised to do a better job following their directions.

---

**FIGURE 4.3.** Original story: "Randy Raindrop."

**CHARACTERS**
Randy Raindrop
His parents
His friends

Describe your main character:

Randy Raindrop likes to play with his friends.

**SETTING(S)**
A cloud.
The ground, a hill, and a river.

Describe your main settings:

The cloud is big, white, and fluffy at first, but then becomes dark.
The river moves quickly.

**STORY OUTLINE/PLOT**
How does the story begin?

Randy is playing with his friends and goes too far from his parents.

What happens next?

The cloud shakes and Randy falls to the ground.

Climax:

Randy is lost and falls into a gushing river.

Describe how your character feels:

He feels sad and scared.

**RESOLUTION**
Ending:

Randy finds his parents.

What was learned?

It's best to do what your parents say.

**FIGURE 4.4.** Completed story recipe, using "Randy Raindrop."

## CONCLUSION

Teachers can feel confident that the time put into planning and implementing the strategies presented in this chapter will help students understand and remember what they read. Students with LD are likely to improve their reading comprehension if teachers:

- Teach strategies that have been documented as effective in promoting reading comprehension.
- Design instruction based on effective principles of direct instruction and strategy instruction.
- Provide modeling, support, guided instruction, practice, attributional feedback, and opportunities to practice across text types.
- Monitor students' progress and make adjustments accordingly.

Stories of students who feel actively engaged in reading for meaning remind us of the importance of supporting students in their text comprehension. Students tell us that they want to understand what they read, and they like it when they are given the tools to do so. In a classroom recently, we asked students what they thought of the new reading comprehension strategies their teacher was using. A quiet student with a reading disability slowly raised her hand and responded, "Before, my teacher did all the talking. Now I know ways to figure it [what I read] out on my own, and I can tell *her* what the story is about."

# CHAPTER FIVE

# Effectively Using Text to Promote Reading Comprehension

## THE IMPORTANCE OF TEXT IN READING COMPREHENSION

What students read is closely related to how well they comprehend. We all know that our comprehension drifts when we are reading about topics that we do not find interesting or know very little about. In addition to text content, students benefit from learning about how authors organize texts and why some texts follow certain structural patterns. As experienced readers, we know the flow of a recipe, or a letter, or an instruction manual. We can easily determine when a newspaper article is going to present an opinion or to report on an event, and we understand if a textbook chapter is presenting information in a cause–effect format or as a sequence of events. Expert readers are also quite flexible in their understanding of text structures. We can follow the flow of a fictional novel if chapters are numbered, named, or when there are no chapter delineations at all. Years of experience with a wide variety of texts helps us to almost automatically identify the ways texts are structured in familiar and unfamiliar formats and to use that information to read with purpose and for meaning. This chapter addresses three important components of text as they relate to reading comprehension instruction: text levels, text selection, and text structure. Specific levels of texts support different aspects of reading instruction and practice. Text selection is focused on the teacher and how to support teachers to identify appropriate texts for their students. Text structure is also a consideration in text selection, but here we emphasize ways to teach skills to students to help them use text organization to support their understanding.

## TEXT LEVELS AND READING COMPREHENSION INSTRUCTION

With so many skills to be learned and so many texts to choose from, how can educators select appropriate texts that will develop their students' reading comprehension? There are three different types of texts to consider for reading comprehension instruction: *independent-level texts, instructional-level texts,* and *stretch-level texts.* The Educator's Practice Guide *Providing Reading Intervention for Students in Grades 4–9* recommends using both instructional-level and stretch-level texts when working on reading comprehension (Vaughn et al., 2022). Next, we explain the different levels and how teachers can use text levels to support reading development.

### Independent-Level Texts

These are texts that a student can read and understand easily on their own, with little to no assistance, fluently and with few errors and high comprehension. Independent-level texts are not typically used to teach reading comprehension because minimal processing is needed to understand them. These texts can be used to learn about topics of interest, for enjoyment, and to develop comfort with (and maybe even a love for) reading. However, be aware that some texts may be easy for a student to read but difficult to understand. Such texts may have challenging vocabulary, complex ideas, or unfamiliar structures that make comprehension difficult. These texts would most likely be considered instructional, in terms of reading comprehension instruction, even though students can decode them fluently.

### Instructional-Level Texts

To support the development of reading comprehension skills and strategies, teachers should select texts that are at a student's instructional level, meaning that the text provides an appropriate level of challenge without feeling frustrating. When texts are too easy, comprehension is often automatic, and students don't need to utilize strategies to figure out what the text is about. When texts are too challenging, reading becomes frustrating, and strategies may not be effective at supporting understanding. Consider, for example, the strategy of using context clues to figure out the meaning of an unknown vocabulary word. If the text around the unknown word is too difficult, then a reader may not be able to use semantic clues to help figure out the meaning or check if a possible definition makes sense. In most cases, instructional-level texts are useful to introduce the strategies provided throughout this book.

### Stretch-Level Texts

It is important for students to have exposure to high-level vocabulary, varied sentence structures, and complex ideas, which are more likely to be found in stretch texts. For students with reading difficulties, stretch texts will often be at or just below grade level. These texts can be engaging for students and help to build their world knowledge. Stretch texts can also foster critical thinking, provide multiple perspectives, and help build confidence for reading in other settings, such as content classes (Vaughn et al., 2019). Students should work with stretch texts two to three times each week for about 6–10 weeks with extensive support from the teacher. Then students can take a break for a few weeks to focus on applying their skills with instructional-level texts. The following recommendations (Vaughn et al., 2022) can help teachers design and teach lessons using stretch texts.

#### Prepare for the Stretch-Text Lesson

- **Select the text:** Identify the stretch text along with supports that will be needed. The text should be interesting to students and connected to curriculum when possible. Texts that work well are those that present new ideas, introduce multiple perspectives, and raise questions that spark discussion. Sequence the stretch texts so they gradually increase in length and difficulty. Remember, these are texts that are just above the instructional reading level. If they are too difficult, students will become frustrated. By increasing difficulty over time, students will become more comfortable and will be more likely to gain confidence and stick with the challenge (Barth & Elleman, 2017; Kim et al., 2017). Some teachers select a content standard or theme and create a text set with three or four texts that build on the same or a similar topic. You can find stretch texts in grade-level curricula materials, supplemental texts that go along with intervention curricula, and websites such as *newsela.com* or *readworks.org.*

- **Identify key vocabulary:** Once you have selected the text, identify key vocabulary to preteach and to follow up on throughout the week. These terms will include complex vocabulary ideas; multisyllabic words that can be used to practice skills students are learning (e.g., specific prefixes); proper nouns; and other essential words to discuss before, during, and after reading (see Chapter 3 for ideas about supporting vocabulary learning).

- **Determine stopping points:** Read through the text to determine stopping points where you can ask questions, clarify understanding, and help students make connections. Just as you will increase the difficulty of the text over time, you can also gradually lengthen the amount of text students read before pausing. See Figure 5.1 for an example of teacher preparation for a stretch-text reading about Louise Erdrich.

#### Provide Support

Provide significant support before, during, and after reading stretch texts, rather than having students read on their own or with a partner. You can determine the amount of support, both in advance and during the lesson, based on the difficulty of the text

---

**Louise Erdrich Wins Pulitzer Prize in Literature**

The Pulitzer Prize is one of the highest awards that writers can receive. In June 2021, the novelist Louise Erdrich won the award for her novel *The Night Watchman*. *The Night Watchman* is based on the life of her grandfather, who fought to ensure the Ojibwe tribe could keep their land.

Erdrich writes frequently about life on and near the reservations. Louise's mother was Ojibwe. Although her father was not Ojibwe, both her parents attended a boarding school run by the Bureau of Indian Affairs. The boarding schools were intended to assimilate Native American children in the "American way of life" and to train them for low-paying jobs.

Erdrich won the equally prestigious National Book Award for her novel *LaRose*. Like all her novels, *LaRose* explored the rich traditions of Ojibwe people and the struggle of children being forced to attend boarding schools many miles from their families. The novel explored the cruelty of separating children from their families and their traditions.

Erdrich's books describe horrors but are also full of humor. They include many fascinating people. Some are very wise and caring, some thoughtless, and many in between.

---

The teacher marks the following sections and words before reading with the group. This is grade-level material for a seventh-grade English language arts class.

**Stop points and discussion starters:**
- Stop after paragraph 1—What is this paragraph about?
- Stop after paragraph 2—What was the purpose of the boarding schools for Native Americans?
- Stop after paragraph 3—What happened in her novel *LaRose* that was disturbing?
- Stop after paragraph 4—What are some positive aspects of Erdrich's novels? What do you think the author means when describing people who fall in between being wise and thoughtless at the same time?

**Proper nouns:**
- *Pulitzer Prize*
- *Louise Erdrich*
- *Ojibwe*
- *Bureau of Indian Affairs*
- *Native American*

**Multisyllabic words using previously taught word-reading skills:**
- *frequently*
- *reservation*
- *attended*
- *assimilate*
- *traditions*

**Essential words:**
- *novel*
- *reservation*
- *assimilate*
- *boarding school*

**FIGURE 5.1.** Teacher preparing to read a short selection from a grade-level text about noted novelist Louise Erdrich. From Vaughn et al. (2022). *Providing Reading Interventions for Students in Grades 4–9* (WWC 2022007). Washington, DC: National Center for Education Evaluation and Regional Assistance (NCEE), Institute of Education Sciences, U.S. Department of Education. Retrieved from *https://whatworks.ed.gov*.

and students' understanding in the moment. Prior to reading, display and introduce two to three key vocabulary terms and any proper nouns that might be difficult or will provide context for the reading. To read the text, the teacher can read out loud while the students whisper read along with the teacher. The group can read out loud together, or the students and teacher can take turns, with the teacher reading one or two sentences and the students reading the next sentences and so on. Discuss words and phrases that are difficult and continue with stopping points to ask questions that clarify confusing parts of the text, prompt students to summarize information, or require them to make inferences. Teachers should also encourage and support students to persist even though reading can feel challenging. If students seem overly frustrated and start to shut down, that is a sign that the text may be too difficult, and adjustments should be made with text selection and or supports.

### Increase Independence

When students become more confident and competent at using strategies with stretch texts, teachers can increase independence, while still providing support. Examples include rereading challenging texts students have previously read, working with students to select text of high interest, and having students work in small student-led groups where they can support one another to apply strategies and make sense of what they are reading. A teacher can lead the preview of the text, by introducing the reading, preteaching key vocabulary terms, and contextualizing important proper nouns. Then, using a graphic organizer with predetermined stopping point questions, students can read and discuss the text together. Even though students are leading the discussion, the teacher is still present to facilitate, to clarify understanding, and to increase support as needed. For instance, after several weeks of teacher-directed practice with stretch texts in a reading intervention class, students read a grade-level text aligned to a social studies standard on technology and the global economy, titled "Meet Your New Co-Worker," about the types of jobs robots can do along with challenges of shifting roles in the workplace. The text was challenging for students to read, but they were motivated to understand it because the topic was engaging and relevant and they saw connections to what they were learning in social studies. Prior to reading, the teacher introduced the text, pretaught a couple of key vocabulary terms (e.g., *automation, transformation, reinventing*) contextualized several proper nouns, and provided encouragement to students. Students then read the text together in small groups and stopped to answer questions on their graphic organizer. The teacher remained with the group, interjecting only as needed to support students. After reading, the teacher facilitated a lively conversation in which students discussed the pros and cons of robots in the workplace and used evidence from the text to support their thinking.

## SELECTING APPROPRIATE TEXTS

We've talked about the types of texts to use with students during reading comprehension instruction and practice, but how do teachers know which texts will be instructional or stretch texts for their students? Research suggests that teachers can find the process of selecting appropriate texts quite illusive and may attend to some features (e.g., font size, illustrations) over other, more important features, such as the multidimensional factors related to vocabulary (Hodgkinson & Small, 2018; Lammert et al., 2022). Beyond whether a student can read with few errors, how can teachers identify which texts will be more or less challenging for their students? *Text complexity* refers to how challenging a text is to read for a particular reader; it is the extent to which text features such as vocabulary and sentence length contribute to how challenging a text will be to comprehend. In addition, the familiarity with and interest in a topic, text structure, and author's style can all make a text more or less difficult to read for students. Teachers may use text complexity ratings provided by publishers as a guide (e.g., Lexile level of 840 or a guided-reading level K), but as noted by Hiebert (2014):

> Teachers need to examine texts themselves, attending to features such as prior knowledge, text structure, vocabulary, and purpose in relation to their own students. Publishers can give useful guidelines (e.g., the number of words that are challenging, the demands of prior knowledge) but teachers need to develop skills at identifying the features that require attention for their students. (pp. 5–6)

To select appropriate texts for students, educators should begin with information they have about a student's reading level, their interests, and their world and word knowledge. Text levels provided by publishers can be helpful but do not provide enough information about important factors that influence text difficulty. Teachers can also use the following guidelines (Brown & Dewitz, 2013; Hodgkinson & Small, 2018) to determine which texts are appropriate for reading comprehension instruction.

- Does the author follow a text structure that students are familiar with?
- Are there visuals or illustrations that help clarify the meaning of the text?
- Are main ideas explicitly stated or implicit?
- Are themes simple and straightforward or complex and interconnected?
- How challenging is the vocabulary (e.g., multiple meaning words, content-specific terms, rare words)?
- Are language conventions clear or abstract (e.g., literal language, figurative language, metaphorical language)?
- Can students determine the meaning of unknown words using morphemic analysis or context clues?
- What level of background knowledge of the topic is needed to understand the text?
- Is the topic relatable to students?

Selecting texts for reading comprehension should not be an afterthought, but should be built into unit and lesson preparation. As we have mentioned, although student assessment data and publisher-provided levels are helpful, teachers also need to consider individual reader characteristics along with the goals and content of instruction when selecting reading materials. Thoughtful preparation of text contributes to the effectiveness of instruction. Next, we describe ways to support students to understand the organization of texts teachers have selected, and to use that information to support comprehension.

## TEXT STRUCTURE

An important comprehension skill is the ability to make use of text structure. *Text structure* refers to the way ideas in a text are organized and includes the relationship among ideas, and the vocabulary used to convey meaning (Bogaerds-Hazenberg et al., 2021). Text structure offers important clues about how information is organized, and these clues influence how a reader approaches reading in a particular situation. Some texts are written with more reader-friendly text structures than others. When students are familiar with the way a text is structured, this knowledge can help them (1) form expectations about what they will read, (2) organize incoming information, (3) judge the relative importance of what they read, (4) improve their comprehension, and (5) enhance their recall (Meyer, 1984). Many students develop a keen understanding of how stories are structured without ever receiving explicit story grammar instruction. However, when the structure of a text is different from what the reader expects, comprehension can break down. Students with poor comprehension tend not to use text structure to guide their reading and this can negatively impact reading comprehension (Rapp et al., 2007). They may not be good at certain tasks, such as selecting important information, making inferences, and identifying story themes. Several reviews of research have demonstrated the positive impact of explicit text structure instruction for students across grade levels and reading abilities with both narrative and expository text (Bogaerds-Hazenberg et al., 2020; Hebert et al., 2016; Pyle et al., 2017).

### *Narrative Text Structure*

Texts are organized in different ways. Narrative text typically follows a single, general, structural pattern, often called a story grammar (Mandler & Johnson, 1977). Story grammar includes characters, settings, problems, solutions to the problems, and feelings. Storytelling patterns are often culturally specific. For instance, Native American stories may progress in a nonlinear fashion (Sharifian, 2002), while Japanese stories tend to have more details but more implicit information than stories written by U.S. authors (Westby et al., 2002). Thus, explicit instruction in common story grammar used in U.S. texts can also support students from diverse language and cultural backgrounds. Table 5.1 shows ways to interact with common elements of narrative stories.

#### *Narrative Intervention*

Zipoli and Merritt (2022) offer a six-step model in the category of narrative intervention strategies. In this model, the teacher reads a text aloud and relies on oral participation as a way to build students' knowledge of narrative text structure. Students

**TABLE 5.1.** Interacting with Narrative Story Elements

| | |
|---|---|
| *Setting:* | Note where and when the story takes place. |
| *Characters:* | Identify the protagonist, major characters, and minor characters. Analyze and describe individual characters, their relationships, and their motivations. |
| *Plot:* | Analyze individual episodes and the overall plot (problem, response to the problem, action taken to solve the problem, outcome). |
| *Theme:* | State the message or main idea of the entire story. |
| *Point of view:* | Identify who is telling the story (first person or third person) and why. Consider why the author wrote the story and what message they are trying to convey. |

with comprehension difficulties along with students with narrative difficulties (e.g., children who have difficulty retelling what happened in a story they read or sharing a story from their day) benefit from narrative intervention strategies. Teachers first select a grade-appropriate narrative story or portion of a story for instruction. Instruction follows a six-step routine:

1. *Read the text aloud to a small group of students, pausing to clarify meaning, check for understanding, and help students connect with the story.* Teachers should also think aloud to model the way a reader makes sense of text.

2. *Teach narrative structure and story grammar relationships.* Provide explicit story grammar instruction (e.g., plot, setting, characters, problem, solution, feelings) using visual cues to show the overall organization as well as the way story elements relate to one another.

3. *Teach temporal ordering and cause–effect/problem–solution relationships.* Make visible (using a story map or other graphic organizer that matches the narrative story structure) the causal relationships of episodes in the story (e.g., *first, next, meanwhile, finally*).

4. *Model and scaffold ways to retell the story using the narrative story structure of an episode.* Use the visual display and emphasize the story grammar elements as you retell an episode and then ask students to practice retelling.

5. *Co-construct parallel narratives.* Once students are familiar with a narrative story structure, prompt them to generate their own stories. Use the story maps or other graphic organizers as a guide. Encourage students to share how characters feel and what motivates them.

6. *Monitor student progress.* Keep track of student progress (e.g., number of story elements used in retelling or story generation) and adjust instruction accordingly.

*Theme Scheme*

A theme is the underlying meaning of a story. It can be explicit (stated in the text) or implicit (suggested). Williams (2005) provided at-risk primary-grade children with explicit instruction in different text structure strategies and found that their comprehension improved and that they were able to transfer the strategies they learned to novel texts. The first approach she investigated was the "Theme Scheme," which includes the following steps:

- *Introduction and prereading discussion:* In the first part of the lesson, the teacher defines the concept of theme, discusses the value of understanding themes, and introduces the background of the specific story for that lesson.
- *Reading the story:* The teacher reads the story aloud, interspersing the text with questions designed to encourage students to process the text actively (e.g., make connections with prior knowledge).
- *Discussion using organizing (theme scheme) questions:* The teacher and students discuss eight questions.
  1. Who is the main character?
  2. What is the main character's problem?
  3. What did the main character do about the problem (solution)?
  4. And then what happened?
  5. Was that good or bad?
  6. Why was it good or bad?
  7. The main character learned that they should _____.
  8. We should _____.
- *Transfer and application of the theme to other story examples and to real-life experiences:* The teacher introduces a one-paragraph vignette that provides another example of the same theme. The teacher and students discuss the example using the eight questions, plus two additional questions:
  1. When is it important to _____?
  2. In what situation is it easy/difficult to _____?
- *Review:* The teacher reviews the eight organizing questions and asks students to think about other examples.
- *Activity:* The teacher leads the class in a follow-up enrichment activity, such as writing, drawing, discussion, or role playing.

*Story Maps*

A helpful way to identify narrative story structure is through graphic organizers, charts, or maps. Studies have shown that visualization of text structure is an effective way to help students understand text structure and remember information from a story (Bogaerds-Hazenberg et al., 2020; Pyle et al., 2017). For narrative story structures, students are given a story map, which is a diagram of key words that represents the flow of the story. Students complete the map with key information as they read a story. The story map could include a diagram with spaces for setting, goal, plot, and outcome, or it could be focused on one character's problem, response, action, and solution. The map can have multiple uses, including monitoring and supporting comprehension during reading, discussing after reading, writing summaries, remembering elements of the story later on, and as an example of a specific text structure that can be applied to stories in the future. Studies have shown that a key to using story maps or other text structure visualizations is that students are actively engaged in completing the maps for themselves (Bogaerds-Hazenberg et al., 2020). While teachers may provide the map with categories and boxes and arrows, students need to fill in information as they read either on their own, with a partner or small group, or as a class. Chapter 4 provides additional examples of graphic organizers that can be used with narrative texts.

### *Information Text Structure*

Expository texts, also referred to as information texts, come in a variety of different organizational patterns, and these can be more difficult to comprehend than narrative texts. Some of the reasons that expository texts can be challenging are the tendency for these texts to include technical vocabulary, facts, unfamiliar content, and complex and cognitively demanding concepts (Denton et al., 2015; McCormick & Zutell, 2015). There are several common expository text structures that may be associated with signal words (Meyer, 2003).

- *Description.* Describes characteristics, information, and/or setting. The main idea is the who or what.
  - Signal words or phrases: *for example, for instance, in particular, specifically, such as, characteristics of, qualities of, looks like, sounds like*
- *Sequence.* Ideas are presented by sequence or time. The main idea is the procedure or order of events.
  - Signal words or phrases: *long ago, before, recently, first, to begin with, next, afterward, later, last, finally, in the end*
- *Cause–effect.* Relationships and the main idea are presented with cause-and-effect–linking ideas.
  - Signal words or phrases: *if . . . then, the reason, caused, because, led to, so, thus, therefore, moreover, caused, as a result*
- *Problem–solution.* Offers a problem and solutions. The main idea often has two parts: the problem, challenge, or obstacle and then the solution, resolution, or answer.
  - Signal words or phrases: *problem, question, puzzle, issue, trouble and solution, answer, a reason for the problem is, response, resolution*
- *Compare and contrast.* Ideas are related based on similarities and differences. The main ideas organize the components of the comparison.
  - Signal words or phrases: *alike, have in common, share, resemble, are similar to, in contrast to, but, instead of, however, unlike, differ, differentiate, whereas, although, despite*

- *Listing.* Can occur with other structures, but organizes information in a series.
  - Signal words or phrases: *first, second, third, then, next, furthermore, also, in addition to, moreover*

As with the other strategies shared throughout this book, students with reading difficulties benefit the most when expository text structure instruction is explicit. Students start by identifying the structure of an expository text. They can then use their knowledge to select and organize key information from expository texts, for instance by selecting the graphic organizer that best matches the text structure of the article they are reading. Knowledge of expository text structures also provides the basis for summarizing and writing expository texts. Roehling and colleagues (2017) offered the following evidence-based ideas for teaching expository text structures.

### Identification Strategies

One way to teach students to recognize expository text structures is to provide exposure to specific text structures and to explain how these structures are used outside of written texts. To introduce various structures, have students share and discuss examples of a structure and then relate the examples to the written format. For instance, for the description text structure, have students practice describing various items and settings. Then introduce the sequence text structure. For the cause–effect text structure, ask students to share some of the ways weather affects our activities, or some of the reasons that people prefer certain activities over others. It's important for students to generate their own ideas first. Then, present the name of the text structure, and read models in expository text.

### SIGNAL WORDS

As noted previously, expository text structures often include signal words (also called key words or cue words) that identify the text structure for the reader. Begin with a shared reading of one text structure type. Highlight and note the signal words. You may want to generate a shared list with students that is displayed in the classroom. This same process can be used with various text structures. However, note that signal words need to be used with flexibility. Some words are used across multiple text structures and some words are common to all kinds of texts and appear without any connection to a particular text structure. They signal a specific text structure when a number of words appear in the text and meet the purpose of the text structure.

Once students are familiar with text structures, teachers can provide practice distinguishing one from the other (Bohaty, 2015). For instance, a teacher can introduce problem–solution and compare–contrast, identifying signal words and the structure and purpose of each. Students can then read texts and classify which text type is used and why the author might have chosen that structure. The teacher can then support students to discriminate between text types.

*Organization Strategies*

Roehling and colleagues (2017) emphasized that understanding how an expository text is organized is in service of using that information to support comprehension. It is not sufficient to teach text structures without connecting with and practicing the ways to use text structure identification to learn new ideas and content in expository text. Once students are familiar with expository text structures, engage them in practice activities that deepen their understanding.

QUESTIONING

Teachers can ask guiding questions that focus students on structural elements of a text, such as cueing students to look for the problem and solutions while reading. For instance, in a reading connected to a chemistry unit on separating liquids from solids, students in an eighth-grade reading intervention group read an article about how scientists worked to clean up an oil spill in the Gulf of Mexico. To use text structure to support comprehension, engage students in the following steps:

1. Present the text structure (or ask students to identify it): *This text is about an oil spill and follows the problem–solution expository text structure.*
2. Have students read the text, stopping at designated places to mark signal words related to problem–solution text structure.
3. Ask the students questions at each stopping place: *What <u>problems</u> did the oil spill create? What <u>solutions</u> were presented to clean up the oil spill? Which <u>solutions</u> were the most effective and why?*

GRAPHIC ORGANIZERS

Similar to the use of visualizations for narrative text, students can create content visualizations related to expository text structures. Teachers can apply graphic organizers that are blank or partially filled in or students can create their own. There are many possibilities for visual representations. A few common ones include:

- *Topic web:* A center circle with additional circles branching out
- *Compare–contrast:* Might include boxes with arrows that indicate how ideas are related
- *Matrix:* Consists of the topic in a row on top, with categories listed in columns below
- *Venn diagram:* Overlapping circles illustrate the relationships across ideas
- *Linear string:* Boxes in a line with arrows can be used to show a progression of ideas in a sequence text structure

Graphic organizers can also include evidence from the text or key details. Graphic organizers can be used for many purposes and not all are intended to support awareness of text structure. For instance, a graphic organizer can be appropriately used to help students identify and keep track of hierarchal information of the main idea and supporting details. Be sure that whichever system you use meets the purpose for the activity, aligns with the text students are reading, and provides ample space for students to display their understanding. Adjustments should be made depending on students' fine motor skills and the amount of information needed to create a coherent and useful representation of the text. Some students may find that creating a graphic organizer electronically is more efficient. This also provides the flexibility for teachers to differentiate (e.g., filling in varying amounts of information) according to individual students' needs. As with any note-taking system, graphic organizers are best when they continue to have value after reading. Students can use information as a guide to discuss or debate a topic, to write a summary, or to remember new information. Graphic organizers can also be reorganized. For instance, descriptive text graphic organizers from two different readings can be combined to compare and contrast information that represent ideas from both texts.

## CONCLUSION

The more a teacher knows about the interplay between the reader, the text, and the purpose for reading instruction, the better they will be at using their professional judgment to select texts that are appropriate for the activity at hand. As teachers develop understanding about how texts work and what makes texts more or less challenging for students, text selection can be more purposeful. Text selection provides an excellent opportunity to collaborate with colleagues and also with students, as teachers seek to identify texts that can be used for multiple purposes. Using a wide variety of resources—including curriculum materials, libraries, and websites—teachers can attune to their students and develop rich and effective reading comprehension instruction for them. In addition to common activities such as teaching text structure, developing reading comprehension skills, fostering discussion, and deepening content knowledge, texts can and should inspire students to keep reading.

# CHAPTER SIX

# Promoting Content-Area Literacy

**STUDY GROUP PROMPTS**

1. Consider how content-area literacy can be integrated into your current teaching practices. Identify a content-area literacy practice you intend to implement soon.

2. Consider the range of content-area instruction (e.g., science, history, social studies). Identify the reading demands in each of these content areas and how you might promote students' content and disciplinary literacy.

3. Observe one or more students with a reading difficulty during a content class. Note the strengths and challenges that students exhibit during reading activities. Consider collaboration between special education and content teachers to help students transfer skills across settings.

Many teachers are familiar with the adage that first students *learn to read* and then they *read to learn*. Reading to learn is an essential part of developing knowledge that facilitates understanding. This knowledge building or background knowledge provides a critical foundation that promotes overall reading comprehension. Reading to learn is asked of students in science, social studies, language arts, and mathematics. However, while reading is not new in content classrooms, what is changing is the emphasis on how teachers approach reading. Teachers are expected not just to ask students to read for understanding, but to teach the general and domain-specific reading skills in social studies, science, mathematics, and language arts that will facilitate both content and disciplinary literacy. We focus here on the aspects of literacy that pertain specifically to reading.

## WHAT IS CONTENT-AREA LITERACY?

Content-area literacy refers to the ability to read and understand content-area texts. These are generalizable skills and strategies that can be applied across content areas to facilitate metacognition and understanding before, during, and after reading (see Chapter 4). Examples include making connections to prior knowledge before reading, learning to use a main idea strategy to synthesize information during reading, and creating a concept map of ideas to summarize and make connections after reading. There is evidence that students with reading difficulties require explicit instruction in a variety of reading strategies that will allow them to "read to learn" with content-area texts. Further, for students to transfer and apply reading strategies, instruction cannot occur only in language arts, reading, and special education settings, but strategies must also be taught and supported in content classrooms, most often within content-area instruction. Content literacy seeks to create readers who can successfully navigate content but does not necessarily attend to techniques for reading that may be unique to the texts in a particular content area (Shanahan & Shanahan, 2012, 2017).

The need to infuse reading strategies into content-area teaching is articulated in progressive state standards, including the Common Core State Standards, representing a shift in the role of content-area teachers, who are being asked to be more intentional in their use of texts and the skills needed to understand them (National Governors Association Center for Best Practices & Council of Chief State School Officers [NGA & CCSSO], 2010). For example, the CCSS include a section on reading instruction in content areas that calls for devoting more class time to reading complex texts, explicitly teaching reading strategies, increasing time for student discussions, and building students' academic vocabulary.

## WHAT IS DISCIPLINARY LITERACY?

Disciplinary literacy refers to the specialized set of skills and understandings that are unique to a specific discipline (e.g., how science writing reflects that discipline). It expands the notion of content literacy to include routines, language, skills, and uses that encourage a more nuanced application of reading in the content areas that necessarily have an application related to the specific content. For example, discipline-specific science reading skills are likely to be more applicable in science than in social studies. The theory behind disciplinary literacy is that reading demands vary by subject and, as such, should be taught across content areas and in different ways (Shanahan & Shanahan, 2008, 2017). Most students require explicit instruction, scaffolding, and many opportunities to practice. Furthermore, whether a general or discipline-specific strategy is taught in a content-area classroom, there is a need to contextualize for students by making explicit connections between the strategy and its use and purpose with the content for which it is being taught and applied (Conley, 2008; Pratt et al., 2023). Special education and reading teachers are encouraged to collaborate with content-area teachers to plan and provide instruction in disciplinary literacy.

To illustrate the differences between content literacy and disciplinary literacy, let's explore the following example related to previewing text. There are general strategies that can be taught to introduce text to students. For example, before reading, teachers might teach the general reading strategy of connecting to prior knowledge. A teacher might ask students to brainstorm what they already know about a topic. This could happen in math class ("What do you already know about quadratic equations?"), in social studies ("What did you learn in the last unit about why the United States entered into World War II?"), or in science ("What do you know about kinetic energy?"). This is a general strategy that prompts students to make connections to what they already know before reading. Brainstorming is used to activate background knowledge for the student, and the process reveals misconceptions and identifies the areas in which a teacher might need to build background knowledge. The brainstorming strategy is not content-specific and can be taught to students to increase content literacy and can be applied broadly to a variety of text types for many purposes. In general, it is helpful to connect to prior understanding before reading an unfamiliar text. Students can add this strategy to their tool kit and transfer it to a variety of reading activities inside and outside of school. Other general previewing strategies are discussed in more detail in Chapter 4 but include such activities as predicting what you will learn and asking questions before reading.

Recall that disciplinary reading strategies are specific to each discipline and thus call on more specialized skills that might apply to one content area and not another. For example, imagine that students in a science class have completed a lab on chemical reactions. They used indicators to tell whether or not a chemical reaction had taken place. In the next lesson, students will compare their lab results with the results gathered by "real" scientists performing the same experiments by reading a section of their textbook called "Making Connections." Thus, a preview activity might entail organizing and reviewing lab results and making predictions about the extent to which students perceive their results will match those from the experiments conducted by professional scientists. The domain-specific literacy skills developed include organizing data to summarize understandings and making predictions based on those data. In addition, one goal of such an activity meets the science content standard of "analyzing and interpreting data" (Next Generation Science Standards, 2012, p. 2).

In one regard, these previewing activities share a similar purpose: to help students make connections to what they already know in preparation for learning from text. In the science example, the activity has been tailored to embed reading strategies in a specific science context. One might presume that in this scenario, the discipline-specific preview strategy would be more powerful than asking students to recall what they know about chemical reactions, preview the text features (pictures, headings, and charts), and predict what they think the text will be about. However, there are times in science when a general reading strategy would also be effective. Consider, for example, the same science class studying chemical reactions. The students are going to read an article about how chemical reactions cause pollution in the world using a reading from the text called "Chemical Reactions and Pollution." In this case, the general reading strategy of brainstorming is appropriate. To make connections to what students already know, a teacher might ask students to recall what they know about how chemical reactions might influence the environment. In addition, to peak students' interest and to focus in on the content of the reading, the teacher would ask students to scan the text and look at charts, graphs, subheadings, pictures, and captions. Based on the brief preview, the teacher asks students to predict what they think they will learn about the chemical reactions and pollution. These are general reading strategies that would be useful preparation for meeting the reading goals in this science class.

Both general content literacy and domain-specific literacy are important, and general reading strategies are often considered a prerequisite to effectively refining disciplinary literacy skills (Hinchman & O'Brien, 2019). General strategies transfer across contexts and provide building blocks for students who struggle with comprehension; discipline-specific strategies focus on the skills and strategies used in particular content areas. Yet, despite recent interest in disciplinary literacy, researchers caution that these discipline-specific reading strategies are not a replacement for instruction in general reading strategies (Faggella-Luby et al., 2012). Struggling readers who lack the foundational reading strategies that will allow them to learn from text still require instruction in general reading strategies. For educators, we think about how and when to incorporate both general and domain-specific strategies to increase reading proficiency and understanding in all content areas.

In a review of reading and writing strategies for struggling learners, only 12 of 150 studies included disciplinary literacy practices (Faggella-Luby et al., 2012). Next, we recommend a few research-based instructional strategies but focus our instructional considerations on helping teachers develop an understanding of the literacy demands that are present in the content areas, with suggestions for areas to consider while organizing and delivering instruction.

## READING IN THE CONTENT AREAS

While much of this book has focused on foundational general reading strategies, the next sections provide an outline of discipline-specific reading demands and instructional considerations. In some lessons, it may make sense to focus a general reading strategy on the content at hand, whereas in other lessons more discipline-specific strategies can be taught. Content-area teachers play an important role because they understand the unique literacy demands required to read and understand in their disciplines. Yet content teachers, who are traditionally more focused on teaching content than teaching students how to read about content, may require support to teach reading strategies and skills to students. Likewise, special education and literacy teachers also need to learn more about discipline-specific reading demands and purposes in order to teach and support reading with various texts and across multiple settings. For instance, a special education teacher might instruct students to evaluate texts written from different perspectives in advance of instruction that will occur in social studies. This individualized instruction in discipline-specific reading practices can prepare students with disabilities to be more successful in content-area classes. Working together with content-area teams, teachers can agree on general and discipline-specific reading strategies to teach that are in line with standards and student needs. Students learn to transfer strategies across content areas and to adapt to discipline-specific reading demands.

## Reading in Science

Reading science texts for understanding and learning requires that students understand the language of science and how science concepts are represented in texts and that they are able to use this information to develop science knowledge (Cervetti & Pearson, 2018; Pearson et al., 2010). Several significant factors continue to complicate teachers' abilities to promote reading in their science classes. First, there is a concern that science teachers will become focused on reading at the expense of providing hands-on, inquiry-based learning experiences, particularly when such reading is not part of the adopted curriculum. On the other hand, many teachers who have tried to increase the focus on reading have been faced with science texts that are too difficult, are of poor quality, have a great deal of technical vocabulary, and are uninteresting for many students (Fang, 2006; Guthrie et al., 2012). Furthermore, teachers may lack the skills to teach students how to read and learn from science texts. Finally, the climate in many schools focuses on content coverage, thus encouraging teachers to provide the information needed rather than having students acquire the knowledge through text. With much to cover and a lack of understanding of how to teach students to read in science in ways that support content learning, teachers may opt for what seems to be a more efficient way to deliver the curriculum. As Pearson and colleagues (2010) have noted, "reading about science may be replaced by listening to someone talk about science" (p. 460). Reading is possible and productive in science and can be integrated into science classrooms at all levels.

### Recommendations for Instruction

- *Use reading to supplement, not supplant, inquiry-based learning in science.* Text can be a form of scientific inquiry and students can learn to read like a scientist. Students can approach science texts similarly to how they interact with an experiment or other inquiry investigation by learning reading skills that focus on gathering data, coming to consensus, understanding multiple representations, and presenting findings based on evidence (Pearson et al., 2010).

- *Embed reading strategy instruction in science content.* Reading and strategy instruction should not be an add-on to content reading (Snow & Moje, 2010). Several reading strategies using focused models have been effective for meeting the needs of struggling readers in science classrooms. For example, Concept-Oriented Reading Instruction (CORI) teaches reading strategies through interdisciplinary science themes. Each unit embeds strategy instruction into the science content. Similar to the multicomponent strategy instruction models described in Chapter 9, CORI instruction includes hands-on inquiry-based activities, inquiry with text, explicit reading strategy instruction, collaborative group work, and features to increase motivation

(Guthrie et al., 2012). The focus for strategy instruction in science is connecting the unique purposes of text and its features with the application of strategy use.

• *Connect meanings of a variety of representations within and across texts.* Science texts often include graphics, formulas, diagrams, and other visual representations along with text. While reading, scientists integrate the text features with the written words and go back and forth between these various sources to make meaning (Shanahan, 2012). Students can also be taught to manage text and text features while reading science texts. In addition, students should read a variety of science texts to gather information about concepts; these could include textbooks, newspaper articles, lab notes, and scholarly studies (Pearson et al., 2010).

• *Separate important information from unimportant information.* In a study of how scientists read in science, scientists surveyed noted the importance of being able to distinguish between important and unimportant details while reading (Shanahan, 2012). Similarly, students can learn strategies that help them focus on important topics and the portions of text that support them. Several of the main idea strategies outlined in Chapter 4 include components that help students determine important information while reading. An example of applying main idea strategies in science is provided in Figure 6.1.

• *Teach science vocabulary, including important prefixes, suffixes, and roots.* Science is its own language, and reading in science includes understanding technical and content-specific terms. Affixes are especially important and provide a key to word meaning (e.g., hydrogen dioxide = 1 hydrogen atom and 2 oxygen atoms = water). Shanahan (2012) recommended the use of a vocabulary notebook that includes the vocabulary term, a definition, an example, a diagram, and additional information as needed, such as the scientific formula and related terms. Content-specific affixes can be created in specific science courses, such as biology or physical science, and in subjects other than science as well. Figure 6.2 provides metric prefixes that are very useful in chemistry, physics, and math. Often, common affixes relate to words in different content areas. For example, the prefix *mal-* (bad) is used in words such as *malformation* or *malignant* in science but would be found more commonly in words like *malcontent* or *malicious* in social studies. Ellery and Rosenboom (2011) provide a list of common affixes with content-specific examples that demonstrate how affixes are applied in different content areas. Additional general vocabulary strategies in Chapter 3 can be adapted for learning science vocabulary.

• *Use graphic organizers to display the key science constructs and how they are related before reading.* There is growing evidence of the value of graphic organizers as a mechanism for teaching key constructs and how they relate providing necessary background knowledge for reading science text with understanding (Roman et al., 2016).

### Reading in Social Studies

Social studies educational reform has increased the diversity of texts that are used to teach history. In addition to textbooks, social studies curricula frequently include

Teaching students to distill the big ideas while reading is a general reading strategy. However, determining the key ideas can be particularly challenging in science, where text is often filled with unfamiliar vocabulary as well as many facts and examples that can obfuscate the key points. The practice and application of generating a summary can be tailored to science texts through the use of graphic organizers.

The purpose of using a general main idea strategy: Identify the most important information in a section of text (this strategy is described in more detail in Chapter 4).

1. Identify the most important *who* or *what* that the section is about.
2. Identify the key ideas about the *who* or *what*.
3. Generate a brief main idea statement.

### Application of the Main Idea Strategy in Science

For some concepts, generating definitions and examples may be a more useful way to synthesize understanding than writing a main idea statement. In addition, science texts often introduce multiple concepts at once. For example, it is common to introduce kinetic energy and potential energy in one or two sections of text. Students need to understand each concept and to explain the relationship between the two types of energy. In this strategy, teachers provide a graphic organizer that aligns with the structure of the text and use important information to come up with a summary statement after reading. Rather than identifying main idea statements for each section, students complete a targeted graphic organizer. The following graphic organizer helps students to identify the important information about each concept and to write down examples. Once students complete the reading and the graphic organizer, they create a summary statement that focuses on the essential learning. To focus on the science content, teachers can scaffold the review statement. Here, rather than asking, "What was the most important information in this text?" the teacher focuses students on the relationship between the two types of energy by asking them to write a summary statement that explains the *relationship* between kinetic energy and potential energy. As students become more experienced using graphic organizers to identify and remember important information, they can select or create their own organizers while they are reading.

### Comparison of Kinetic and Potential Energy

| Kinetic Energy | | Potential Energy | |
|---|---|---|---|
| Definition: | | Definition: | |
| Example | Example | Example | Example |

Write a summary statement that explains the relationship between kinetic energy and potential energy. _____
_____
_____

**FIGURE 6.1.** Identifying important information in science text.

| Prefix | Value |
|--------|-------|
| *peta-* | quadrillion |
| *tera-* | trillion |
| *giga-* | billion |
| *mega-* | million |
| *kilo-* | thousand |
| *hecto-* | hundred |
| *deca-* | ten |
| *deci-* | tenth |
| *centi-* | hundredth |
| *milli-* | thousandth |
| *micro-* | millionth |
| *nano-* | U.S. billionth |
| *pico-* | U.S. trillionth |
| *femto-* | U.S. quadrillionth |

**FIGURE 6.2.** Metric prefixes.

biographies, primary source documents, and historical fiction. Often, multiple sources are used to analyze one historical event, with the purpose of deepening the understanding of history. Multiple perspectives are explored, and work is done to evaluate bias. In many classrooms, the textbook is no longer the definitive expert source but has become one of many sources to sift through (VanSledright, 2012). There is also an increased use of project-based learning that incorporates these various texts. While reading comprehension is essential to understanding and general reading strategies can be supportive, especially for struggling readers, researchers have argued that reading in social studies must combine essential comprehension strategies with higher-level discipline-specific skills that are essential to developing historical literacy. In other words, understanding the text is just one aspect of reading in social studies. Some of the skills that are needed to read in history include developing content knowledge, organizing information, evaluating bias, determining cause and effect, developing intertextual understanding (i.e., comparing and contrasting information from various sources), constructing arguments based on evidence, and gaining the critical-thinking skills that allow students to evaluate and to reason historically (e.g., De La Paz, 2005; MacArthur et al., 2002; Taboada et al., 2015; VanSledright, 2012).

By studying how expert historians read, we can see the varied and complex reading skills that are required to learn from text in social studies. Examples of reading strategies used by historians that can be taught to students include evaluating the reliability of various accounts of a single event, revising interpretations, assessing the perspective of the author given the historical context, asking important historical questions, and "exercising historical imagination to fill in evidentiary gaps" (VanSledright, 2012, p. 212).

### Recommendations for Instruction

• *Teach reading and note-taking strategies that develop understanding of historical concepts and information.* Historical understanding includes knowledge of historical events, concepts, and groups of people as well as how these factors shape history. Students need to learn how to read and remember a great deal of information in history. Using graphic organizers and note-taking strategies allows students to distill what is important and to keep it for later reference and study. In one case (Harmon et al., 1999), students used a prediction strategy to categorize section headings in the text to determine if the sections would be about a person, event, or place, and then took notes that addressed questions related to each category. Students also clarified important words as they read. The focus of the strategy was gaining content knowledge, making cause-and-effect connections within and beyond the text, and learning how specific information gathered during reading added to a larger understanding of historical concepts.

• *Embed strategy instruction in domain-specific tasks.* In social studies, as in science and other content areas, the use of explicit strategy instruction with scaffolded support can be effective in meeting domain-specific reading goals for students who are struggling readers. For example, the "get the gist" main idea strategy can help students develop understanding as they read, and questioning strategies, such as QARs, may help students move beyond recall of facts to developing critical understandings by synthesizing information, understanding relationships, and making inferences (see Chapter 4). Figure 6.3 describes how one teacher used her social studies curriculum and a unit on the American tradition of protest to increase content learning and to meet a literacy standard in social studies: Determine the meaning of words and phrases as they are used in a text, including vocabulary specific to domains related to history/social studies.

Other programs integrate a set of reading strategies into content teaching. In Promoting Acceleration of Comprehension and Content through Text (PACT; Vaughn et al., 2013, 2015a, 2015b), both discipline-specific and general reading strategies are taught within the content of history units. In a recent study, five eighth-grade social studies teachers taught their content to some of their classes with the PACT model and taught the same content in other classes without PACT strategies. The instructional cycle includes five components that are taught within 10-day units. Teachers provide explicit instruction linked to content with embedded supports focused on increasing content learning, vocabulary, and use of reading strategies (see Chapter 8). Students receiving PACT instruction scored significantly higher than their peers who had received typical instruction in measures of content comprehension, general reading comprehension, and content learning (Vaughn et al., 2013). These findings were replicated for students with reading difficulties, English learners, and in large-scale

Henry David Thoreau was a writer and philosopher who lived in the mid-1800s. His writings about nature are still pondered by those who are interested in the environment today. Impelled by his beliefs, he also greatly opposed the slave trade. Thoreau not only wrote that keeping slaves was immoral, he also took action by speaking out against the government and by refusing to pay taxes. Thoreau was imprisoned for one night for not paying tax and famously wrote about this as a form of protest against the state's support of slavery.

Using this excerpt in a unit on peacekeepers around the world, Ms. Foster taught her students to apply the click-and-clunk strategy (see Chapter 9) to first identify unknown words and then to use context clues and word parts to figure out their meanings. In this reading, students identified *pondered*, *impelled*, *slave trade*, and *imprisoned*. After Ms. Foster modeled the strategy, students worked together in partners, rereading the text to find clues that would help them determine the meaning of the difficult words, breaking words apart, and checking definitions in the text. Students wrote their definitions in the margins of the text as part of their note-taking system. Students applied this strategy in subsequent texts with additional scaffolding as needed.

**FIGURE 6.3.** Identifying unknown words and using fix-up strategies in social studies.

effectiveness studies (Roberts et al., 2023; Vaughn et al., 2015a, 2015b). Furthermore, teachers implementing PACT were more likely to engage students in interactive instructional practices (Toste et al., 2019).

 • *Teach students how to evaluate and connect multiple sources.* Many students read all texts in the same way by trying to learn and remember as much as they can. Indeed, reading for understanding is an essential reading goal and one that many students will struggle with throughout their lives and that they get relatively little practice doing in content-area classes (Murray et al., 2022). However, in social studies (and in science as well as other disciplines), reading requires a critical evaluation in addition to a literal understanding. For example, how does the author of the text (e.g., a slave, a slave owner, or a textbook writer) influence the point of view and the "facts" that are presented? Students need to be taught how to read and evaluate multiple sources and how to judge an author's veracity.

In a study of historical reasoning, students were taught to evaluate the bias in text, to determine how information was presented differently depending on the source—newspaper, opinion essay, textbook—and to write opinion essays using textual evidence (De La Paz et al., 2007). The general education and special education teacher worked together to help students learn note-taking and reading strategies with primary-source documents that enabled them to engage in historical thinking. The role of the special education teacher was to focus on supporting the domain-specific reading goals and included such activities as reteaching strategies and concepts, helping students apply the strategies they were learning, and providing extra time in the special education setting to engage in collaborative discussion about the text and to complete assignments.

A similar strategy was recommended by De La Paz and Felton (2010). Students were taught to employ the following strategies to read and respond to a text:

1. Consider the author.
2. Understand the source.
3. Critique the source.
4. Create a more focused understanding.

For each strategy, there was explicit instruction and multiple opportunities to practice. Students then repeated this reading procedure with various historical concepts.

• *Support the reading and writing connection.* Social studies standards depend on using information gained in reading to reflect, to synthesize, and to defend arguments in writing (Hwang et al., 2022; Taboada et al., 2015). In a study by De La Paz (2005), students first learned to read and take notes in preparation for a writing task in which they would write opinion essays based on their reading and interpretation of text. Regardless of their initial reading and writing skills, students with and without disabilities who mastered the discipline-specific reading strategies wrote higher-quality persuasive essays that were more historically accurate. Note that the connection between reading and writing is relevant in all content areas and can be tailored to needs in specific content areas. For example, in science, students can be taught to gather and evaluate information from various texts in order to make a scientific claim or come to a consensus. Follow-up writing activities can be based on evidence gathered from reading and other activities. Regardless of the focus content area, it is essential to make connections explicit for students and to teach them how to use information from reading to support writing tasks.

### Reading in English Language Arts

English language arts (ELA) teachers, particularly in secondary settings, are often viewed as reading teachers. And indeed many ELA teachers are well versed in the types of general and domain-specific instructional strategies that support students in developing content and disciplinary literacy in English. Yet there are several challenges that present themselves in ELA classrooms. First, researchers who have observed ELA classrooms for all grade levels have found more often than not that teachers ask students to demonstrate essential reading skills and strategies, such as generating a main idea statement or writing a summary after reading, without providing explicit instruction in how to do so (e.g., Pressley, 2006; Stevens et al., 2019). Thus, while teachers may understand essential strategies, they may be less practiced at teaching them. A second tension in ELA classrooms is that in addition to teaching students how to understand and learn from text, teachers are required to teach much more, including but certainly not limited to, characterization, plot, setting, figurative language, symbolism, theme, tone, and a host of skills related to evaluating texts. Third, many language arts classes include an entire curriculum around writing, limiting the time available to focus on reading—with often minimal time allocated for reading texts (Murray et al., 2022). Fourth, the adoption of progressive state standards has signaled key shifts, including an emphasis on reading expository text, that may also impact instruction in ELA classrooms. Inasmuch as these standards apply to instruction in ELA classrooms, as noted earlier, there is a stated focus on application of standards across the content areas. Finally, in addition to the elements articulated in the standards, experts in ELA also encourage the teaching of critical literacy. Proponents of critical literacy posit that "teachers must invite their students to actively critique and challenge existing notions of what it means to both produce and consume texts" (Hicks & Steffel, 2012, p. 129). Thus, like other content teachers, ELA teachers may feel pressed for time and resources in their effort to address all that is required of them.

### Recommendations for Instruction

Consider the following for improving reading comprehension within ELA.

- *Teach students to read texts from a variety of genres, including contemporary and classic works.* Using a balance of fiction and nonfiction texts is emphasized, as is the integration, analysis, delineation, and evaluation of knowledge and ideas. We expect that grade-level texts will be more challenging for all students, and especially for struggling readers and students with LD.
- *Provide structured opportunities for using "stretch texts" or more challenging texts for students to read.* The recent Institute of Education Sciences Educators Practice guide on improving reading outcomes for students with reading difficulties in grades 4–9 recommends the use of stretch texts, text reading that is at grade level for students with reading difficulties, as one source of the texts that they read (Vaughn et al., 2022). These texts are selected because they align with the classroom instruction, and while they are above the reading level of the students, small-group teacher-led support is provided to make these texts accessible. Of course, they are not the only texts that students read, but they give students an opportunity to see how the strategies that they are learning to comprehend text can be utilized to support their access to more challenging texts.
- *Develop skills that allow students to interpret and analyze text craft and structure.* Students will be asked to understand nuances of text craft, beginning in the early grades. These initially include being able to understand various text types and move quickly into interpretation, analysis, and the ability to make connections. Further, students will need to be able to determine how an author's purpose is conveyed through point of view and how words, phrases, and larger sections connect with each other and to a larger meaning (Haager & Vaughn, 2013; LaRusso et al., 2016).
- *Increase knowledge about content and the world through texts.* Improving reading comprehension occurs through expanding knowledge, as background knowledge contributes extensively to reading comprehension across the age ranges (e.g., Francis et al., 2018; Lonigan et al., 2018). The process of "close reading" is intended to develop such skills as determining key ideas and details and going back to the text to provide textual evidence to support thinking. There is also an emphasis on

integrating knowledge and ideas initially by relating text to text features (e.g., illustrations, titles, and headings), and later by making higher-level connections within and across texts.

• *Provide challenging and complex texts.* Create time and space for students to access grade-level text with particular attention to the multiple dimensions of text complexity. Teachers are required to use texts that are increasingly complex as students progress through grade levels. The CCSS provide detailed guidelines for ways to evaluate text complexity, including considerations of qualitative aspects (e.g., depth of concept meaning, structure, and language difficulty), quantitative sources (e.g., readability measures), and matching the reader to the text and the task (e.g., motivation, experience with subject matter, goals for reading) (NGA & CCSSO, 2010). The focus on text complexity may be particularly challenging for struggling readers, and this is an excellent area for collaboration with specialists as they work together with ELA teachers to determine ways to help students access challenging texts in general education classrooms.

• *Engage students in rich discussions about text using textual evidence to ground conversations.* During large-group discussions, teachers may need to support students in ways that can increase participation of struggling readers by altering discussion formats. In small-group discussion formats, students may need to develop group work skills such as turn taking, sharing ideas, and providing feedback to group members. In addition, students may need to be taught how to use textual evidence to support their ideas during discussions. Teachers can also integrate cooperative learning strategies such as increasing individual accountability during group work, helping students feel that their ideas are valued in the group, and reinforcing that students are part of a team that will learn more together than they can on their own (Kent et al., 2015). In summary, if students are going to participate in high-level discussions about text, they will need to be taught skills and strategies to engage productively. A sample mini-lesson is provided in Figure 6.4. In this lesson, students as a whole class or in small groups are given a discussion prompt with accompanying discussion stems. Discussion stems can change according to the goals for the content learning or the types of discussions skills being developed. In just a few minutes, this type of discussion can support students at all levels to engage meaningfully in discussions.

• *Develop critical literacy skills.* Teach students to read texts in an active and reflective manner, with opportunities to make connections to the larger world, to question the text, and to develop an understanding of the text that goes beyond basic comprehension. Critical literacy includes higher-order thinking skills involved in such actions as inferring, and exploring how texts define identities and how perspectives are shaped by culture and power structures. Students are thus able to evaluate and make judgments as they read, becoming more informed and discerning consumers of text.

• *Embed general strategy instruction in the teaching of literature.* Incorporate reading strategies that are geared to the needs of the learners. This will mean teaching general reading strategies in addition to more discipline-specific literary strategies.

| | *Band members have a special bond. A great band is more than just some people working together. It's like a highly specialized army unit or a winning sports team. A unique combination of elements that becomes stronger together than apart.* —Steven Van Zandt (musician) |

**MAKING A COMMENT**
- From my background knowledge, I know this person . . . and it may have influenced them to think . . .
- I think this quote means . . .
- In my own life, I think my teacher might be showing us this quote because . . .
- I'm wondering . . .
- I imagine my teacher chose this picture to illustrate this quote because . . .

**RESPONDING TO OTHERS**
- To add on to what _____ said, _____.
- I agree with _____ because _____.
- I respectfully disagree with _____ because _____.

**FIGURE 6.4.** Three-minute discussion. Quote retrieved from *www.brainyquote.com/quotes/quotes/s/stevenvanz514981.html*.

Attention to how strategies are taught and supported is particularly important. Teachers should not discuss the strategies or ask students to use them without first offering guidance. Strategies need to be explicitly and intentionally included in ELA instruction, with opportunities to practice and to refine application. If students continue to struggle, teachers should be prepared to scaffold and to provide additional instruction as needed.

## Reading in Math

As with any content area, the primary focus of teaching math literacy is to increase knowledge and understanding of math vocabulary, skills, and concepts. Mathematics is generally thought to comprise three areas: computational fluency, conceptual understanding, and mathematical processes. Yet some have argued that the focus on teaching literacy in mathematics classrooms may undermine the development of math understanding (Siebert & Draper, 2012) by being overly focused on reading texts that don't support math learning. Thus, the first question to ask is: Does reading belong in the mathematics classroom? The concern is that reading looks different in math classrooms and that traditional texts just aren't a good fit. The reading of text might support certain math concepts, such as reading the picture book *How Much Is a Million?* (Schwartz, 1985) as kindergartners are working to conceptualize large numbers. But we caution that simply adding in more reading for reading's sake may not be the right approach.

Yet reading is required in math. Consider the following math problem, which is similar to those found in fourth-grade textbooks:

Cinderella's wicked stepmother wanted to put wall-to-wall carpeting in her den. She gave Cinderella $275. The room measures 10 feet by 12 feet. The carpet costs $4.50 per square foot. Luckily, Cinderella found a half-off sale. How much did Cinderella have left over after paying for the carpet?

To answer, a student needs to sift through quite a bit of text (e.g., fairy tales, deals, measures, wall-to-wall carpeting, half-off sale, square foot) to get to the core of the problem. And this is math class. Mathematics textbooks can also challenge struggling readers. In general, math textbooks are designed with descriptions, problems, graphs, charts, and examples, and it takes a skilled reader to navigate the variety of forms in which information is presented. In addition, sidebars or boxes that may be unrelated to the topic are often included. These sidebars might contain review concepts, additional skills practice, or a graph or fact intended to connect the text to the real world (Metsisto, 2005). Scenarios that are intended to peak students' interest (e.g., calculating speed in a bicycle race) are presented, but they may lack explicit connections with the mathematical concepts. Students read through a narrative that tells a story, and if they don't make the expected connections, the story can be both confusing and distracting. Hughes et al. (2016) recognized that word-problem solving is challenging because it involves reading the problem, understanding the context, identifying important versus extraneous information, choosing an approach to solving problems, and solving the problem correctly (Hughes et al., 2016; Powell et al., 2019).

In addition, attention to how common words change meaning in math is important for struggling readers and ELs. Metsisto (2005) points out how common words can cause confusion in math. See Figure 6.5 for examples of how common words such as *of, off,* and *a* have very different and specific meanings in math. Multiple meaning words are also problematic. Consider the word *square,* which has multiple meanings in math (e.g., square root, a square shape, and a number squared), additional meanings outside of math (e.g., town square, to square off in a fight), and can be a noun, a verb, and an adverb. Adding vocabulary instruction to math interventions is associated with improved outcomes (Stevens et al., 2023).

We have thus far been referring to "reading to learn." A consideration in math and in some other content-area reading relates to "reading to *do.*" A student is not asked just to understand a math word problem, but to interpret the meaning of the word problem so that the student can "do" the associated math thinking and problem solving specified in the text. In short, math reading cannot be approached in the

---

- The words *of* and *off* can be confusing in percentage problems. The percent *of* something is different from the percent *off* something.
- The word *a* can mean "any" in mathematics. When asking students to "show that a number divisible by 6 is even," we aren't asking for a specific example, but for the students to show that all numbers divisible by 6 have to be even numbers.
- To take the area "of" a triangle includes understanding that this is the space "inside" the triangle.

FIGURE 6.5. Confusion caused by small words.

same way as reading expository or narrative text in other content areas. So what can teachers do to support content literacy in mathematics? Unfortunately, there is little research that defines how to develop math literacy (Siebert & Draper, 2012). Thus, in lieu of specific considerations, we recommend a close collaboration between general education mathematics teachers and reading specialists to analyze the reading demands in a particular math course and to identify areas that need support. For example, special educators can help students develop math vocabulary and work with students to preview and practice how to explain their thinking. In addition, specialists can offer suggestions for scaffolding instruction to allow access to mathematical material that has a high reading demand.

## CONCLUSION

The debate about general strategies versus disciplinary strategies is not a new one. As early as 1922, researchers began to study the ways in which individuals varied their approach to reading depending on the type of reading material and began calling for the teaching of skills that were subject specific (Moore et al., 1983). The issues of whether to teach discipline-specific or generic reading strategies continues to be raised, and many researchers agree that both general reading skills and domain-specific skills are needed for reading success. We offer the following final suggestions.

- *Teach general content-area literacy skills.* Faggella-Luby and his colleagues (2012) reminded educators and researchers that students who have yet to develop basic or general literacy skills require instruction well beyond elementary school. They noted that "disciplinary literacy, a potentially powerful idea, cannot replace general strategy instruction for all adolescent learners because adolescents who struggle with reading and writing do not possess the foundational skills and strategies necessary to learn proficiently" (p. 69). Further, general strategies can be used to help students make connections and provide multiple opportunities for them to practice as they apply similar strategies across content areas. Content literacy is a building block that allows students to learn and apply disciplinary-specific literacy skills. Teachers should intentionally embed general strategy instruction for content areas that is reflective of students' needs.

- *Teach discipline-specific strategies, including adapting general strategies in content-specific ways.* Sometimes, relatively small tweaks to general strategies are effective in tailoring a strategy to a particular content area. At other times, discipline-specific strategies allow students to delve more deeply into the content to meet discipline-specific reading goals. Attending to the skills required to complete a reading task and teaching these explicitly will support students in using domain-specific strategies.

- *Collaborate with specialists to plan and develop explicit instruction in reading strategies.* Finally, collaboration is especially important if teachers are to address the complex reading demands and requirements set forth in the era of educational reform articulated in new standards such as the CCSS and the Next Generation Science Standards. Special education teachers and reading specialists are uniquely equipped to collaborate with content-area teachers to address literacy needs within content demands. Such collaborations can be leveraged to plan and deliver instruction that supports both discipline-specific and general strategy instruction in content-area classrooms (Kennedy & Ihle, 2012). Further, general education teachers are challenged to incorporate more explicit instruction in both content and disciplinary literacy. Working together to meet the needs of all students across content areas is both a challenge and an opportunity.

# CHAPTER SEVEN

# Supporting English Learners with Learning Difficulties

The school-age population in the United States is becoming increasingly diverse. If you have been teaching for a long time, you may have students from a wider variety of backgrounds in your classroom than in previous years, including English learners (ELs).[1] The term *English learners* is a designation given to those students who are in the process of acquiring English as a second or additional language and who have not reached English proficiency, as measured by a school-based English proficiency assessment process. By law, ELs are offered supports in school to develop English language skills and to access grade-level content. ELs are the fastest-growing segment of the student population. In the United States, about 5.1 million, or 10.4%, of public school students are ELs (National Center for Education Statistics [NCES], 2022). In previous decades, ELs were concentrated in specific areas of the United States, but now school districts across the country serve ELs. The largest proportion of ELs are in elementary grades (e.g., 15% of kindergarten students were ELs in 2019). More

---

[1] We use the term *English learners* (Els) because it is the term used by the U.S. Department of Education. We also recognize other culturally affirming names, including *multilingual learner, emergent bilingual,* and *dual language learner.*

than 75% of students learning English in school speak Spanish as their primary language (NCES, 2022).

As a group, ELs tend to underachieve in comparison with fluent English-speaking peers on tests of literacy administered in English. Data from the 2019 National Assessment of Educational Progress (NAEP) indicated a 33-point discrepancy between ELs and non-ELs in fourth-grade reading achievement scores, and a 45-point gap at eighth grade (NCES, 2022). These gaps in scores indicate how imperative it is to attend to ELs when planning and delivering reading comprehension instruction. Yet many educators are not fully prepared to meet the needs of their EL students (Ortiz & Robertson, 2018). Teachers report being "challenged to help these children reach the level of proficiency required for learning sophisticated academic content through English" (Dixon et al., 2012, p. 6). As local and state standards emphasize increasingly complex texts, it is more imperative than ever to use effective reading comprehension instruction that attends to the unique needs of ELs.

## WHO ARE ELs?

ELs vary in many ways. For instance, immigration status, generation of family in the United States, and number of years in the country differ. More ELs are born in the United States than in other countries; as of the last decade or so, 82% of the ELs in grades PreK–5 and 65% in grades 6–12 were born in the United States (Mitchell, 2016). ELs born in the United States are more likely to be simultaneous bilinguals, meaning that they started to learn both their home language and English simultaneously at a very young age, before starting school. ELs who were not born in the United States are more likely to be sequential bilinguals (Baker, 2006), because they may have started to learn English as an additional language later, often when they began attending school. Regardless of whether ELs are simultaneous or sequential bilinguals, the language and literacy learning processes differ in important ways from learning to read and write in only one language. Prior knowledge, oral language skills, and literacy in their home language and in English affect ELs' learning in English.

ELs vary in their English proficiency from beginning to advanced levels. Depending on their prior experiences and when and how they learned the various languages they speak, ELs show different profiles of relative strengths and weaknesses across language and literacy domains. For example, those who acquire a language in a natural setting are more likely to excel in spoken language, whereas those who learn a language in a more formal setting, such as in school, are more likely to excel in the written aspects of language. ELs can vary in their knowledge of vocabulary and grammar, and how they understand the rules of language usage (e.g., Proctor et al., 2017). ELs might be stronger in English in subjects such as science, which they learned in school, and stronger in another language in other topics. Students' background knowledge, instruction, context, motivation, and need to use each language all affect the language acquisition process.

To avoid making erroneous assumptions about their backgrounds, knowledge, and competencies, teachers need to consider the many differences among ELs. We have heard about ELs who were studying advanced mathematics (e.g., calculus) in their home countries but then were placed in remedial classes when they started school in the United States and stagnated. If teachers understand the variability among ELs, then it is more likely they will make suitable pedagogical decisions to meet their ELs' needs by providing challenging, appropriate, and high-quality instruction. Perhaps most important is that along with the variation previously noted, English learners are not two monolinguals in one person, turning on a switch to activate one language or another. Bilingualism is holistic. This means that each individual engages in flexible and principled language use and can learn the most when they are able to draw on their full linguistic repertoire.

### ELs with Learning Disabilities

About 14% of the ELs in the United States are considered to have a disability, which is about the same percentage as non-ELs. Among ELs with a disability, about half are identified with a learning disability, and 21% are identified as having a speech and language impairment (U.S. Department of Education, 2022). ELs with disabilities are less likely to be included in general education and have a lower graduation rate than their peers with disabilities who are not ELs (Cooc, 2023). Determining whether an EL has LD can be quite challenging. The assessment team must rule out language acquisition as the primary reason for a student's learning difficulties (Individuals with Disabilities Education Improvement Act [IDEA], 2004). This does not mean that the team must wait until the student is fully proficient in English to determine if a student has a disability. Rather, it means that they must establish that the student exhibits behaviors characteristic of *both* LD and language acquisition and that the student is struggling in their first language as well as in English. The team must also determine that the student has received an adequate opportunity to learn through suitable instructional practices. Yet, making these judgment calls is not easy (Castro & Artiles, 2021; Klingner et al., 2006). Some ELs are mistakenly placed in special education when they do not actually have LD; others are overlooked and do not receive the special education support that could benefit them. The characteristics of language acquisition can appear to mirror those of LD on the surface, so it is very important to consider alternative explanations for each behavior (see Klingner & Eppolito, 2014, for more information).

ELs with LD are typically taught by special educators who have not received adequate preparation in their teacher education programs on how to meet students' language and literacy needs (Barker & Grassi, 2011). Another challenge is that many ELs lose access to specialized language instruction, such as through English language development (ELD), English as a second language (ESL), or bilingual education programs, when they are placed into special education (Kangas, 2018). Yet special education and ELD services should not be thought of as "either/or." ELs with LD are entitled to a full range of seamless and coordinated services designed to meet their language and learning needs.

# FACTORS THAT INFLUENCE COMPREHENSION FOR ELs

Many factors affect ELs' reading comprehension, including oral language proficiency, the ability to use comprehension strategies, knowledge of different text structures, level of interest and motivation, and background knowledge about the topic of the reading. ELs often comprehend more of what they read in English than they are able to convey when they are asked to demonstrate their understanding in English only. For instance, many activities ask students to read a text and respond in writing. Responses may indicate an issue with reading comprehension when the challenge is being able to express ideas in writing. Therefore, providing ELs with alternative ways to show what they know or encouraging them to respond in a combination of English and other languages can help students express what they know.

# RECOMMENDED INSTRUCTIONAL PRACTICES
# TO SUPPORT ELs WITH READING DIFFICULTIES

Did you know that learning to read in a second (or additional) language differs from learning to read in one's first language in some important ways? Although there certainly are many similarities, there also are notable differences (August & Shanahan, 2006; Hall et al., 2019; Proctor et al., 2017). It is important for teachers to understand these differences as well as the similarities and to use the most up-to-date information to design and deliver instruction based on the individual needs of the ELs they serve. In this chapter, we describe what we know from research about vocabulary and comprehension instruction in particular, drawing from recent research on ELs with reading difficulties (e.g., Hall et al., 2019) and an Institute of Education Sciences (IES) Practice Guide focused on teaching academic content and literacy to ELs (Baker et al., 2014).

## *Vocabulary*

Vocabulary knowledge plays an indispensable role in students' comprehension of text (Proctor et al., 2017). ELs' familiarity with English vocabulary often lags behind their word-reading ability, negatively affecting their comprehension (Lesaux & Kieffer, 2010; Mancilla-Martinez & Lesaux, 2011). Many ELs have extensive vocabularies but still need support to develop depth in their vocabulary knowledge. For instance, they might know the most common meaning of words with multiple meanings but not know the less common or more abstract meanings (such as thinking of *run* as the act of moving quickly on one's feet but not knowing the more expansive aspects of the definition, such as tears that *run* down one's face or for colors to *run* together) (August & Shanahan, 2006). Also, ELs can be puzzled by prepositions, pronouns, cohesion markers (to connect clauses or ideas; e.g., *perhaps, similarly, as shown by*), anaphora (repetition of a word or phrase at the beginning of successive phrases), figurative language, and idioms. It is important for teachers to consider that although textbooks typically provide explicit definitions for key vocabulary terms in the text, perhaps in the margins or with bolded font, it is actually the meanings of words with multiple definitions, figurative language, conjunctions, or prepositions that may be harder for ELs to understand than words that have difficult or complex meanings (see Chapter 5 for more examples).

Teachers should also keep in mind the substantial difference between English words for which ELs already understand the underlying concept and know the word in their native language and words that are altogether unfamiliar (August & Shanahan, 2006). When ELs already understand what a word means in another language, access to a translation or telling them what the word is in that language should be adequate. When ELs do not know the concept in any language, they will need instruction in what the word means (e.g., *photosynthesis* or *democracy*). For example, consider the English word *anodyne*. Telling you that the Spanish translation is *anodino* (a cognate) is not going to help if you do not already know what *anodino* means. In this case, a synonym should do the trick: *painkiller*. But consider the word *dulosis*. That is more complicated—it is the practice by some ants of enslaving other ants to collect food for them. If you do not already know what *enslaving* means, then understanding this word will be more challenging. No simple explanation will do.

### Vocabulary Instruction

Several approaches to helping improve the vocabulary of ELs can be effective. Vocabulary should be emphasized before, during, and after reading and throughout the day, during language arts as well as in the content areas. Vocabulary instruction should be a focus in prekindergarten through postsecondary classrooms. Instruction should help ELs access background knowledge (using all their language resources), make critical content connections, and develop higher levels of word knowledge. The IES Practice Guide recommends teaching a set of vocabulary words intensively across several days using a variety of instructional activities (Baker et al., 2014).

#### EXPLICIT VOCABULARY INSTRUCTION

1. Select a short, engaging piece of informational text that includes academic vocabulary. It's best if the text connects with content instruction (e.g., a social studies or science unit), has ideas that are worth discussing, and provides examples and details that support comprehension. This text can be used as the base for vocabulary instruction for the week.

2. Identify about five to eight academic vocabulary words from the text for in-depth instruction. These may be words that are used frequently in the text and that appear in other content areas. Consider also choosing words that have multiple meanings, contain affixes, and that are cognates (e.g., association—*asociación* in Spanish).

3. Teach academic vocabulary in depth using multiple modalities (writing, speaking, listening) with many opportunities for students to engage with words. Examples include providing student-friendly definitions and then applying these definitions to

the content of the target text and using examples and nonexamples with images to deepen understanding of each word. To increase interaction with new words, facilitate discussions in which students use and discuss meanings of new words and ask questions that encourage students to demonstrate nuances in word meanings.

4. Teach word-learning strategies to help students independently figure out the meaning of unknown words. Students can learn to figure out the meaning of new words using context clues, morphemic analysis (word parts), and cognates. Provide opportunities for students to discuss how they are figuring out words and to check that their definitions make sense in the context of the target text. See below for additional detail on word-learning strategies.

### SHARED BOOK READING

Shared book reading is one promising approach for enhancing young children's vocabulary, both in the home (Collins, 2010) and at school (Fitton et al., 2018). A popular practice for ELs and non-ELs, in shared reading an adult reads with a child or a group of children, using interactive techniques to engage children, and to clarify words or ideas. Providing rich explanations of key vocabulary words improves students' understanding and vocabulary. Also important is providing children with opportunities to talk about the story and try out the new words they are learning. Use open-ended questions rather than yes/no questions, and make sure to provide students with enough time to respond. Consider the difference between asking a student, "Did you like the story?" (a question that can be answered with a *yes* or *no* response) and "Tell me two things you liked about the story" (which requires much more talking). Or be even more specific: "What does a chrysalis do?" Ask for clarification or elaboration frequently.

### BRIDGING

Bridging is a useful technique for supporting ELs' vocabulary learning during shared book reading. Bridging means to embed Spanish (or other language) vocabulary in English-language lessons using a word or explanations in Spanish to help students understand the meaning of a new English word (Lugo-Neris et al., 2010). Students with strong skills in their home language seem to benefit the most.

### COGNATES

Cognates, or words with common meanings and similar spellings in two or more different languages, can also enhance comprehension (Montelongo et al., 2011; Nagy et al., 1993). Teachers ask students if they can think of any similar words in another language. As part of an EL adaptation of collaborative strategic reading (CSR; Klingner, Vaughn, et al., 2012), teachers cue students to think about similar words they know in another language and provide them with lists of cognates to refer to while they are reading.

## MORPHOLOGICAL ANALYSIS

Morphological analysis, or figuring out word meanings based on an understanding of roots, prefixes, and suffixes, is another powerful way to improve vocabulary learning. In this approach, students look at word *parts* to try and figure out what they mean and use the meanings of those chunks to help them determine the meaning of unknown words. Morphological analysis can be better than the more commonly used practice of learning definitions and writing words in sentences (Carlo et al., 2004). In one study, Kieffer and Lesaux (2008) found that fifth-grade ELs with more morphological awareness had higher vocabulary knowledge and reading comprehension than peers with less morphological awareness.

## CONTEXTUALIZED VOCABULARY INSTRUCTION

To support ELs to build vocabulary, vocabulary instruction should occur across content areas. This means using content-focused texts in support settings such as ELD instruction, reading intervention, or other small-group instruction, and it also means providing explicit vocabulary instruction as part of content lessons such as math, social studies, and science. Using the contextualized vocabulary instruction or the intensified vocabulary instruction framework during science lessons, Taboada and Rutherford (2011) explored two instructional frameworks that varied in the explicitness of academic vocabulary instruction, comprehension strategy instruction, and supports for student autonomy with fourth-grade ELs. Teachers integrated comprehension strategies with instruction in science vocabulary and practices designed to promote autonomy and motivation. Results indicated that students improved in the area(s) emphasized in the intervention and for which they received explicit instruction.

## MULTICOMPONENT VOCABULARY INSTRUCTION

Multicomponent vocabulary instruction may be the most effective for helping ELs to learn new words. For instance, in one study, Vaughn and colleagues (2009) provided ELs in seventh-grade social studies classes with multicomponent instruction that included explicit instruction in words and their definitions, graphic organizers, and videos to build background knowledge and conceptual understanding. Students spent some time during each lesson working collaboratively with peers and discussing new content. Their vocabulary knowledge and content learning improved. Vaughn et al. concluded that the combination of explicit vocabulary and concept instruction promoted students' vocabulary and understanding of content.

In a different study, this time with sixth-grade ELs in language arts classrooms (Lesaux et al., 2010), students read short, interesting passages with targeted academic words. They engaged in an array of vocabulary activities, such as brainstorming definitions; discussing contextual information and new words in pairs and with the whole class; creating class definitions; sketching representations; engaging in morphology practice; playing word games; using the words in new contexts; and writing, editing, and sharing paragraphs. Their vocabulary knowledge and comprehension improved significantly.

Using a multicomponent program called Quality English and Science Teaching (QuEST), August and colleagues (2009) helped ELs in middle school science classes to improve their science knowledge and academic language. QuEST lessons included explicit vocabulary instruction, visuals such as pictures and diagrams, graphic organizers, hands-on experiments, demonstrations, modeling, discussions among teachers and students, and guided reading activities. ELs learned general academic vocabulary, such as the words *structure* and *function,* as well as discipline-specific vocabulary, such as the words *organism* and *cell* (see Chapters 5 and 8).

Word Generation (WordGen) is another multicomponent academic language model that has been beneficial for ELs across many settings (Kim et al., 2018; Snow et al., 2009). For instance, researchers taught students WordGen to middle school students. Participants included ELs and also fluent English speakers. It was the ELs who were most successful with the program. WordGen focuses on words students need to know to be successful in school, which the developers of the program refer to as "all-purpose academic words" (p. 326). The main criteria for selecting the target words were that they must be high-utility, high-functional, and cross-disciplinary. WordGen presents target words in semantically rich contexts, provides frequent exposures to each word, includes explicit instruction in word meanings and word-learning strategies, such as morphological analysis and cognates, and offers multiple opportunities to use words orally and in persuasive writing.

## MULTIMEDIA

Multimedia also offers promising ways to support ELs' vocabulary learning. One interesting program is called Improving Comprehension Online (Dalton et al., 2011; Proctor et al., 2011), which is a web-based scaffolded text environment designed to improve monolingual English and bilingual students' vocabulary learning and reading comprehension. The approach includes informational texts and several folktales available in both Spanish and English. The program adjusts for reader factors, such as word recognition skill and fluency, so that they no longer function as gatekeepers to the text. The reader has the option to listen to the text through audio-recorded narration or with a text-to-speech read-aloud tool. As part of a research study, fifth graders read eight multimedia folktales and informational texts and completed embedded activities, researcher-developed measures of comprehension and vocabulary, and standardized reading achievement tests. Improving Comprehension Online students outperformed comparison students on vocabulary measures, but not on comprehension measures.

Many teachers have turned to apps to teach vocabulary to ELs, as a way to supplement instruction. A recent study that used a tool to evaluate the quality of apps to deliver effective vocabulary instruction showed that most of the 53 apps they evaluated did not adhere to guidelines of effective instruction (Northrop & Andrei, 2019). The authors provided the following guidance when selecting apps to enhance or supplement vocabulary instruction for ELs:

1. Test out the app looking for key features:
   a. Can teachers select the words?
   b. Does the app give definitions?
   c. Is the app interactive with games or other ways to practice?
   d. Are there features specific supportive of ELs (e.g., narration, translating into a students' home language, visuals)?
2. Look for apps that allow teachers to create and individualize word lists.
3. Match the app to the instructional needs of the ELs who will be using it. A student who is just beginning to learn English will benefit from different features than a student who is more proficient in English.

In summary, research studies have added to our understanding of what it takes to improve ELs' vocabulary learning. It appears that ELs benefit from multicomponent approaches as well as explicit instruction. We list different aspects of vocabulary instruction that research indicates are beneficial to ELs for enhancing vocabulary and improving comprehension.

- Engage students in shared book reading with definitions of target words and opportunities to discuss text.
- Help students access and connect with background knowledge.
- Use videos, demonstrations, and actual experiences (e.g., a common field trip) to build relevant new knowledge.
- Supply "bridges" to a first language using words and definitions from that language.
- Connect new learning with content.
- Offer sufficient support to build conceptual understanding.
- Make use of technology and multimedia sources when available.
- Teach strategies for figuring out the meanings of unknown words.
- Build students' morphemic and semantic awareness.
- Help students identify cognates and use their knowledge of words in another language to figure out new words in English.
- Focus on vocabulary before, during, and after reading or engaging in other instructional activities.
- Provide meaningful opportunities for students to discuss content using the new words they are learning, with peers and/or with the teacher.
- Facilitate the use of students' multilingual resources.
- Scaffold students' attempts to use new words; provide feedback.
- Prioritize words that students are likely to see across academic content areas.
- Teach discipline-specific meanings when they vary across content areas.
- Provide multiple exposures to target words in a variety of ways.
- Offer various opportunities for meaningful practice, such as through word games, skits, debates, and other engaging activities.
- Use graphic organizers (e.g., semantic webs, concept maps), pictures, diagrams, and real objects when teaching new words.
- Encourage writing using new words, such as persuasive essays.

### *Reading Comprehension*

As complicated as reading comprehension is for readers in their first language, it is even more complex for readers in a second or additional language who are not fully proficient in English (Phillips Galloway & Uccelli, 2019; Snow, 2002b). The reason is that ELs are dealing with all of the same cognitive and metacognitive processes as their fluent English-speaking peers, plus they are doing so in a language with which they are not entirely familiar. English proficiency makes a difference. In a longitudinal study of ELs' English reading comprehension throughout elementary school, Mancilla-Martinez and Lesaux (2011) found that variations in students' English skills accounted for the variance in their English reading comprehension. The students had received instruction in an English-only environment. Instruction had focused on word identification and phonics. Their word-level reading was adequate but their reading comprehension was quite low, at about a second-grade level. These researchers and others have stressed the importance of focusing on vocabulary and oral language instruction to improve comprehension (Cho et al., 2019).

In addition, teachers rarely spend enough time actually teaching strategies and other techniques to ELs to improve their reading comprehension (August & Shanahan, 2006). Rather, it is much more common for them to ask lower-level rote questions about facts instead of questions that require higher-level thinking skills such as synthesizing, making connections with prior knowledge or across subjects, or applying information in a passage to real-life situations. Teachers seem to expect students to know how to answer challenging questions or apply comprehension strategies without teaching them how to do so.

### *Reading Comprehension Instruction*

There are many different ways to help improve ELs' reading comprehension. In the previous section, we discussed vocabulary as one essential component. ELs also benefit from comprehension strategy instruction that helps them to develop their metacognitive and cognitive skills (e.g., Garcia & Godina, 2004; Genesee & Riches, 2006). Promising practices for ELs include reading the whole text for the gist and self-monitoring for understanding; transactional literature circles with collaborative conversations (McElvain, 2010); cooperative learning; instructional conversations (Goldenberg, 2013); and providing multiple ways for students to demonstrate understanding.

Comprehension strategy instruction can help ELs become better readers (August & Shanahan, 2006; Garcia & Godina, 2004; Goldenberg, 2013; Riches & Genesee, 2006). Strategies should be taught in the context of helping students learn new content or of reading fiction rather than in isolation. For example, in Figure 7.1, the teacher is helping students distinguish between the main idea and subordinate ideas or important details from the grade-level curriculum text using a concept map. This type of instruction helps students organize information into a main idea statement. It is important to keep in mind that comprehension strategies help students understand what they read and provide them with tools for figuring out and remembering challenging text, but they are not the end goal by themselves.

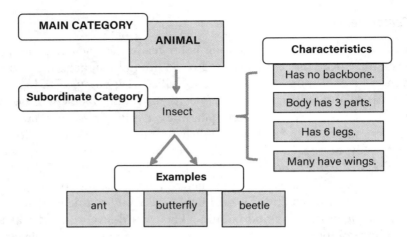

**FIGURE 7.1.** Concept map. *Goal:* In this type of lesson plan, ELs are encouraged to distinguish between main categories ("animals") and subordinate categories ("insects"). Next they are supported in thinking of examples ("ants" and "butterflies") and characteristics ("Has no backbone," "Body has three parts"). If time permits, they are encouraged to come up with different examples.

## STUDENT-GENERATED QUESTIONS

One useful strategy is generating questions about a text (see also Chapter 4). Students might develop questions before reading and then try to answer them during reading, as Berkeley, Marshak, and colleagues (2011) did when they taught a self-questioning strategy in inclusive seventh-grade classes, 23% of whose students were ELs. Berkeley et al. found that self-questioning improved ELs' reading comprehension and content learning of grade-level social studies.

Or students might generate questions after reading. In two related studies, Taboada and colleagues (2012) examined student-generated questions about science text. First, they looked at the impact of student questioning in relation to general vocabulary knowledge in English-only speakers and ELs and found that questioning predicted both groups' reading comprehension, although with different patterns in general vocabulary. Next, they explored the questioning-generating instruction that ELs with varying reading levels received and found that the instruction improved their questioning skills. Together, the two studies indicated that text-based student questioning is a reading strategy that contributes to ELs' reading comprehension and conceptual knowledge in the content area of science.

## MULTICOMPONENT MODELS

Researchers have successfully implemented various multicomponent instructional models with ELs. These models focus on teaching and developing a combination of skills. There is strong support that models that include both vocabulary and comprehension instruction have greater comprehension benefits for ELs than either comprehension or vocabulary instruction on their own (Hall et al., 2019). Focusing on features of instruction, Proctor and colleagues (2021) worked with teachers and students over a 3-year period to develop a multicomponent approach to EL literacy development, including reading comprehension. They identified key features of instruction that teachers can use as a guide when selecting approaches.

- Provide explicit instruction and opportunities to practice and reflect on language and metalinguistic awareness (e.g., semantics, syntax, morphology).
- Encourage student talk, facilitating discussion about language and text.
- Use multimodal texts and scaffolds to support comprehension, writing, and oral expression.
- Encourage students to access and use all their multilingual resources.

In terms of specific models, modified versions of reciprocal teaching (Palincsar & Brown, 1984) can help enhance ELs' reading comprehension (see the description of reciprocal teaching in Chapter 9). Klingner and Vaughn (1996) adapted reciprocal teaching and used it with seventh- and eighth-grade Spanish-speaking ELs with LD in their social studies classes. The researchers added a brainstorming step before reading to help students access and connect with their prior knowledge. They added cooperative learning and peer-tutoring components in their implementation of the model, and they encouraged students to use Spanish as well as English to discuss reading passages. Findings showed that students' reading comprehension improved significantly. Results from other CSR studies that included ELs have demonstrated that students are more likely to engage in student-led discussions about what they are reading than when teachers used their business-as-usual approaches (Boardman et al., 2017). Discussing text provides an opportunity for ELs to develop oral language and increase comprehension with structured supports they learn to apply through models such as CSR.

Hall and colleagues (2020) used a different multicomponent approach focused on inferencing with small groups of middle school students with reading difficulties, the majority of whom were ELs. Teachers modeled the strategies by thinking aloud, asked inference-eliciting questions during reading, and taught students to use graphic organizers to scaffold the inference process. Students in this study improved both their reading comprehension and their ability to make text-based inferences. In this approach, students learn to notice gaps or points in the text that are unclear, to identify clue words or phrases, and to make connections between what they already know and what is in the text. The teacher identifies points in the text where the meaning lacks coherence or where making an inference would clarify understanding. At the stopping points, the teacher asks inference questions. Students learn to look for evidence and discuss their reasoning as they answer the questions. Read more about inference instruction in Chapter 9.

## CONCLUSION

These are exciting times to be a teacher of ELs. Research sheds light on the cognitive benefits of bilingualism (Bhattacharjee, 2012): "Being bilingual . . . makes you smarter. It can have a profound effect on your brain, improving cognitive skills not related to language and even shielding against dementia in old age" (para 1). Whenever bilingual individuals speak, both (or all) languages are active. Rather than causing interference, as previously believed, the challenge of figuring out how best to communicate one's message actually strengthens the brain, in a sort of "cognitive workout."

What does this mean for teachers? If our goal as a nation is to produce high school graduates who are ready to compete in the global economy, then we should consider that students who begin school already knowing a language besides English have a head start. If we nurture their bilingualism and capitalize on their strengths, helping them to feel "smart" rather than inferior, as, unfortunately, still seems to be the case in many classrooms, then we are enriching their school experiences as well as our own. We can do this by implementing the instructional approaches outlined in this chapter, focusing on vocabulary and comprehension, and making sure that our ELs have every opportunity to interact with peers and use academic language, engage in higher-level thinking, and contribute in their classrooms in meaningful ways.

All teachers, not only ESL and bilingual specialists, must become knowledgeable about how best to support the language acquisition and learning of ELs. Teachers should understand the wide diversity in EL populations; the possible variability in students' backgrounds; and the language proficiency, academic, and literacy competencies of ELs in both or all of their languages. They also should recognize and appreciate the linguistic and cultural resources that ELs bring into their classrooms from their homes and communities. ELs, even those who sometimes struggle with reading, need teachers who can provide challenging but appropriate learning opportunities that integrate them into the classroom and that match their needs and capabilities.

# CHAPTER EIGHT

# Intensive Interventions for Students with Significant Reading Comprehension Difficulties

1. Conduct an informal survey of the various programs and other resources that are used to provide "intensive intervention" in reading to the students in your school. Determine the aspects of these programs that align with research and the parts that appear to be less well connected to research. Establish a plan for how your school will select and use research-based interventions.

2. How are data used to identify students for intensive interventions? Consider whether the practices for identification are clearly specified. How is progress-monitoring used to determine students' responses to these intensive interventions?

3. Consider the profiles of the students in your class who have significant reading comprehension difficulties. Prepare a plan that describes the amount of instructional time each week in which they will be given word study, vocabulary, fluency, and reading comprehension instruction.

4. Select one or more of the sample lessons provided for improving reading comprehension that you think would be beneficial for your students with significant reading difficulties. Work with your colleagues to describe ways to make the lesson more systematic, explicit, and intensive so that it meets the needs of your target students.

## HOW TO ACCELERATE THE PROGRESS OF STUDENTS WITH SIGNIFICANT READING COMPREHENSION DIFFICULTIES

Significant reading comprehension difficulties may be explained by one of several causes, including poor early reading instruction, underdeveloped word reading skills, inadequate background knowledge about the text, overall low vocabulary knowledge that interferes with understanding, inadequate practice in reading for meaning, and insufficient or inadequate instruction. Students may also have significant learning difficulties because they have *cognitive processing difficulties* that interfere with successful learning. These learning difficulties in reading include executive-function or self-regulation problems. Promising research suggests that integrating strategies that support cognitive processing through academic instruction may accelerate academic progress. Moreover, students may exhibit pronounced learning difficulties because the learning environment does not provide opportunities for teachers to align instruction with students' learning needs. Learning can be increased for students who have significant reading comprehension difficulties when instruction is delivered in *smaller learning groups* and in one-on-one settings, and students are given *additional time* with appropriate instruction, practice, and feedback. Finally, students may demonstrate significant difficulties with reading comprehension because the *instructional delivery* does not meet the learning needs of students who typically require more explicit and systematic instruction. In this chapter, we discuss each of these considerations with an aim to providing improved reading comprehension instruction for students with the greatest needs. To make instruction more individualized, teachers need to:

- Target the reading areas of highest need (e.g., word study, fluency, comprehension).
- Provide additional opportunities to practice until word or phrase reading is automatic and error free.
- Gradually increase the amount of text (e.g., from phrases to paragraphs) that students read orally and silently.
- Create multiple opportunities for students to select easy and difficult texts of high interest to them.
- Provide feedback and further instruction to ensure success.

## IMPLEMENTING STRATEGIES THAT ENHANCE COGNITIVE PROCESSING

Students with significant reading difficulties and disabilities display very low performance in reading. In the early grades this low performance is exhibited as difficulty remembering the names of letters, connecting sounds to letters, segmenting sounds, and reading words. As students get older, their very low performance is manifested in slow and inaccurate word and sentence reading as well as very low comprehension of text. Since this book focuses specifically on reading comprehension, we will highlight intervention practices for students with specific and intractable reading comprehension problems.

For some of these students, their low performance in reading comprehension is related to their demonstrated difficulties with *cognitive processing.* These include difficulties with executive functions, self-regulation, and an array of cognitive processes that affect and influence memory; with attention; and with the generation, selection, monitoring, and implementation of learning strategies (Follmer, 2018).

One can conceptualize these as the "control processes" that manage goal direction for learning and overlap with other cognitive and behavioral processes, such as language, short-term memory, processing speed, and nonverbal reasoning. A growing research base associates executive functions with learning in reading (Cutting et al., 2009; Locascio et al., 2010; Souvignier & Mokhlesgerami, 2006; Swanson & Howell, 2001; Was & Woltz, 2007) and writing (Altemeier et al., 2008; Hooper et al., 2006; Santangelo et al., 2007; Sesma et al., 2009). Research also suggests that executive functions influence general academic outcomes (Barnett et al., 2008; Blair, 2002; Blair & Razza, 2007; Diamond et al., 2007).

How might we consider these "control processes" as they relate to students with reading comprehension difficulties? We know that students with reading comprehension difficulties are more likely to have problems with inhibition and working memory and that they consistently demonstrate overall lower ability to utilize cognitive flexibility. Cartwright and her colleagues (2017, 2019) have conducted studies in which they have provided cognitive flexibility training to students with reading comprehension difficulties, resulting in overall improved reading comprehension outcomes. Cognitive flexibility is also referred to as attention shifting, as it largely refers to successfully shifting between tasks. How might cognitive flexibility be related to reading comprehension? One possibility is that much of reading comprehension requires making strong inferences, and therefore we think flexibly about the text and put pieces together that are not directly stated. Thus, it may be useful to have inference-making tasks integrated within our intensive interventions. For examples of inference-making tasks, see Figure 8.1.

You may recall the research decades ago on processing problems of students with learning disabilities that focused on neurological models of learning based on models of brain injury (Johnson & Myklebust, 1967; Kirk & Kirk, 1971). One assumption was that students with significant learning problems had cognitive processing problems much like individuals who suffered brain trauma. A second assumption was that treating these underlying cognitive processes was both possible and necessary prior to academic learning. Although some students may have underlying neurological or information-processing disorders, research does not support the notion that practitioners can identify these disorders (e.g., auditory processing disorders) and then treat them in isolation (e.g., training a child in auditory processing apart from their academic learning; Lyon, 1985; Mann, 1979). Reliably identifying strengths and weaknesses of academic learning has been challenging. Moreover, treatments provided independently of academic learning have not improved academic outcomes in reading. As a result, in the last 2 decades, educators have put considerable emphasis on imparting effective, systematic, and explicit instruction to identify and address students' academic instructional needs in reading.

In summary, current research on cognitive processing such as executive functions and self-regulation has advanced our understanding of learning in two fundamental ways. First, executive functions and self-regulation are based on theoretical frameworks with a robust empirical base (e.g., Pintrich, 1995; Zimmerman, 1989). Second, these conceptualizations of executive functions and self-regulation have been integrated into academic instruction and not remedied separately as a precursor to academic learning.

1. **Text-connecting inferences.** Text-connecting inferences are referential inferences that successful comprehenders make all of the time. These types of inferences connect two pieces of information from the text. One type of text-connecting inference may be anaphor resolution or lexical inference in which the reader connects noun phrases to secure meaning. Another type is when the reader reads around the word to gather the meaning of an unknown word. This is particularly useful when reading information text. For example, "The scientist was particularly interested in how *mitosis* was proceeding with these cells, since they were dividing and replicating themselves at a more rapid rate than expected." By reading this sentence carefully the meaning of the word *mitosis* can be inferred.
2. **Knowledge-based inferences.** These are inferences in which background knowledge helps make an inference that supports understanding. For example, "Cynthia took an extra aspirin and decided to refrain from any more difficult work that day." We can infer, from what we know about taking an aspirin and stopping work, that Cynthia is not feeling well.
3. **Pronoun referent.** Many students with reading comprehension difficulties have trouble with pronouns and to whom or what they refer. The pronouns *it, them,* and *they* can be particularly confusing. For example, "The boys decided to give up on their pursuit of finding the missing ear buds and instead moved on to playing games on their computers. When their mom brought them downstairs they were gratified." What does *them* refer to in the sentence. We infer that it refers to the "earbuds," and thus we now know that the earbuds were found.

**What are some effective practices for improving inference instruction?**

1. Help students to identify clues or key words in the text and to use these words to derive inferences. Perhaps help students to ask questions that require using the text inferentially to answer.
2. Facilitate students using their background knowledge to make connections and resolve inferences.
3. Find "gaps" in the text and help students use this information to generate inferences and to make connections as they read further.

**FIGURE 8.1.** Teaching inference making. From Hall and Barnes (2017). Reprinted by permission.

### *How Do Cognitive-Processing Difficulties Impede Reading Comprehension?*

Most teachers are aware that many students with significant reading comprehension difficulties also have poor memory. For example, students with poor memory often have difficulty recalling the key ideas in a sentence that they just read, the names and descriptions of characters in text, and previous learning that relates to what they are currently reading (Swanson et al., 2009). Of course, struggling to remember what was read makes reading comprehension difficult, particularly because readers must remember ideas across multiple sentences and paragraphs. Imagine trying to write the main idea of two paragraphs you just read while not being able to hold in memory the key ideas or connect them in a meaningful way. Working memory, the ability to make inferences, and comprehension monitoring are predictive of reading comprehension (Cain & Oakhill, 2006; Fletcher et al., 2018). Students with reading difficulties have disadvantages in all memory tasks, and these disadvantages are associated with poor performance in the foundations of reading (i.e., phonological awareness, word reading), as well as in reading comprehension (Swanson et al., 2009).

Students' difficulties with cognitive processing are consistent with poor executive-function and self-regulation abilities: setting learning goals, monitoring success in meeting these goals, using language to self-talk through difficult elements of completing tasks, and regulating language and memory to facilitate learning. Executive functions exert considerable influence on success in reading for understanding. For example, students who struggle to regulate their thinking and behavior consistently demonstrate lower academic learning and cognitive and motivational processes (Dembo & Eaton, 2000; Krouse & Krouse, 1981). Further, students who acquire self-regulatory skills experience improved academic achievement and increased self-efficacy (Zimmerman, 1989; Zimmerman & Bandura, 1994; Zimmerman et al., 1996; Zimmerman & Risemberg, 1997).

### Why Should Teachers Integrate Self-Regulation Practices and Motivation into Their Reading Comprehension Instruction?

Self-regulation instruction can be integrated within cognitive and motivational processes to advance reading comprehension (Boekaerts & Cascallar, 2006). For example, two meta-analyses of effective instructional practices (Hattie et al., 1996; Rosenshine et al., 1996) showed that learning skills training was effective when students were metacognitively aware and used self-regulation strategies to support their learning.

Another example related to self-regulation is attribution—a person's beliefs about the causes of their academic failures and successes. Students with maladaptive attribution may think that failure is due to stable, internal causes that cannot be changed, and that success is due to unstable causes such as luck. Accurate attribution is associated with small to moderate improvements in academic outcomes, including reading (Robertson, 2000; 20 studies reviewed). In studies designed to improve reading comprehension, training students to attribute learning outcomes to their own effort has resulted in small benefits (Berkeley, Mastropieri, et al., 2011; Borkowski et al., 1988; Bosnjak et al., 2017; Carr & Borkowski, 1989; Chan, 1996). Integrating attributional training with interventions for students with significant learning difficulties seems promising, because these students are prone to a maladaptive attribution style. Last, without attributional training aligned with instructional practices, students may experience low motivation to perform well academically (Fulk & Mastropieri, 1990).

### How Can Teachers Instruct Their Students to Use Self-Regulation Strategies When Reading?

One of the things teachers can do to make their thinking "visible" to students is to show them how to consider comprehension and integrate it with text. Teachers can use think-alouds to demonstrate how successful readers approach text comprehension, reflect on text, answer questions, or give themselves feedback. Students with reading comprehension difficulties benefit when their teachers provide ongoing monitoring and feedback regarding independent use of self-regulation strategies. Students can be taught to monitor their own learning by using "awareness" to identify "breakdowns" in understanding. One way to integrate self-monitoring into academic learning is by teaching students to ask themselves questions to determine if they understand the big ideas and can put the ideas together to make sense. If you notice students struggling, model how you self-monitor.

For example, ask a student to read aloud to you. When the student misses a word, wait until they finish reading and then ask them to tell you the words they missed. If the student does not know, point out the missed words. In either case, ask the student, "What do you do when you don't know how to read a word?" After the student responds, show them effective strategies for reading the missed word (e.g., teach the student the phonics elements needed to read the word and/or ask the student what would make sense).

Teachers can integrate the same strategies regarding the comprehension of ideas and concepts. For example, when reading, ask students to stop and think about ideas they did not understand. Then ask students to reread and figure out how to "repair" their problems. Making inferences when reading sentences, paragraphs, and multiparagraph texts can also enhance self-monitoring. Ask students to read the text aloud and think about what the author is saying. If students have trouble figuring out the author's intention, ask them questions about previous or subsequent text and show them how to put ideas together to make an inference.

### How Can Teachers Enhance Students' Memory and Self-Regulation While Engaged in Reading Comprehension Practices?

Typical practices that teachers use to enhance students' memory include taking notes, rehearsing what they need to remember out loud, developing a mnemonic device to remember information, using graphic organizers and other text organizers to remember what they read, identifying and recording important concepts in their lecture notes (Boyle, 2010), and labeling parts of a story web with key ideas (Kim et al., 2004). Teachers can improve self-regulation in students by providing them with feedback about reading comprehension that is specific to the task rather than the person, with statements such as, "You organized your response to the text by summarizing the author's key ideas, and then you discussed the aspect of the author's ideas you thought were confusing." Feedback like this helps students attribute successes to their effort and work. Teachers can also help students link their work behaviors to outcomes—for example: "You reread the text with the question in mind and adjusted your answer so that it more accurately reflected the text." Use the Making Inferences in Science lesson in the Appendix as a guide to teaching the self-regulation and cognitive strategies that enhance reading comprehension. Useful internet resources on self-regulation and cognitive strategy instruction include the following:

- Cognitive Strategy Instruction website, University of Nebraska–Lincoln (*https://cehs.unl.edu/csi*)
- Online modules from the IRIS Center for Faculty Development
  - SRSD: Using Learning Strategies to Enhance Student Learning (*https://iris.peabody.vanderbilt.edu/module/srs*)
  - SOS: Helping Students Become Independent Learners (*https://iris.peabody.vanderbilt.edu/module/sr*)
  - Improving Writing Performance: A Strategy for Writing Persuasive Essays (*https://iris.peabody.vanderbilt.edu/module/pow*)

As you think about the role of self-regulation as a mechanism for improving reading comprehension, consider the following key constructs and the role that they play:

- *Working memory:* This term refers to the way we manipulate the information that we have stored in memory recently—so when reading, we are referring to remembering what is previously read and making connections.
- *Shifting:* This term, also referred to as cognitive flexibility, refers to how students switch between tasks, goals, and mental activities.
- *Inhibition:* This term refers to how students learn to suppress an immediate response in order to stop and think about an alternative response.
- *Planning:* This term refers to setting goals and thinking about how to conduct the task or activity.
- *Monitoring:* This element may be thought of as thinking about thinking in a way that allows students to focus attention on the goal and to determine how they are proceeding toward achieving the goal.

## INTENSIFYING INSTRUCTIONAL DELIVERY

### What Considerations Are Important When Implementing Intervention?

The purpose of implementing an intervention is to accelerate the progress of the student. That is why considerations about time, training of the interventionist, materials used, and progress monitoring are important to facilitate effectiveness. Use the time during the intervention to improve student learning by:

- Teaching additional skills and strategies
- Providing additional practice opportunities with feedback
- Delivering more explicit, systematic (step-by-step) instruction
- Offering more opportunities to read a range of texts with support
- Monitoring student progress in the interventions to ensure that the additional learning time increases student mastery of skills

There are several research-based practices for intensifying reading comprehension instruction for students with significant reading difficulties, such as reducing group size; adjusting the frequency, length, and duration of the intervention; and making changes in instructional delivery.

### How Can Group Size Be Adjusted to Provide a More Intensive Intervention?

One of the most practical methods for intensifying intervention for students with reading difficulties is using small-group instruction (Foorman & Torgesen, 2001). Instruction in smaller groups—when possible in pairs or one on one—can improve student outcomes (Elbaum et al., 1999; Morris, 2023; Vaughn et al., 2003).

Previous research has indicated that students receiving instruction in small groups of 3 to 4 students outperform those receiving instruction in large groups of 8 to 10 students (Lou et al., 1996; Vaughn et al., 2003, 2010). In addition, Vaughn et al. (2003) reported students receiving one-on-one instruction also made considerably more gains on several reading measures than did students receiving the same instruction in groups of 10 students. However, students receiving one-on-one instruction made gains similar to students who received the instruction in groups of three. Thus, students benefit from one-on-one and very-small-group instruction more than from large-group instruction.

The general trend of scores favored students in the smaller groups. Because fewer intervention studies on adolescents with significant academic difficulties are available than studies on younger students, additional research is needed in grade 4 and higher to more systematically define effective grouping practices for intervention.

As with increasing intervention time, coupling smaller group size with carefully designed, effective instruction can accelerate progress. When you decrease group size, you can divide your attention among fewer students and increase the potential for individualized instruction, more student response and practice, and timely teacher feedback.

### How Can Adjusting Frequency, Length, and Duration of the Intervention Improve Learning?

One of the most effective ways of improving learning is to provide appropriate instruction for a longer period of time (Torgesen, 2000). Of course, time is a precious commodity in schools, so deciding how best to increase intervention time is essential. Educators can increase intervention time in several ways. First, one can increase the *frequency of intervention.* For example, an intervention that is provided 5 days a week may be more intensive than an intervention that is provided 3 days a week. Educators can also increase the frequency of intervention by delivering more than one session of intervention per day (e.g., Torgesen et al., 2001; Wanzek & Vaughn, 2008). For example, with younger students (kindergarten, first grade), shorter-duration interventions, several times a day, can better capitalize on young students' attention and interest. Second, one can increase the *length of the instructional sessions.* If a student currently receives 20 minutes of instruction per intervention session, providing 40 minutes may intensify the intervention if student engagement remains high. Increasing both the frequency of intervention and/or the length of the instructional sessions allow struggling students to receive additional, targeted instruction and increased opportunities for practice with feedback.

Only a few studies have examined the effects of increasing the amount of time in intervention on student outcomes, and most of these studies focus on reading at the elementary level. For example, Denton and colleagues (2006) found positive gains in word reading, fluency, and comprehension when first- to third-grade students with significant reading difficulties received 1 to 2 hours of daily intervention over 8–16 weeks. Torgesen et al. (2001) demonstrated that many third- to fifth-grade students with learning disabilities who received an intensive intervention during two

50-minute sessions per day for 8 weeks improved their reading outcomes to grade-level expectations and maintained the gains 2 years later. Increased instructional time—coupled with carefully designed, effective instruction—can benefit students with learning difficulties.

Although increasing the frequency or length of intervention can improve outcomes for students with learning difficulties, evidence also suggests that some students need interventions over an extended period. A third way to increase intervention time is to increase the *duration of the intervention*. Some students with learning difficulties may require additional weeks or months of an intervention, particularly when the goal is to improve cognitively complex tasks like reading comprehension that are not likely to be remedied quickly. For instance, research studies in which "extensive" interventions of 100 sessions or more across grade levels (kindergarten through middle school) were associated with improved outcomes in reading (Wanzek & Vaughn, 2007; Vaughn et al., 2003). Most of the research on the efficacy of time variation on intervention effects has been conducted at the elementary level. Vaughn et al. (2012) conducted a 3-year, longitudinal study of middle school students with reading difficulties. Although gains in years 1 and 2 were small (Vaughn, Cirino, et al., 2010; Vaughn et al., 2012), by year 3, very low responders outperformed comparisons on a standardized reading comprehension measure by more than one standard deviation. Although more research on older students is needed, these findings suggest that students who continue to struggle with reading into the secondary grades may need substantially more time in intervention than students with reading difficulties in the elementary grades.

## How Can Teachers Intensify Instruction through Changes in Instructional Delivery?

In addition to adjusting group size and intervention time, a valuable way to intensify instruction is to make changes in the instructional delivery. What is instructional delivery? This refers to the materials used, the way the curriculum is customized for the learning needs of the students, and the amount of practice with feedback provided to the learner.

Students' high error rates and difficulties with learning new content are clearly signs that the teacher needs to identify the critical component(s) of instruction. Swanson et al. (1999) found that, across content and grade levels, interventions delivered through direct instruction plus strategy instruction yielded the highest effects. Such interventions include these key components: explicit instruction, systematic instruction, and opportunities for student response and feedback.

### Explicit Instruction

Explicit instruction means making the steps, strategies, processes, or practices "visible" to the learner—in other words, overtly teaching them. Explicit instruction includes teacher presentation of new material, teacher modeling, and step-by-step instruction to demonstrate what is expected so that students can accomplish a learning task. Research has associated interventions incorporating explicit instruction with improved outcomes for students with learning difficulties with both basic skills and higher-level concepts (Baker et al., 2002; Biancarosa & Snow, 2004; Gersten et al., 2008; Swanson, 2000; Vaughn, Gersten, & Chard, 2000; Vaughn et al., 2022). Explicit instruction is not always necessary but is particularly valuable during the initial instruction of new content and when teaching students to generalize known content to new situations (Fuchs et al., 2003). See Figure 8.2 for a list of ways to provide explicit instruction.

Educators can blend self-regulation strategies with explicit instruction of new content. For example, when introducing the use of graphic organizers to facilitate learning and understanding of content in a social studies text, a teacher could:

- Develop students' background knowledge, such as introducing the vocabulary necessary for understanding the text.
- Discuss the importance of the graphic organizer strategy and how it will help increase what students remember.
- Model how to use the graphic organizer and include self-instruction techniques that show students how to talk themselves through the task.
- Help students memorize the steps for completing the graphic organizer and for monitoring their completion progress.
- Support students as they practice using the graphic organizer while applying the self-instruction and self-monitoring techniques.
- Allow students to use the graphic organizer and self-regulation strategies independently. (IRIS Center for Training Enhancements, 2005)

---

1. Break down tasks into smaller, more manageable components to help students build knowledge.

2. Purposefully connect new lessons to previous learning to foster comprehension and achievement.

3. Gradually increase task difficulty to support students' success in independent work.

4. Use modeling or think-alouds in daily practice to address important features of the content.

5. Provide daily opportunities for students to respond and provide feedback on their responses.

6. Provide engaging work that allows students to take control of their learning.

7. Create classrooms where students clearly understand what is expected—including what they are supposed to do, practice, and/or express.

8. Move fluidly from modeling to independent practice when teaching new tasks.

9. Provide feedback that is clear, focused, and directly related to the learning task and that guides the student to continue and/or adjust learning practices.

10. Create purposeful time for students to practice all new skills and refresh learned ones.

---

**FIGURE 8.2.** Ten key policies and practices for explicit instruction. From Meadows Center for Preventing Educational Risk. (2021). Copyright © 2021 University of Texas at Austin/Meadows Center for Preventing Educational Risk. Reprinted by permission.

*Systematic Instruction*

In systematic instruction the teacher considers the complexity of the task and then selects the units or pieces that the student must perform well to accomplish the overall task. Systematic instruction often includes sequencing learning chunks from easier to more difficult and providing scaffolding, or temporary supports, to control the level of difficulty throughout the learning process. For example, systematic phonics instruction is effective when it progresses from smaller to larger units and is sequenced from easier to more difficult sounds and word types. For students with significant difficulties, this approach is more effective than less systematic instruction is in increasing word reading (Zipoli & Merritt, 2022). In fact, across content areas, interventions with the highest outcomes for students provide explicit and systematic instruction together (Fletcher et al., 2018; Swanson et al., 1999).

*Delivering Feedback*

Students with learning difficulties need many opportunities to demonstrate what they know and can do, as well as opportunities to respond, both orally and in writing, to instructional activities. In addition to student response, appropriate teacher feedback is necessary to accelerate learning. Frequent student response can assist the teacher in monitoring student understanding, and teacher feedback during student practice can be a powerful tool for refining and mastering new skills (Hattie & Clarke, 2018; Hattie & Timperley, 2007; Vaughn, Gersten, & Chard, 2000). By using explicit and systematic instruction, educators keep tasks at the appropriate levels for student response and effective feedback.

Hattie and Timperley (2007) reported that although the average effect of feedback was high, they found great variability within and across 12 meta-analyses: Average effects ranged from 0.12 for an analysis of research on teacher praise to 1.24 for an analysis of research on the effects of feedback for special education students. Table 8.1 lists the 12 meta-analyses that served as the database for the Hattie and Timperley analysis, their context, and the average effect sizes.

Feedback prompts students to continue successful attempts during practice and to remedy errors before they become entrenched. Hattie's (1999) synthesis of more than 500 meta-analyses of student achievement reported that feedback was one of the top three influences on student outcomes.

## WHAT IS THE MOST EFFECTIVE TYPE OF FEEDBACK?

Feedback is most effective when it relates to student goals and conveys information on how to complete tasks more effectively (Hattie & Clark, 2018; Hattie & Timperley, 2007). Researchers have noted lower effects for feedback that consists of only praise, rewards, or punishment (Kluger & DeNisi, 1996). Effective feedback on student responses is clear and precise, communicating specifically which aspects of the task students performed correctly or incorrectly. This type of feedback is known as process-directed feedback. Specificity is key in helping students understand what

**TABLE 8.1.** Summary of Effect Sizes from 12 Meta-Analyses Assessing
the Influence of Feedback

| Study | Context | Number of effects | Effect size |
|---|---|---|---|
| Skiba et al. (1985–1986) | For special education students | 35 | 1.24 |
| Lysakowski & Walberg (1982) | Cues, corrective feedback | 54 | 1.13 |
| Walberg (1982) | Cues, motivational influences, and reinforcement | 19 | 0.81 |
| Tenenbaum & Goldring (1989) | Cues, participation, reinforcement, feedback, and correctives | 15 | 0.74 |
| Rummel & Feinberg (1988) | Extrinsic feedback rewards | 45 | 0.60 |
| Yeany & Miller (1983) | Diagnostic feedback in science | 49 | 0.52 |
| Kluger & DeNisi (1996) | Feedback | 470 | 0.38 |
| L'Hommedieu et al. (1990) | From student ratings | 28 | 0.34 |
| Moin (1986) | Feedback | NR | 0.29 |
| Bangert-Drowns et al. (1991) | From testing | 40 | 0.28 |
| Kulik & Kulik (1988) | Immediate versus delayed | 53 | 0.28 |
| Getsie et al. (1985) | Rewards and punishment | 89 | 0.14 |
| Wilkinson (1981) | Teacher praise | 14 | 0.12 |

they did correctly and how they might better complete the task. Simply providing praise ("Good job"), rewards, or statements of incorrect responses (e.g., "That's not the answer I expect") is not associated with improved academic outcomes. For the greatest effect, tie feedback directly to the student's actions and the learning goals.

## WHEN IS FEEDBACK MOST EFFECTIVE?

Feedback is more effective when offered as close to the students' response as possible. For example, if a student is responding to text the student read and gives an answer that does not make sense, feedback should follow immediately. As soon as the student responds, say, "Reread the bottom of page 8 again and see how you might adjust your answer." Return after the student has reread the passage and assist in reframing a more accurate response. Provide feedback immediately for discrete tasks (e.g., writing the spelling of a word), and after a brief delay for more complex tasks (e.g., writing a paragraph) to allow students to think through the process first. Offering feedback immediately after a student answers a question or completes a task is more likely to yield future correct responses for a student with significant learning difficulties than waiting until after the lesson. Delaying feedback beyond the instructional session is less valuable for students. When there is a significant delay between the student's response and your feedback, the student may not be able to associate the feedback with the response or thought process, and the student may have already practiced the task incorrectly several times. Use timely feedback to prevent inaccurate practice, increase the rate of student mastery, and ensure successful, efficient learning.

## When Is It Effective to Have Students Practice Independently and Deliberately?

One final component of instruction to consider is independent practice. Independent practice for students with significant reading problems is most effective when students are practicing reading tasks in which they have demonstrated high levels of success when working with the teacher. For example, it makes sense for students to have opportunities to practice making inferences independently with text after they have demonstrated that they are able to successfully make inferences with increasingly reduced teacher assistance.

Vaughn and Fletcher (2021) identify the practice gap in reading as an explanation for why many struggling readers are challenged to "catch up" to grade-level reading expectations. As in most skilled areas (e.g., playing chess, golf, or cooking), practice is an essential ingredient for expert performance.

Ericsson (2008) describes expert performance as resulting from *active engagement* in *deliberate practice* with teachers or coaches monitoring the deliberate practice. Critical to understanding expert performance in reading requires applying the two constructs of *active engagement* and *deliberate practice*. When we observe active engagement in students, we see them motivated to learn, interested in succeeding, and focused on specific goals. For example, students may read in a more engaged manner when asked to write questions for others to answer that relate to their reading.

Deliberate practice is also a necessary component of expert performance and is different from what we might think of as typical practice. Deliberate practice has specific goals with related tasks and activities and is conducted with teacher or coach feedback and additional practice. This additional practice may be repeated reading for a deliberate purpose, for example, practicing reading challenging words correctly or improving speed of reading a designated phrase, sentence, or chunk of text. Figure 8.3 provides examples of how teachers might support deliberate practice using fluency routines.

There are four components to deliberate practice: (1) well-defined goals, (2) interest in achieving specified goals, (3) feedback, and (4) opportunities for additional practice. As we think about developing opportunities for deliberate practice for our students, consider the above-mentioned components and how you might ensure that they are represented within your instructional routines. Since interest in achieving specific goals is a necessary component, it may be useful to secure students' interest in achieving specific goals and then to identify the well-defined goals that are expected. This goal setting can lead to goal monitoring (progress monitoring), which serves as a built-in feedback loop to keep students engaged and on track.

Using findings from two syntheses of the research on reading fluency as a guide (Chard et al., 2002; Stevens et al., 2017), the following fluency practices are associated with improved reading performance for students with reading difficulties.

1. **Repeated word and phrase reading.** Use deliberate repeated word-list and phrase reading to improve students' fluency of reading challenging words independently and in text.
2. **Repeated reading with a model.** Select a text that is challenging but not too difficult and model reading the text fluently and with expression. Ask student(s) to then read the same passage in the same way with you. Then ask students to read the same passage to a partner, providing feedback for missed or challenging words. Finally, ask students to read the passage to themselves, identifying any words that are challenging and providing feedback so that they can practice those words.
3. **Set performance criteria for rate and accuracy of reading.** With the student, establish a challenging but achievable goal for the rate and accuracy of reading. Practice reading appropriate passages providing feedback and measuring students' performance toward the established goal.

**FIGURE 8.3.** Effective fluency practices.

Teachers of students with reading difficulties need to consider many elements of learning to read, with perhaps the most important being opportunities to utilize deliberate practice to build the reading brain. Deliberate practice includes setting goals, monitoring these goals, and providing specific and well-defined reading tasks that are practiced with teacher feedback and support. Deliberate practice targets students developing reading skills and also provides opportunities for reading extensively.

## CONCLUSION

This chapter describes research-based practices for intensifying reading comprehension instruction for students with significant reading difficulties. Evidence for integrating strategies that support cognitive processes with academic instruction, that reduce group size, that increase instructional time, and that intensify instructional delivery is described. These practices, thoughtfully integrated, can complement each other. For example, when the group size is reduced, students' opportunities to respond increase. Intensive interventions for students with reading difficulties are complex; Figure 8.4 lists resources that support your knowledge and expertise.

**Resources from the Center on Instructional RMC Research Corporation**

- Effective Instruction for Adolescent Struggling Readers—Second Edition
  *www.centeroninstruction.org/effective-instruction-for-adolescent-struggling-readers---second-edition*
- Extensive Reading Interventions in Grades K–3: From Research to Practice
  *www.centeroninstruction.org/extensive-reading-interventions-in-grades-k-3-from-research-to-practice*
- Synopsis of "Improving Comprehension of Expository Text in Students with Learning Disabilities: A Research Synthesis"
  *www.centeroninstruction.org/synopsis-of-improving-comprehension-of-expository-text-in-students-with-learning-disabilities-a-research-synthesis*
- Synopsis of "The Power of Feedback"
  *www.centeroninstruction.org/a-synopsis-of-the-power-of-feedback*
- Synopsis of "Writing Next: Effective Strategies to Improve Writing of Adolescents in Middle and High School"
  *www.centeroninstruction.org/synopsis-of-writing-next-effective-strategies-to-improve-writing-of-adolescents-in-middle—high-schools*

**Resources from The Meadows Center for Preventing Educational Risk**

- AIM Schoolwide PACT Lessons: A Tiered Approach to Improve Reading among Sixth- through Eighth-Grade Students with Disabilities
  *https://meadowscenter.org/resource/aim-schoolwide-pact-lessons*
- Establishing an Intensive Reading and Writing Program for Secondary Students (Revised)
  *https://meadowscenter.org/resource/establishing-an-intensive-reading-and-writing-program-for-secondary-students-revised*
- Meeting the Needs of English Learners with and without Disabilities: Grades 3–5 Practice Brief Series
  *https://meadowscenter.org/resource/meeting-the-needs-of-english-learners-with-and-without-disabilities-grades-3-5-practice-brief-series*
- Partner Reading: An Evidence-Based Practice Teacher's Guide
  *https://meadowscenter.org/resource/partner-reading-an-evidence-based-practice-teachers-guide*
- Sample Lesson Plans for Elementary Struggling Readers, Grades 1–5
  *https://meadowscenter.org/resource/sample-lesson-plans-for-elementary-struggling-readers-grades-1–5*
- What Dyslexia Looks Like in Middle School and What You Can Do to Help Your Child
  *https://meadowscenter.org/resource/what-dyslexia-looks-like-in-middle-school-and-what-you-can-do-to-help-your-child*

**Resources from Other Organizations**

- Doing What Works
  *www2.ed.gov/nclb/methods/whatworks/edpicks.jhtml*
- Online modules from the IRIS Center for Faculty Development
- RTI (Part 5): A Closer Look at Tier 3
  *http://iris.peabody.vanderbilt.edu/rti05_tier3/chalcycle.htm*
- CSR: A Reading Comprehension Strategy
  *http://iris.peabody.vanderbilt.edu/csr/chalcycle.htm*
- Foundational Skills to Support Reading for Understanding in Kindergarten through Third Grade
  *https://ies.ed.gov/ncee/WWC/PracticeGuide/21*
- High-Leverage Practices for Students with Disabilities
  *https://highleveragepractices.org*
- Literacy Sample Lessons to Support Intensifying Intervention
  *https://intensiveintervention.org/implementation-intervention/literacy-lessons*
- Provide Reading Interventions for Students in Grades 4–9
  *https://ies.ed.gov/ncee/WWC/PracticeGuide/29*

**FIGURE 8.4.** Resources for supporting students with intensive learning needs.

# CHAPTER NINE

# Multicomponent Approaches to Strategy Instruction

In this chapter we describe instructional approaches designed to help students become strategic readers by applying a set of strategies before, during, and after reading. Teaching students to apply a combination of comprehension strategies, often referred to as multicomponent reading strategy models, can improve reading comprehension for struggling readers and students with LD in kindergarten through third grade (Denton et al., 2022; Shanahan et al., 2010) as well as in the upper grades (Donegan & Wanzek, 2021; Filderman et al., 2022; Edmonds et al., 2009; Vaughn et al., 2016; Wanzek et al., 2013). Note that comprehensive reading interventions should include instruction in the various components of reading, including reading comprehension, but can also incorporate other core components of reading, such as decoding and fluency. In this chapter, we highlight three comprehensive approaches: reciprocal teaching, collaborative strategic reading (CSR), and multistrategy inference intervention. These multicomponent approaches combine aspects of the different methods for promoting reading comprehension we have already described in this book. We present them here because they offer a way to tie everything together and help students apply comprehension strategies while they are learning content from expository text or reading novels, short stories, or other narrative texts. Additional multicomponent strategies are presented in Table 9.1.

Reciprocal teaching and CSR rely on peer discussion as a catalyst for improving comprehension and facilitating the independent application of reading strategies (Lawrence & Snow, 2011). Because multistrategy inference intervention is typically enacted with teacher-led small groups, the discussion for that model usually involves teachers and students together. As just one example of the ways discussion supports comprehension, McCallum and colleagues (2011) compared student reading

**TABLE 9.1.** Additional Multicomponent Reading Strategies Models

Concept-Oriented Reading Instruction (CORI)

*Overview*: CORI is an instructional program that combines reading strategy instruction and conceptual knowledge in science with support for student motivation. CORI organizes instruction in content-based units in which the following elements are emphasized: developing self-efficacy, creating relevant learning experiences, valuing the importance of reading, creating opportunities for collaboration, and offering choices.

*Reading strategies*: inferencing, summarizing, concept mapping, discussion

*For further information*: *www.corilearning.com*; Guthrie et al. (2012)

Peer-Assisted Learning Strategies (PALS Reading)

*Overview*: In this structured classwide peer tutoring model, students read together in pairs, taking turns being the "coach" and the reader. As the reader reads, the coach provides corrective feedback. Points are awarded for good reading and coaching. The first- through sixth-grade version of PALs emphasizes reading fluency and comprehension.

*Reading strategies*: partner reading, main idea generation, predicting, retelling

*For further information*: *www.kc.vanderbilt.edu/pals*; Fuchs et al. (1997); Rafdel et al. (2011)

Promoting Acceleration of Comprehension and Content through Text (PACT)

*Overview*: PACT includes five connected components that are embedded in 10-day units of instruction in social studies. The PACT cycle includes a comprehension canopy, essential word routines, critical reading of content text, and team-based comprehension checks. PACT incorporates explicit instruction with individual and team-based learning opportunities.

*Reading strategies*: connection to background knowledge, question generation, graphic organizers, concept mapping, peer discussions

*For further information*: Vaughn et al. (2013)

Students Achieving Independent Learning (SAIL)

*Overview*: An application of transactional strategies instruction, the SAIL program promotes extensive reading of children's literature and encourages students to set their own purposes and goals for reading, to ask questions while reading, and to apply a menu of reading comprehension strategies as they are needed. A prominently displayed chart serves to remind students of the questions they can ask themselves as they read.

*Reading strategies*: predicting, questioning, visualizing, clarifying, summarizing, text structure analysis, story grammar analysis

*For further information*: Bergman (1992); Pressley, Schuder, et al. (1992); SAIL faculty and administration, Bergman, & El-Dinary (1992)

comprehension outcomes among students who either were permitted or were not permitted to discuss with a peer the story they were reading. Results showed that students in the peer discussion group had higher reading comprehension scores than students who used comprehension strategies without discussion. Similarly, eighth graders who reported having more frequent class discussions about text scored higher on average on the National Assessment of Educational Progress (NAEP) than students who reported having discussions less frequently (National Center for Education Statistics [NCES], 2011).

## RECIPROCAL TEACHING

Developed by Palincsar and Brown (Oczkus, 2018; Palincsar, 1986; Palincsar & Brown, 1984; Palincsar et al., 1987), reciprocal teaching was originally designed to improve comprehension for middle school students who could decode but had difficulty comprehending text. Students learn to use the four strategies of prediction, summarization, question generation, and clarification and to apply them while discussing text with the teacher and their peers. First, the teacher models how to implement the strategies. Next, through prompts, questions, and reminders, the teacher supports students' efforts to use the strategies while reading and discussing text. As students become more proficient, the teacher gradually reduces this assistance. The premise is that teaching students to use the four strategies collaboratively in a dialogue will help them bring meaning to the text as well as promote their internalization of the use of the strategies—thus ultimately improving their reading comprehension.

### Theoretical Foundation

Brown and Palincsar (1989) described three related theories that explain the effectiveness of reciprocal teaching: the zone of proximal development, scaffolding, and proleptic teaching. In the zone of proximal development (Vygotsky, 1978), the focus is not on what students can do independently but on how students' emerging skills and knowledge can be enhanced with guidance provided through interactions with others. The manner in which support is provided within a student's zone of proximal development is based on the theories of scaffolding (Wood et al., 1976) and proleptic teaching (Rogoff & Gardner, 1984). Brown and Palincsar (1989) described scaffolding as a means of providing "adjustable and temporary supports" (p. 411) through which the expert guides the learner to solve a problem that the learner would not be able to complete independently, much as a construction scaffold provides temporary support to builders. In order to successfully assist the learner, the expert must be aware of where the child's abilities lie on a continuum from novice to expert and be able to adjust instruction accordingly. Proleptic teaching means setting high expectations for all students, regardless of their current level of functioning. In this approach the teacher acts as the expert while the child takes on an apprentice role.

Reciprocal teaching is also firmly grounded in cognitive views of learning and development (Brown & Palincsar, 1989). Students are presented with multiple models of cognitive processing, through explanations and think-alouds, from the teacher and their peers. In addition, each of the four reciprocal teaching strategies can be explained in terms of cognitive psychology: prediction (Stauffer, 1969), question generation (Manzo, 1968), clarification (Markman, 1985), and summarization (Brown & Day, 1983). Similarly, the idea of using metacognition to monitor one's use of strategies and understanding of what is being read comes from cognitive psychology (Flavell, 1979).

## Research Support

In their first pioneering study, Palincsar and Brown (1984) taught comprehension strategies to seventh graders who were adequate decoders but poor comprehenders. Students participated in approximately 20 sessions. Each session included strategy instruction as well as an assessment of how many questions they could answer accurately after reading a short passage. Students in a control condition took the same pretests and posttests as did the strategy-instructed students but received no strategy instruction or daily assessments. Students who participated in the reciprocal teaching intervention outperformed comparison students on all measures of text comprehension and memory.

Since Palincsar and Brown's (1984) initial study, there have been more than 150 studies of reciprocal teaching, with most reporting positive outcomes for students. In comparison with traditional methods, reciprocal teaching has been found to be more effective, using both narrative and expository texts, with a wide range of students: middle school ELs with LD, including low decoders (Klingner & Vaughn, 1996), high school students in remedial classes (Alfassi, 1998), and average and above-average readers at various grade levels (e.g., Okkinga et al., 2018; Spörer et al., 2009; Rosenshine & Meister, 1994). Rosenshine and Meister (1994) reviewed 16 studies on reciprocal teaching and found that it consistently yielded statistically significant findings on different measures of reading comprehension. An important finding was that reciprocal teaching was more successful when it included direct teaching of the four comprehension strategies. Another notable aspect of reciprocal teaching and other multicomponent strategy models is that it takes time to learn to discuss and apply strategies at a high level. In a study with low readers in high school, students who participated in reciprocal teaching groups for 12–26 sessions had significant gains in reading comprehension, while there was no difference in posttest scores between students who were in the reciprocal teaching short-term groups of six to eight sessions and students in the comparison group (U.S. Department of Education, 2010; Westera & Moore, 1995). Studies have also found that implementation matters. For instance, in a study of low-achieving adolescents, Okkinga and colleagues (2018) reported that reading comprehension gains occurred for students only in classes with high-quality implementation of reciprocal teaching.

In other studies, researchers have combined reciprocal teaching with other approaches, adapted it, or compared it with different methods. For example, Marston et al. (1995) compared six research-based teaching strategies, including reciprocal teaching, and found that student achievement was highest with the following three approaches: computer-assisted instruction, reciprocal teaching, and one of two direct instruction conditions. Johnson-Glenberg (2000) trained third- through fifth-grade adequate decoders who were poor comprehenders for 10 weeks in either reciprocal teaching or a visualization program. The reciprocal teaching group excelled on measures that depended on explicit, factual material, whereas the visualization group did best on visually mediated measures. A small group of elementary ELs and students with LD increased engagement and academic achievement while using internet reciprocal teaching. Klingner and Vaughn (1996) studied 26 seventh- and eighth-grade students with LD who were ELs. Students learned a modified version of reciprocal teaching that included an emphasis on accessing background knowledge. Students read English text but were encouraged to use both Spanish (their native language) and English in their discussions. An important finding was that a continuum of students, rather than just those students who were adequate decoders but poor comprehenders, benefited from reciprocal teaching. In other words, students who had comprehension levels higher than their decoding skills also made gains in reading comprehension. In addition, Klingner and Vaughn reported that students continued making gains even when they worked in small groups or in tutoring dyads without the immediate presence of the researcher as teacher.

### How to Implement Reciprocal Teaching

Reciprocal teaching includes three essential components: dialogue, comprehension strategies, and scaffolding. The dialogue begins after students read a paragraph from the assigned text. The teacher or a student in the role of "dialogue leader" then begins a discussion structured around the four reading strategies. The dialogue leader is responsible for starting the discussion by asking questions and helping the group clarify any words or concepts that are unclear. Answering questions, elaborating or commenting on others' answers, and asking new questions are the responsibility of everyone in the group. The dialogue leader then provides a summary of the paragraph and invites the group to elaborate or comment on the summary. The dialogue leader also gives or asks for predictions about the upcoming paragraph. Through this process the group is able to move beyond merely restating the information in the text to develop a collective meaning for the passage. After the dialogue is finished, the process begins again with a new section of text and a new leader.

At the heart of the dialogue are the four strategies: predicting, clarifying, summarizing, and questioning. Palincsar and Brown (1984) selected these strategies because they are the tactics good readers use to make sense of text. Figure 9.1 provides a description, rationale, and method for each of the four strategies.

The scaffolding of instruction is integral to reciprocal teaching. The teacher guides students in using the strategies and gradually turns over this responsibility of strategy application to the students themselves. First the teacher explains the purpose for learning comprehension strategies, telling students that the primary goal is for them to become better readers (i.e., more "strategic" and better comprehenders). Following this purpose-setting statement, the teacher models the entire process of reading a passage and applying the strategies by using think-alouds so that students

**Predicting**
1. *Description*: Predicting involves finding clues in the structure and content of a passage that might suggest what will happen next.
2. *Rationale*: Predicting activates prior knowledge and motivates students to continue reading the passage to determine if their predictions were correct.
3. *Method*: To learn this strategy, students are instructed to use the title to make initial predictions about the story and then to use clues in the story to make additional predictions before reading each new paragraph or section of text. Students share predictions with one another.

**Clarifying**
1. *Description*: Clarifying involves discerning when there is a breakdown in comprehension and taking steps to restore meaning.
2. *Rationale*: Clarifying assures that the passage will make sense to the reader.
3. *Method*: To learn this strategy, students are instructed to be alert to occasions when they are not understanding the meaning of text, and when this occurs to process the text again. For instance, if a word did not make sense to the student, they would be instructed to try to define the word by reading the sentences that precede and follow it. Students are also taught to attend to words such as *or*, which may signal the meaning of an unfamiliar word, and to be certain they know to what referents such as *them*, *it*, and *they* refer (anaphora). If, after rereading the passage, something is still not clear, students are instructed to request assistance.

**Summarizing**
1. *Description*: A summary is a one- or two-sentence statement that tells the most important ideas contained in a paragraph or section of text. The summary should contain only the most important ideas and should not include unimportant details. A summary should be in the student's own words.
2. *Rationale*: Summarizing can improve understanding and memory of what is read.
3. *Method*: Students are instructed to locate the topic sentence of a paragraph. If there is no topic sentence, they are taught to make up their own topic sentence by combining the sentences they have underlined as containing the most relevant ideas. Students are then instructed to locate the most important details that support the topic sentence and to delete what is unimportant or redundant. Finally, they are instructed to restate the main idea and supporting details in their own words.

**Question Generating**
1. *Description*: Questions are constructed about important information in the text, rather than about unimportant details.
2. *Rationale*: Question generation allows readers to self-test their understanding of the text and helps them to identify what is important in the story.
3. *Method*: To learn this strategy, students are instructed to select important information from the paragraph and use the words *who, how, when, where*, and *why* to make up questions. Students are taught to ask questions about the main idea of the passage, questions about important details, and questions for which the passage does not provide the answer.

**FIGURE 9.1.** Reciprocal teaching strategies.

can see "the big picture." The teacher may next choose to provide direct instruction in each of the strategies before proceeding. The teacher and students then use the strategies while reading and discussing the text in small groups. The teacher offers a great deal of support as students try to implement the strategies. The teacher must be skillful at assessing the students' zone of proximal development and adjusting support accordingly, using scaffolding techniques such as prompts, elaborations, modifications, praise, and feedback. The teacher is the first dialogue leader, but as students develop proficiency in applying the strategies, they then take turns leading discussions. This approach sets high expectations for all the students—a basic feature of proleptic teaching. By about the eighth day of reciprocal teaching, in their alternating roles as students and dialogue leaders, students typically can implement the strategies with minimal assistance from the teacher. See Figure 9.2 for a step-by-step guide for implementing reciprocal teaching. Note that this model includes direct instruction in the strategies. Figure 9.3 illustrates an excerpt from a reciprocal teaching lesson in action.

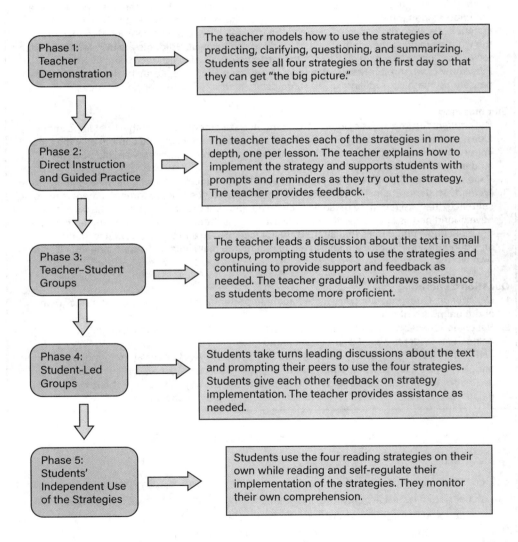

**FIGURE 9.2.** How to implement reciprocal teaching. Data from Palincsar and Brown (1984) and Quezada et al. (2006).

---

**Section 1: Roles**

Mateo—Questioner
Vicky—Clarifier
Cynthia—Summarizer
Jack—Predictor

The students have just read a section of a text on sea otters.

MATEO [questioner]: OK. I am the questioner. Let me find a good one. Hold on. Why do otters get all tangled up in seaweed?

CYNTHIA: Oh, I know this. They are really holding on to the kelp and seaweed so they don't float away. The seaweed is like an anchor on a boat.

MATEO: Yup.

VICKY [clarifier]: I don't know *entangle*.

JACK: Tangled is like caught up or messy. My mom sprays "No More Tangles" in my sister's hair when she gets out of the shower so she can comb it.

VICKY: So if the otters are entangled in the seaweed, they are all caught up in it? That makes sense.

VICKY: What is *swirling*?

MATEO: Swirling is like (makes a circular motion with his hand). Sort of going around and around.

JACK: I know that. In the water when it goes around in one place.

CYNTHIA [summarizer]: OK. I'm next. The otters float on their backs, like all the time. They even sleep floating. They sleep wrapped up in seaweed so they don't float away.

JACK: They entangle themselves in the kelp.

CYNTHIA: They eat floating too.

JACK [predictor]: My turn. Let's go to the next part. I make the prediction. I think the next section is going to tell us about what otters eat and how they eat because in the pictures coming up I see the otters with clams and stuff.

The students continue to read, and when they stop to discuss the next section, they shift roles in the group so everyone has a chance to lead various parts of the discussion through the reciprocal teaching roles. Students read the next section and then the discussion continues.

---

**FIGURE 9.3.** Reciprocal teaching in action.

## COLLABORATIVE STRATEGIC READING

With CSR, students learn to use comprehension strategies that support their understanding of expository text (Klingner & Vaughn, 1999; Klingner et al., 2001). The development of CSR was influenced significantly by the approaches of reciprocal teaching and transactional strategies instruction. Initially, the teacher presents the strategies to the whole class using modeling, role playing, and teacher think-alouds. After students have developed proficiency in using the strategies, the teacher then assigns the students to heterogeneous cooperative learning groups (Johnson & Johnson, 1989; Kagan, 1991). Each student performs a defined role while collaboratively implementing the strategies. Hence, with CSR, all students are actively involved, and everyone has the opportunity to contribute as group members learn from and understand the text. See Table 9.2 for a comparison of reciprocal teaching and CSR.

**TABLE 9.2.** How CSR and Reciprocal Teaching Differ

| Reciprocal teaching | Collaborative strategic reading |
| --- | --- |
| Designed for use with narrative as well as expository text. | Designed primarily for use with expository text. |
| No *brainstorming before reading.* | Students *brainstorm to activate prior knowledge as part of preview (before reading).* |
| Students *predict what they think will happen next before reading each paragraph or segment of text.* | Students only *predict as part of the preview strategy (before reading), making informed hunches about what they think they will learn.* |
| Students *clarify words or chunks of text they don't understand by rereading the sentences before and after the sentence they don't understand, and/or asking a peer for assistance.* | Students use "fix-up strategies" to clarify *"clunks" (words they don't understand):*<br>• Reread the sentence.<br>• Reread the sentences before and after.<br>• Break apart the work and look for smaller words you know.<br>• Look for a prefix or suffix you know. |
| Students *summarize the paragraph or segment of text they have just read.* | Students *get the gist of the paragraph or segment of text they have just read, identifying "the most important who or what"* and the most important thing about the *who* or *what.* They say the gist in 10 words or less. |
| Students *generate questions after each paragraph or segment of text they have just read.* | Students only *generate questions as part of a wrap-up after they have read the entire day's selection. Students answer each other's questions.* |
| There is no *review after reading.* | Students *review what they have learned after reading the day's selection.* |
| There are 8 to 12 students, plus the teacher, in the group. | An entire class is divided into *cooperative groups of two to five; the teacher circulates rather than staying with one group.* |
| There are no learning logs. | Students record their previews, clunks, questions, and what they've learned in individual *CSR learning logs.* |
| The "leader" (a student) facilitates the discussion about a paragraph or section of text; this role rotates after each paragraph. | Every student in the group has a meaningful role; one of these roles is to be the "leader." Roles are assigned for an entire lesson (only rotating biweekly in some classes). |
| There are no cue cards. | Students use *cue cards to help them implement their roles and the comprehension strategies.* |

The goals of CSR are to improve reading comprehension and increase conceptual learning in ways that maximize students' participation. Originally developed to help ELs and students with LD become more confident, competent readers in heterogeneous "mainstream" classrooms, CSR has also proven to be a valuable approach for students at varying achievement levels. CSR provides students with a more independent way to interact with grade-level textbooks and learn important content than, for example, a whole-class, teacher-led approach that involves reading the text and answering the questions at the end of the chapter.

We introduce the four strategies students learn as part of CSR here and describe them in more detail later:

1. *Preview.* Prior to reading a passage, students recall what they already know about the topic and predict what the passage might be about.
2. *Click and clunk.* Students monitor comprehension during reading by identifying difficult words and concepts in the passage and using fix-up strategies when the text does not make sense.
3. *Get the gist.* During reading, students restate the most important idea in a paragraph or section.
4. *Wrap-up.* After reading, students summarize what has been learned and generate questions "that a teacher might ask on a test."

## Theoretical Foundation

Like reciprocal teaching (Palincsar & Brown, 1984), CSR is grounded in sociocultural theory and the principles of scaffolding and zone of proximal development (Vygotsky, 1978), and also draws on cognitive psychology (Flavell, 1992). The idea is that cognitive development occurs when concepts first learned through social interaction become internalized and made one's own. Through the collaborative approach emphasized with CSR, both the teacher and the students scaffold. The teacher delivers instruction in strategies, assigns group roles, and provides a guide for reading and discussion. Students then scaffold each other's learning by giving immediate feedback at a level and in a manner that is just right for the others in the group.

CSR capitalized on this theoretical heritage and extended it to reflect knowledge about teaching ELs and students with reading disabilities. One way CSR extended this approach was by helping students tap into their prior knowledge (Fitzgerald, 1995) and make connections with their own lives (Perez, 1998). Also, CSR takes into account that students with LD and ELs benefit from explicit instruction. Therefore, the teacher carefully teaches the strategies using clear explanations and lots of modeling. The teacher provides students with multiple opportunities to practice the strategies in supported situations before asking them to apply the strategies on their own in cooperative learning groups.

## Research Support

CSR has yielded positive outcomes for students with LD and those at risk for reading difficulties, as well as average and high-achieving students and ELs. In the first study of CSR, Klingner et al. (1998) provided instruction in diverse, inclusive fourth-grade classrooms, teaching students how to use CSR while reading social studies texts. Comparison students received typical teacher-directed instruction in the same content. CSR students made statistically significant greater gains than students in a control condition on the Gates–MacGinitie Reading Tests and demonstrated equal proficiency in their knowledge of the social studies content.

Klingner and Vaughn (2000) then implemented CSR with fifth-grade students, many of whom were ELs, while they read and learned from science textbooks in their small groups. Results indicated that students demonstrated high levels of academic engagement and assisted each other with word meanings, main ideas, and understanding the text. In other studies, Bryant et al. (2000) implemented CSR in an inclusive middle school program and achieved gains for students with and without disabilities, and Vaughn, Chard, and colleagues (2000) examined the effects of CSR on fluency and comprehension as part of a third-grade intervention, with positive results.

Studies have looked at the use of CSR in upper elementary and middle school language arts and reading classrooms. Vaughn, Klingner, and colleagues (2011) evaluated the use of CSR in 61 seventh- and eighth-grade language arts classrooms in Texas and Colorado over an 18-week period. Classes were assigned to use CSR two times each week with curriculum reading materials or to continue using typical instructional practices. Students in the CSR condition significantly outperformed their non-CSR peers on a standardized measure of reading comprehension. Using a similar study design in fourth- and fifth-grade classrooms, students with LD who used the CSR model made significantly greater gains in reading comprehension than students with LD in the comparison condition did (Boardman et al., 2016). Focusing on meaningful opportunities to discuss text, Boardman et al. (2018) also found that when compared to typical instruction, during CSR lessons there was a higher amount of talk focused on the text, including a higher ratio of student talk to teacher talk and more text-based discussion among students.

One interesting and feasible adaptation of CSR was a study conducted with middle school students with significant reading difficulties. A computer-adapted approach to using CSR was implemented, in which students worked in pairs to read text on the computer and to respond to the critical CSR strategies (Kim et al., 2006). Computer-based approaches to reading comprehension are becoming more popular, and CSR has shown itself to be amenable to this adjustment in the delivery of instruction.

Additionally, CSR includes critical elements identified in special education as enhancing the performance of students with disabilities, such as (1) making instruction visible and explicit, (2) implementing procedural strategies to facilitate learning, (3) using interactive groups and/or partners, and (4) providing opportunities for interactive dialogue between students and between teachers and students (e.g., Vaughn et al., 2022).

### How to Implement CSR

At the outset, the teacher provides explicit instruction to students to teach the CSR reading comprehension strategies. As with reciprocal teaching, the teacher first conveys the value of learning different comprehension strategies, emphasizing that these strategies are what good readers use to help them understand what they read, and explains that by learning the strategies, everyone can become a better reader. The teacher also emphasizes that reading is thinking. The teacher then uses a think-aloud procedure to model how to use the different strategies while reading a short passage. See Figure 9.4 for an example of how a teacher might model the clunk strategy.

---

**Teacher Actions**

Display fix-up strategies and provide a handout with one or more short but challenging passages for students.

1. Explain finding clunks.

TEACHER: A clunk is a word or an idea that is confusing or that you don't know. As I read this passage, I am going to think about what I am reading and see if anything is hard to understand. Those will be clunks. Then, I'm going to use some fix-up strategies to try to figure out those difficult words or ideas.

2. Read the paragraph out loud, pausing and thinking aloud to show monitoring understanding.

*In the near future the intelligence of machines will exceed or be greater than that of humans.* [Think aloud: *Exceed.* I'm not sure what that word means.] *Within about 25 years, devices such as computers and robots will demonstrate the same or possibly even a more advanced range of human characteristics, such as decision making, emotions, musical creativity, and physical movement.* [Think aloud: *Physical movement.* That's a strange term. Isn't all movement physical? Wow! In 25 years, computers will be able to do what we can do. That could be helpful.]

3. Identify clunks.

I have a clunk in the first sentence. There is a word that I'm not sure I understand. The word is *exceed.*

Does anyone else have any other clunks in this passage? [Make a list of clunks on the board.]

4. Use of fix-up strategies.

Look at the list of fix-up strategies. The first two use context clues, or hints from the passage that might help us figure out the meaning of a confusing word or idea. [Review fix-up strategies 1 and 2.] Let's try the first fix-up strategy with my clunk, *exceed.* It says, "Reread the sentence with the clunk and look for key ideas that might help." OK, I will reread. *In the near future the intelligence of machines will **exceed** or be greater than that of humans.* Now I see that there is a hint. The word *or* makes me think that exceed means the same as *to be greater than.* Let's try that. In the near future, the intelligence of machines will be greater than. . . . Well, you can see that the word *exceed* is defined in the sentence. Just by rereading, I was able to figure out the meaning of a challenging word. Let's look at one of your clunks . . . [modeling continues].

---

FIGURE 9.4. A teacher models how to find clunks.

Again, as with reciprocal teaching, students are exposed to all of the strategies on the first day so that they can get a sense of what CSR-style strategic reading looks like. The teacher then offers additional instruction in each strategy, teaching students why, when, and how to apply each one. The CSR reading strategies include the following (Klingner et al., 2001):

1. *Preview.* The purposes of previewing are to (a) help students identify what the text is about, (b) tap into their prior knowledge about the topic, and (c) generate interest in the topic. The teacher helps the students with previewing by reminding them to use all of the visual clues in the text, such as pictures, charts, or graphs, and to look at the headings and subheadings used throughout the passage. The teacher might help students connect the topic to their own experiences and also preteach key

vocabulary that is important to understanding the text but that does not lend itself to the click-and-clunk fix-up strategies.

2. *Click and clunk*. Students use the process of click and clunk to monitor their comprehension of the text. When students understand the information, it "clicks"; when it does not make sense, it "clunks." Students work together to identify clunks in the text and use fix-up strategies to help them "declunk" the word or concept. The clunk expert facilitates this process, using clunk cards. A different strategy for figuring out a clunk word, concept, or idea is printed on each card:

    a. Reread the sentence without the word. Think about what would make sense.
    b. Reread the sentence with the clunk and the sentences before or after the clunk, looking for clues.
    c. Break the word apart (prefixes, suffixes, roots) or look for smaller words you know.
    d. Does the word have a cognate that makes sense?

Students record their clunks in their learning logs to share with their teacher and peers.

3. *Get the gist*. Getting the gist means that students are able to state the main idea of a paragraph or a section of text in their own words, as succinctly as possible. In this way students learn how to synthesize information, taking a larger chunk of text and distilling it into a key concept or idea. Students are taught to identify the most important *who* or *what* in the section, and then to identify the most important information they read about the *who* or *what*, leaving out details. Many teachers require that students state the main idea in about 10 words or less.

4. *Wrap-up*. Students learn to "wrap up" by formulating questions and answers about what they have learned and by reviewing key ideas. The goal is to improve students' knowledge, understanding, and memory of what they have read. Students generate questions about important information in the passage. They learn to use question starters to begin their questions: *who, what, when, where, why,* and *how* ("the five W's and an H"). As with reciprocal teaching, students pretend they are teachers and think of questions they would ask on a test to find out if their students really understood what they had read. Other students should try to answer the questions. Students are taught to ask some questions about information that is stated explicitly in the passage and other questions that require making inferences or connections (Raphael, 1986). In other words, students are encouraged to ask questions that involve higher-level thinking skills as well as literal recall. To review, students write down the most important ideas they learned from the day's reading assignment in their CSR learning logs. They then take turns sharing what they learned with the class. Many students can share their "best idea" in a short period of time, providing the teacher with valuable information about their level of understanding.

Once students are proficient in using the comprehension strategies with the support of the teacher, they are ready to learn how to implement the strategies while working in heterogeneous cooperative learning groups. According to Johnson and Johnson (1989), cooperative learning should encourage and include:

- Positive interdependence
- Considerable face-to-face interaction among students
- Individual accountability
- Positive social skills
- A self as well as group evaluation or reflection

In cooperative groups, students do not simply work together on the same assignment; each person must have a key role to play, and everyone is responsible for the success of the group. Students are told that they have two responsibilities: to make sure they learn the material and to help everyone else in their group learn it, too.

Students who have not previously worked in cooperative learning groups may need some preparation in order to work productively and effectively in this context. It may be helpful for them to practice skills that are vital for the successful functioning of a group, such as attentive listening, asking for feedback, asking others for their opinion, taking turns, asking clarifying questions, and conflict resolution measures (Klingner et al., 2001; see also Kagan, 1991).

With CSR, students discuss what they have read, assist one another in the comprehension of the text, and offer academic and affective support for their classmates. With CSR everyone has a chance to try out all of the roles. These roles may include (Klingner, Vaughn, et al., 2012):

- *Leader:* Leads the group in the implementation of CSR by saying what to read next and what strategy to apply next; asks the teacher for assistance if necessary.
- *Clunk expert:* Uses clunk cards to remind the group of the steps to follow when trying to figure out a difficult word or concept.
- *Gist expert:* Guides the group toward the development of a gist and determines that the gist contains the most important idea(s) but no unnecessary details.
- *Question expert:* Facilitates the generation of leveled questions about the text and leads the group members to ask and answer each other's questions.

Many teachers provide explicit instruction in each of the roles and spend time establishing expectations and honing students' discussion skills. One way to do this is by preteaching the roles to selected students, who can then model them for their classmates. Also, CSR includes cue cards for every role, with prompts that remind students of what is required as well as sentence frames to guide student-led discussions. For example, the gist expert card offers several dialogue frames including: *How are our gists similar and different? I think* _____*'s gist captures the most important ideas because* _____. Many schools have customized cue cards so that prompts support the types of thinking, discussion, and close reading outlined in the CCSS.

Students use the cue cards when first working together in their small groups, but as they become more confident in how to fulfill their roles, they can be encouraged to set aside the cue cards so that more natural discussions can take place. The cue cards serve an important function in that they help students with LD to be successful in any of the CSR roles, including that of leader.

CSR learning logs are an important component of the model. They enable students to keep track of learning "as it happens" and can be a springboard for follow-up activities. Logs furnish an additional way for all students to participate actively in their groups and provide valuable "wait time" for students with LD and ELs to form their thoughts. Logs might be kept in binders or journals made by folding paper in half and stapling on a construction paper cover. A different learning log can be created for each social studies or science unit; these logs contain written documentation of learning and can serve as excellent study guides. Some special education teachers have even included CSR learning logs in students' individualized education plans (IEPs). See Figure 9.5 for an example of a learning log.

Once the teacher has taught the CSR strategies and procedures to students and they have begun working in their cooperative learning groups, the teacher's role is to circulate among the groups and provide ongoing assistance. Teachers can help by actively listening to students' discussion and, if necessary, clarify difficult words, model strategy usage, encourage students to collaborate with one another, and provide positive reinforcement. Teachers should expect that students will need some assistance learning to work in cooperative groups, implementing the strategies, and mastering the content in textbooks. The focus of students' work should be on learning the material and helping their classmates learn it as well, not merely going through the steps of a given strategy.

## MULTISTRATEGY INFERENCE INTERVENTION

Barth and Elleman (2017) developed a comprehensive, inference-focused set of strategies designed for middle-grade struggling readers called *multistrategy inference intervention*. As with reciprocal teaching and CSR, in the multistrategy inference approach to strategy instruction the teacher provides support and guidance to students as they learn and apply new strategies. The emphasis in the multistrategy inference model is to build content knowledge and learn to generate text- and knowledge-based inferences. Through teacher explanation, modeling, and supported practice, students learn to read like a detective solves a crime. The strategies include (1) using text clues to clarify words and phrases, (2) activating and integrating prior knowledge, (3) understanding character perspectives and the author's purpose, and (4) answering inference questions. We include this model because of the direct attention to the important skill of inferencing, a component of reading that is especially difficult for many students who struggle with comprehension (e.g., Elleman et al., 2011).

### Theoretical Foundation

Multistrategy inferencing aligns with the situation model of reading (see Kintsch, 1988), in which representations of text are influenced by both lower- and higher-level cognitive processes (van den Broek et al., 2015). To understand what they read, individuals need to activate lower-level cognitive processes to quickly gather word-level semantic information, determined by their decoding, fluency, and vocabulary

Today's Topic _____ Date _____ Name _____

Before Reading:
PREVIEW

After Reading:
WRAP-UP

| What I Already Know about the Topic | Questions about the Important Ideas in the Passage |
|---|---|
| What I Predict I Will Learn | What I Learned |

During Reading
CLUNKS

GISTS

FIGURE 9.5. CSR learning log. From *Teaching Reading Comprehension to Students with Learning Difficulties, Third Edition*, by Sharon Vaughn, Alison Boardman, and Janette K. Klingner. Copyright © 2024 The Guilford Press. Permission to photocopy this material, or to download and print additional versions (*www.guilford.com/vaughn3-forms*), is granted to purchasers of this book for personal use or use with students; see copyright page for details.

knowledge. For higher-level cognitive processes, skills such as monitoring understanding, working memory, general knowledge, and importantly, inferencing, support comprehension.

Recent research has pointed to the key role that inferencing plays in text comprehension (e.g., Barth & Elleman, 2017; Hall, 2016). There are two key types of inferences. Text-based inferences connect current information in the text to information that has been read previously. Additionally, knowledge-based inferences link information in the text with the reader's relevant background or world knowledge. Readers can connect with other texts from a class or with their own world knowledge. Barth and Elleman (2017) note that making inferences while reading helps "fill in gaps in the text" (p. 32). Students with reading difficulties in middle and high school tend to have a harder time making inferences to support comprehension, so models that include instruction in how to make inferences may be especially useful.

### Research Support

A small number of studies have looked at the influence of inferencing on reading comprehension. For instance, Elbro and Buch-Iversen (2013) conducted a study with 236 sixth graders who learned to make knowledge-based inferences in eight 30-minute sessions. Students were taught to identify important information in the text and to use graphic organizers to make inferences by connecting what they were reading to relevant background knowledge. The students made gains in both inferencing making and reading comprehension. Barth and Elleman (2017) studied the multistrategy inferencing intervention model described below. Middle school students identified with reading difficulties participated in 10 40-minute sessions in reading intervention settings. When compared to students who received business-as-usual reading intervention, students made significant gains in reading comprehension across both proximal researcher-made and standardized measures of reading comprehension. In a study focused on English language learners with comprehension difficulties, students in reading intervention settings who received 24 40-minute sessions of inference instruction also made significant gains in reading comprehension when compared to a comparison group who did not receive intervention (Hall et al., 2020). These studies are in line with other reviews of inferencing research conducted across grade levels, demonstrating the effects of teaching students to make inferences while reading (see Hall, 2016; Elleman, 2017).

### How to Implement
### the Multistrategy Inferencing Intervention Model

Often taught in small groups of students, instruction is provided in a series of lessons, using an overarching reading detective theme in which students are taught to read like a detective solves a crime. The teacher defines and explains each strategy to students and models its usage. Students practice the strategies with feedback from the teacher in small groups of about three students.

1. *Use text clues for clarification.* First, the teacher identifies target words within a reading, selecting the words based on their importance to understanding the text. Students learn to use clues in the text to make sense of the target words. Students are also taught to stop periodically while reading to ask: Does the text make sense? If it does not, students learn to reread and to look for clues to clarify their understanding. Once students are familiar with finding clues to clarify meaning, as a daily practice while reading, teachers cover a word with a sticky note. When students come to the target word, they apply the text-clue strategy to figure out the meaning.

2. *Activate and integrate prior knowledge (make inferences).* Students learn to make inference connections while reading (a) within the text, (b) between the current text and texts read previously, and (c) between the text and prior knowledge. For each inference, students are asked to justify how their connections helped them understand what they are reading or helped them answer a question about the text. Key to this strategy is teacher feedback to help students understand the relevance of their connections to comprehending the text.

3. *Understand character perspectives and author's purpose.* For narrative texts, students are taught to use clues from the text to make inferences about a character's motive and intent. Teachers ask students to identify and justify why characters behaved in certain ways, based on information provided by the author. For expository texts, students look for the author's purpose or point of view. For instance, in a text with claims and counter claims about global warming, students can be asked, "Although the authors presents claims and counter claims about possible reasons for global warming, what evidence is provided about the authors perspective on this issue?" Teachers may also ask students to look for lengthy explanations (in both narrative and expository text) and to consider why this information is important to the text.

4. *Answer questions.* After reading, students learn to analyze comprehension questions first for question type (main idea, vocabulary, inference question) and then for the strategy needed to answer the question. For main idea questions, students are taught to find the most important information and to explain why it is most important (see gist strategy in CSR above). For vocabulary questions, students apply the text-clue strategy and for inference questions, students learn to determine whether questions require in-text inferences or out-of-text elaborative inferences using the text and background knowledge.

Students begin with short teacher-selected passages that lend themselves to introducing and practicing strategies. During this phase of instruction, for each lesson, teachers lead a review of the four strategies. Teachers then stop at various points in the text to support students to apply the strategies and provide justification for their decisions. After reading, the teacher leads students to review the question types, practicing with two or three questions as a group. Students then apply the strategies with the remaining comprehension questions. The group comes back together to discuss answers and the justifications.

Over time, teachers provide content-focused passages at grade level or at the reading level of the intervention group. To date, this model has been studied in small intervention groups, and results have shown comprehension growth after a short number of sessions. If teachers choose to apply inferencing strategies with larger groups of students, they should ensure that students with comprehension difficulties are provided with regular support and feedback as they learn and apply reading strategies in this, or any, multicomponent reading comprehension model.

## CONCLUSION

This chapter has focused on three multicomponent comprehension-building strategies that are combined into reading routines that teachers and students become familiar with and that they can apply regularly, increasing comfort and familiarity with how the reading process works. Teachers can also incorporate additional reading practices into their reading routines, depending on what students need. (See the lesson plans in the Appendix for additional ideas.)

All three approaches described in this chapter share commonalities, including a focus on explicit instruction in strategies that skilled readers use to support comprehension. With each approach students learn to apply different strategies before, during, and after reading. They learn through modeling, explicit instruction, and guided practice. Each approach has improved the reading comprehension of students with LD as well as other students. At the same time, these approaches can also be challenging for teachers to learn and apply in their classrooms, particularly at the onset. We offer this cautionary note in the hopes that teachers will discuss implementation challenges with their colleagues and support one another in trying out new instructional practices. Teaching strategies to students so that their use becomes second nature requires expertise and commitment on the part of teachers. Yet the results are well worth the effort.

# CHAPTER TEN

# Questions Teachers Ask about Teaching Reading Comprehension

Over the past couple of decades, we have worked with numerous teachers across schools, districts, states, and even countries. We collect these questions as among those that are frequently asked. Hopefully, you will find that many of these questions align with those you have wondered about as well. Consider using these questions in your professional study groups and see how your responses compare with those we provide. Questions are organized around broad topics such as word reading, English learners, and background knowledge. We hope some of these questions align with ones you have asked or been asked over your educational career.

## The Role of Word Reading for Promoting Reading Comprehension

1. For older students (upper elementary and middle school students) who still have difficulty decoding words, how much of reading instruction time should be spent on comprehension strategies versus word reading instruction? How do you find this balance?

   *Response:* Essential to reading comprehension are two very fundamental skills. First, students need to be able to read the words accurately and efficiently (i.e., automatically), which is decoding. Second, students need to know the meaning of the words in the text they are reading, which is vocabulary knowledge. Both are focused on word-level reading. Thus, regardless of the age or grade of the student, knowing how to read words accurately and efficiently cannot be overstated! We simply cannot accomplish the important goal of reading for meaning when students have inadequate word reading. For this reason, a strong instructional focus on word reading is necessary for students who have word-reading and decoding difficulties to develop reading comprehension.

Now, for the rest of your question about how much time is spent on word reading in upper elementary and middle school: A considerable amount of time needs to be focused on decoding/word reading in the service of improving reading comprehension. The decision of how much time is spent on word reading relates specifically to students' level of word reading. Severity of the word-reading problem determines the amount of time. To provide some working guidelines, we suggest approximately 8 minutes per day based on the gap between performance grade and actual grade. Thus, if students' word-reading level is at the third grade and their actual grade is fifth grade, a 2-year gap, it would be 15–20 minutes per day. This is provided as a general working model that teachers would adjust to meet the varying needs of their students.

2. Particularly for secondary students with reading difficulties, how do I balance instruction on flexible decoding strategies with content access via audiobooks or platforms such as podcasts?

*Response:* Teachers frequently wonder how to balance instructional time for students who have word-reading difficulties but who are older and also require extra time for text reading and accessing knowledge in other ways. Unfortunately, there is no simple formula for deciding how much time is used for decoding or word-reading strategies and how much time is used for content acquisition. Consider the previous question and answer that all students with word-reading difficulties require word-reading instruction and that the amount of time for that instruction is directly related to their needs. Also consider the reasons why alternative text sources such as audiobooks or podcasts might be used. The fundamental idea is that alternatives to text reading, such as audiobooks and podcasts, are excellent ways for teachers to provide access to highly informative content knowledge to build background knowledge essential to making progress in content-area classes. However, a steady diet of alternative sources without integration of print-based sources is inadequate. Maybe it would help to think about these various sources in much the way that progressive dieticians ask us to think about what we are eating. They want us to be sure that we have an adequate number of servings of vegetables (perhaps much like we think of text reading) and fruits (maybe word-reading practices) but realize that we also need carbohydrates and protein (e.g., alternative sources of information such as podcasts and audiobooks) to provide a well-balanced diet—or as we think about it—a well-balanced instructional approach.

The "watch-out" in this formula is that we might have a tendency to provide too much time with alternative knowledge sources such as podcasts for students who are our weakest readers—the ones who actually need the most text reading.

3. If I have an hour-long resource room session with a student, should I focus on one aspect of reading comprehension at a time or should I focus on several?

*Response:* Many special education teachers and reading resource teachers have access to students for as little as 1 hour per day. In these cases they have to be sure to utilize every minute as productively as possible. It may be helpful to think about the essential elements of reading that are most conducive to personalized instruction and least likely to be taught in the general education classroom. It is reasonable to think that elements such as word reading, decoding, and fluency are less likely to be customized to a student's needs in the general education classroom and thus may be priorities for the resource room. Additionally, selecting words and texts a student is currently using in the general education classroom may enhance their content learning in the general education setting.

## Secondary Content-Area Teachers and Reading Comprehension

4. For a secondary-level teacher of any content class: Is there anything I could/should do for about 5 or 10 minutes a day consistently throughout an entire school year that would help all of my students improve their reading comprehension?

   *Response:* What a great question! Let's start with words—spend time each day on key words that are valuable for students to recognize automatically and to know the meaning. We can think of these as high-utility words—words that occur with frequency across contexts and subject areas. For example, the word analyze (and its various forms) will occur in language arts, such as in character analysis; math, as in analyzing a word problem; and in social studies, as in an analysis of political events. There are so many words that students need to know and a few minutes teaching them within the context of the unit you are teaching can extend students' reading and vocabulary knowledge. Also, finding ways for students to read text everyday—even for a few minutes—will have an additive value over time.

## Building Background Knowledge

5. How much time should I spend "building background knowledge" and/or connecting a new topic to students' experiences? I spend extensive time on these issues because my students tend to be unfamiliar with the upcoming topics.

   *Response:* Background knowledge is essential to comprehending text. But as you suggest, students may be unfamiliar with topics they are reading about, making it difficult to connect what they are reading with what they already know. We want to spend enough time on background knowledge to give students access to the text they are reading but not so much time that we take away from their opportunity to extend their background knowledge independently by reading. Think about brief (e.g., 5 minutes) and efficient ways to build background knowledge that are not so time consuming, such as short videos, quick overviews of key information (e.g., key personnel or key events), and condensed readings at an easier level that build students' background knowledge. Not all building of background knowledge needs to be done orally by you doing the explaining.

6. How much time should I spend before reading a text with my students, assessing background knowledge and engaging in knowledge-building activities? Is it sometimes good to have students practice making sense of a text for which they *don't* have all the requisite knowledge?

   *Response:* As stated in response to the previous question, there is not one correct answer; however, we certainly don't want to spend as much time "preparing" students to read as they do reading and learning from the target text. Ideally, in a 50-minute class, teachers might spend 10–15 minutes building and extending background knowledge. These activities could include a brief video, pictures, or images that relate to what students are learning, enhancing their understanding of key persons or places, and teaching essential words and their meaning.

## Strategy Instruction and Reading Comprehension

7. I realize that "strategy instruction" works. However, how much time should I spend teaching comprehension strategies and when should this instruction occur?

   *Response:* This answer is taken from Stevens and Austin (2022). Consider carefully how many strategies you teach because strategy instruction may be taxing on students' working memory (Compton et al., 2012). Emphasis on remembering aspects of the strategy and the steps that go with the strategy may occupy students' cognitive processes so heavily that they inadequately grapple with the text. Of concern is when strategies are taught in an isolated manner and not applied to reading for meaning. While we think an overemphasis on strategy instruction is not productive, teaching a few strategies well can improve reading comprehension. Select two or three strategies to use throughout the school year and provide ample practice for students to utilize them across content areas and texts. These practices can be implemented while reading and to support text-based discussions.

8. Strategy instruction takes a lot of time. If I could only choose one or two to teach, which strategies are helpful to every student in my class? Which ones are most powerful?

   *Response:* There are a couple of powerful reading strategies that are associated with improved reading comprehension. Consider teaching students the "get the gist" strategy, which is presented in this book in Chapter 9 (and outlined at length in the Appendix). The get the gist strategy helps students think about the main idea while they are reading. Once students are successful at "getting the gist" or main idea, they can use multiple "gists" to develop a summary statement. Thus, the strategy of summarization becomes an extension of what students learn from the gist. Getting the gist and developing summaries also increases opportunities to write. Another strategy I would consider teaching students is "question generation," where students learn to think about and write questions after reading text. This practice is explained in Chapter 9 and can be a useful way to have students generate questions independently, in pairs or in teams.

## Text Sources and Text Levels

9. How do I think more broadly about what "counts" as reading (e.g., access to print and content via audiobooks and assistive tech verses decoding alone)? Many of my students gravitate toward graphic novels. Should I dissuade students from reading graphic novels? Do graphic novels offer potential benefits for reading comprehension instruction and engagement?

   *Response:* The research on using graphic novels is emerging and preliminarily promising. Anecdotally, graphic novels can be a stepping-stone; that is, they offer support for students who need the visual scaffolds but hesitate to engage with print in a more traditional way. You can use graphic novels to get at comprehension processes, for example, asking students to generate main ideas or make inferences. Some students may feel hesitant to use Learning Ally or other technology-based platforms that they feel stigmatize them among their peers. While we want students to read print, there are many sources of print in nontraditional books, online sources, and so forth. We know that audiobooks are not the same as "reading" a book; however, they offer a valuable source for building background knowledge, vocabulary, and access to information that might be otherwise beyond students' reading level.

10. Is it really not a good idea to teach students using "just-right" texts—that is, to use leveled texts and teach students using a text at their level? I think it's frustrating for students to ask them to read books that are too easy or too hard.

    *Response:* The appropriate level of text for any student is determined based on consideration of several important factors: the purpose of reading the text, the level of support available for the student while reading the text, and the student's background knowledge about the text. Let's start with the purpose of reading the text. If the purpose is related to the student's enjoyment of the text, then allowing students to select texts from a range of levels based on their interest in the book is appropriate. Students may occasionally enjoy reading easier texts and also be willing to struggle with more challenging texts if they choose them and are reading for pleasure. The level of support available to students is also an important consideration. If students are reading without any teacher support, then the text they can read will need to be easier than if they are reading the text with a teacher or with peers. More challenging "stretch" texts that are above level are more accessible to students with ongoing teacher or peer support. The background knowledge of the student also plays an important role in determining whether the text is accessible to them. Some students have very strong background knowledge that aligns with the text they are reading and therefore can read more challenging texts than if the topic was one for which they had very little background knowledge.

11. I know I'm supposed to support my students in reading and comprehending grade-level texts whenever possible. But for my students who have difficulties reading grade-level texts fluently and with comprehension, how do I effectively scaffold their reading of such texts?

*Response:* For many students with reading difficulties, reading grade-level text is really reading "stretch text," or text that is beyond their independent reading level, making it difficult to read the text on their own. With teacher support, it is possible for students with reading difficulties to comprehend when reading beyond their comfortable reading level. There are technology applications that can also support students when reading difficult text, such as read-aloud or word look-up features. The advantage of exposing your students to grade-level text is that they encounter more sophisticated concepts, language structures, and vocabulary, providing an opportunity to build their knowledge and capacity. However, these texts will require teacher support to avoid student frustration. This support entails guiding students through the content and vocabulary, while also encouraging and praising your students when they grasp the content.

One way to support students in challenging text is chunking the text into smaller segments, stopping to discuss words and concepts that are critical to following along and understanding the "big ideas." After reading a segment, such as one or two paragraphs, stop and discuss the important ideas. The "get the gist" strategy discussed in Chapter 9 is a good way to guide your students through text, focusing on the main ideas. When preparing to use stretch texts with your students, mark any important words that may be challenging to your students. You can preteach these words before reading so the words will be more familiar when you reach them. You can also mark the stopping points where you will discuss the key ideas and help your students connect them as you move through the text. Proper nouns and multisyllabic words are likely to pose challenges and are often essential to understanding the text. Stopping to discuss them will help your students grasp the text. Another recommendation is to build interest and motivation as you read these texts. Your students will be more willing to accept the challenge of difficult text if they are genuinely interested in what they are reading. We recommend using stretch text two to three times per week and using easier text at your students' actual reading levels at other times.

## Independent Reading, Reading Silently, and Reading Comprehension

12. I've heard I shouldn't provide my students with independent-reading time (i.e., that it's a waste of instructional time). But I loved independent-reading time when I was in school—and my students seem to love it, too. Should I really not provide students with independent-reading opportunities?

*Response:* There are many opportunities to support students to read independently. Promoting the idea of reading as a valuable and ongoing part of a daily routine is extremely important. Using independent reading as a choice for students who have completed their assigned work is also valuable. Our current knowledge about "dedicated, independent-reading time" or what may be referred to as "sustained silent reading (SSR)" is that it is not associated with improved overall reading outcomes. This does not mean that it has no value—just that if the goal of the SSR is to improve reading outcomes, there is currently no evidence to suggest that will be the outcome. The value of independent-reading time may lie in increasing your students' interest and motivation, as well as the development of good reading habits.

13. What should independent reading look like? I think teachers would specifically appreciate guidance around a couple of issues related to independent reading: Is it ok for students to read any book of their choosing or does the book need to be at their independent-reading level? Can students read on tablets, e-readers, and the like? Can independent-reading time be better spent on direct instruction or things like phonics practice or computer-assisted instruction?

*Response:* As discussed above, independent-reading time provides students opportunities to explore interests and feel empowered by having a choice of reading materials. Independent-reading time should not take away from valuable instructional time focused on important reading concepts and processes. It should be an opportunity to practice reading and explore topics and text types. Reading from various sources, including books, tablets, or other devices, would certainly provide such opportunities. Independent-reading time is enhanced if your students have opportunities to share what they are reading, with the whole class or a partner. When your students discuss what they are reading, you will gain insight into their reading interests and habits. As for the level of text, we know that students need opportunities to read at a comfortable pace, which means reading at their independent-reading level, to build fluency and good reading habits. Stopping to sound out too many difficult words or complex language may lead to frustration. However, sometimes students are highly motivated to read a text that is difficult because they are very interested in it. For example, students may really want to read popular books, such as the Harry Potter series, and be willing to struggle through it. Or, they may want to read a nonfiction book about a topic they want to learn more about, such as soccer or types of animals. Teaching students a few ideas about text selection can help. Discuss with your students the importance of selecting books that seem interesting and are at a comfortable level. Ask your students to give a new book a trial run, reading one or two pages and then stopping to think about whether it is a good fit. Students can use their fingers to count how many difficult words they encounter in the first page or two. If they encounter five difficult words, that is, five fingers, it is likely too difficult. However, the exception to that rule is if their interest is high and they are comprehending despite the word difficulty. Involving students in this process of selecting and trying out texts is building the habit of reflecting on their own reading.

14. How much should I have my students read aloud (vs. reading silently)? What factors should influence my decision making (e.g., age, reading accuracy/fluency)?

   *Response:* The answer to this question is contingent upon the grade level of the student and the purpose for reading. Students in the early grades (kindergarten through second grade) like to read aloud, and in the early stages, it is helpful for the teacher to observe how the reading process is developing in your students. Students benefit from opportunities to read aloud or to subvocalize, that is, read silently while moving their lips or whispering. As students become more proficient readers, we encourage them to reduce their vocalizations until they are successful at reading silently. No matter what grade, it is important for all students to have regular opportunities to read aloud. For example, when students are performing oral-reading fluency activities, they often read aloud so that the teacher can record the number of words they read accurately per minute. Oral reading—even with older students—provides a valuable window into students' accuracy and prosody while they read.

15. I've heard "round robin reading" is not an evidence-based practice. Why is it bad? What format should I use, instead, to give my students opportunities to practice reading aloud with accuracy and fluency?

   *Response:* "Round robin reading" refers to the practice of students taking turns reading segments of text in a continuous fashion. Typically with "round robin reading" students know when it will be their turn to read and then they may not pay as much attention to following along when others are reading aloud as they would if they were responsible for reading the entire text. Another issue with round robin reading is that many students with reading difficulties are uncomfortable reading aloud. They recognize that they are likely to make errors and this may be embarrassing to them. Reading aloud "alone" and in front of others is also an anxiety-producing exercise for many students that we would want to avoid if possible. When asking students with reading difficulties to read aloud, be sure that the setting is comfortable for them. Teachers use round robin reading to get a whole class through a text passage without burdening any one person with reading the whole thing. The main objective is to keep all students engaged in reading the passage. There are several alternatives to accomplish this goal. Partner reading involves two students taking turns reading chunks of text, making their way through the whole passage. It is important for the students to have a goal or task to keep them accountable and focused, such as creating one or two questions they will answer or a graphic organizer to complete. Another alternative routine would be choral reading, meaning that every student reads together. This routine can be cumbersome, so it may be helpful to alternate formats; for example, the teacher reads one or two paragraphs aloud, then the class chorally reads the next segment, stopping to discuss. Small-group reading, with each group member taking a turn, a sort of small-group round robin, may eliminate the anxiety that struggling readers experience, especially if the teacher models how to provide peer support and encouragement.

## Motivation and Reading Comprehension

16. How can I build student motivation to read—particularly for students who have lost their interest in reading?

    *Response:* Reading motivation is an important and often overlooked piece of the reading puzzle. Research has documented positive associations between intrinsic motivation, amount of time spent reading, and reading comprehension. In other words, the more internally motivated your students are and the more time they spend reading, the better their comprehension will be. It helps a lot when your students like reading. Intrinsic motivation is the idea of being motivated to do a task for internal reasons; in the case of reading, internally motivated students read for the joy of it or the self-satisfaction of doing something well. Extrinsic motivation comes from external sources, such as seeking teachers' praise or achieving a reward. External motivators, such as rewards for reading books, can jump-start unmotivated readers, but should be used in tandem with encouraging self-awareness and self-satisfaction when doing so.

    Self-concept is an important component. When students view their own reading ability positively, they are more likely to be motivated to challenge themselves with reading. This points to the importance of setting your students up for success. When students feel competent, they are more likely to stay engaged and try to attain reading goals. Setting reading goals and discussing students' progress toward them fosters intrinsic motivation. One way to set reading goals is to use progress-monitoring data, such as reaching a fluency goal. However, we do not want to overfocus on reading speed. There are other, more motivating, types of goals, such as reading a certain number of books, moving up a reading level, becoming an "expert" on a topic by reading, or improving comprehension. Offering choice is another motivating factor, such as letting students choose books or topics, or choosing which assignment to complete. Engaging read-alouds and discussions are also motivating for students.

17. How much "struggle" should students experience reading to promote comprehension but also keep them motivated to read?

    *Response:* Basic learning theory helps us to answer this question. Teaching involves getting the level "just right." When tasks are too easy, students are not challenged and may disengage. When tasks are too difficult, students experience frustration and develop negative self-perceptions of their competence. Students need a mix of easy and difficult tasks. Vogotsky called this the "zone of proximal development," setting up learning tasks that are just a little beyond the reach of what a student can do easily and automatically. Striving to reach a challenge can be motivating, and it builds self-efficacy to accomplish something difficult. So, applying this concept to the reading process, your students will need some opportunities to read at their independent-reading level, a level at which they can read comfortably and unassisted, but they will also benefit from some challenges, with appropriate teacher support and encouragement to reach attainable goals.

There is no formula for how much struggle is enough. You have to observe your students, sense when they are reaching frustration, and be ready to increase support or change the task when that happens. For example, teachers might observe, "Well, that had some difficult words in it, but you got through most of them. Next time it will be a little easier for you!" You also need to celebrate accomplishments when your students successfully meet the challenge.

# Lesson Plans

The lesson plans in this Appendix offer ideas and examples for implementing the research-based strategies described in this book. Lesson plans should be used as building blocks in the classroom, adapted for unique contexts and individualized for students. Lessons are divided into before, during, and after reading, though some lessons may be applicable at different points in the reading process.

Lesson Plan titles followed by an asterisk (*) are adapted with permission from The Meadows Center for Preventing Educational Risk (*meadowscenter.org*), 2012–2022. Copyright © The Meadows Center.

## BEFORE-READING LESSON PLANS

**TEXT PREVIEW**

### Grade Levels

All

### Purpose

To introduce a new text, engage students, and focus reading.

### Materials

- Grade-level text from curriculum materials
- Prepared preview

### Lesson Routine

1. Provide a context for the new reading and its relation to what students have already learned. This information activates prior knowledge about the subject and guides students to make explicit connections between what they already know and what they will learn.
2. Provide a quote or bit of interesting information from the reading to motivate readers to find out more about the topic.
3. Ask one to three focus questions to guide readers to attend to the important information during reading.

Following is an example of a teacher preview in a sixth-grade social studies class.

### Context

*In this unit we have been studying the civil rights movement and looking at ways that people use words and actions, instead of fighting, to get their ideas to be heard. We have talked about Dr. Martin Luther King, Jr., and read several biographies and speeches. Today we are going to learn about another important man who used nonviolent ways to help people. His name is Mahatma Gandhi. Some of you may have heard of him; there are many books and even a few movies about him. Today we will read a story about Gandhi's life and his influence in India and in the world.*

### Engage

*Here is a famous quote from Gandhi that is part of your reading today: "In the empire of nonviolence, every true thought counts, every true voice has its face value."*

*Questions*

*While you are reading, I want you to think about this quote and the following questions:*

1. *What are examples of nonviolent ways that Gandhi influenced people?*
2. *What might have happened if Gandhi had used fighting and violence?*
3. *What does it mean when he says, "every true thought counts, every true voice has its face value"?*

### *Ideas for Providing Additional Support*

1. For students who struggle with auditory processing or remaining focused during reading, provide an outline of the teacher preview and guiding questions.
2. Adjust the number of focus questions for students. Whereas some students may be able to attend to several key questions while reading, others should focus on just one important question that is specific to individual skills, such as remembering factual information, making a personal connection to reading, or drawing conclusions.
3. Students who would benefit from additional practice reading can preread the selection and prepare a "teacher preview." The teacher collaborates with students to prepare the class teacher preview. Students benefit by having an additional opportunity to read. Their preread is focused when they attempt to situate the reading, find an engaging piece of information, and ask their own questions.

## VOCABULARY MAPS*

### *Grade Levels*

Third grade and up

### *Purpose*

Students will increase academic vocabulary knowledge using vocabulary maps before reading.

### Materials

- One vocabulary map per word to be taught
- Text students will read containing the words

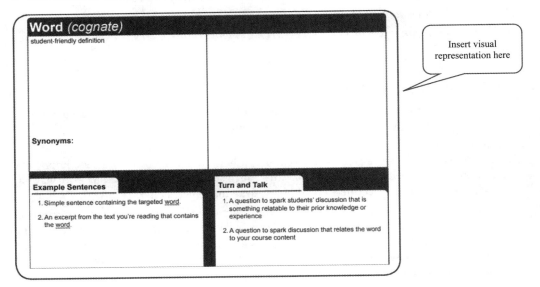

### Lesson Routine

1. Prepare to use vocabulary maps.
   a. Select a passage and identify the key ideas you want students to learn.
   b. Select two or three vocabulary words that support understanding of the key ideas. These words should be academic words that are used frequently in academic text, are essential to the meaning of the text, and cannot be easily grasped from the context.
   c. Create a vocabulary map for each word and prepare to display before reading the passage. Using the vocabulary map template, include the following:
      - Vocabulary word
      - Student-friendly definition of the word
      - Cognate or translation of the word, as appropriate
      - Visual representation of the word
      - Synonym(s) of the word
      - Example sentences using the word
      - Turn-and-talk prompts for students to practice using the word and for you to monitor student understanding
2. Explicitly teach words *before* reading the passage using vocabulary maps.
   a. Explicitly teach the word, stating the word, its definition, and the visual representation.
   b. Review and discuss synonyms.
   c. Read and discuss the example sentence.
   d. Engage students in turn and talk.
3. Read the passage, stopping to notice the words as they occur and how they are used.
4. Provide additional practice with words on subsequent days.

*Example*

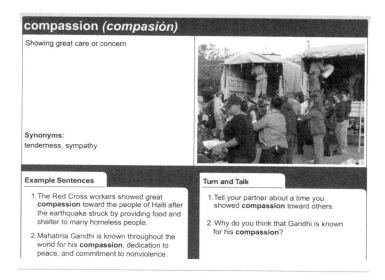

compassion *(compasión)*

Showing great care or concern

Synonyms:
tenderness, sympathy

**Example Sentences**

1. The Red Cross workers showed great **compassion** toward the people of Haiti after the earthquake struck by providing food and shelter to many homeless people.

2. Mahatma Gandhi is known throughout the world for his **compassion**, dedication to peace, and commitment to nonviolence.

**Turn and Talk**

1. Tell your partner about a time you showed **compassion** toward others.

2. Why do you think that Gandhi is known for his **compassion**?

# SEMANTIC MAPS

*Grade Levels*

All

*Purpose*

Create a semantic map to show how words that relate to a key concept are connected to each other.

*Materials*

- Semantic mapping chart, chalk board, or overhead

*Lesson Routine*

1. Brainstorm words associated with a key concept.
   - *As a class, have students brainstorm all the words that are associated with a key concept or idea. You may also have several key words that you would like to highlight, and you can add them to the class list.*
2. Create a semantic map.
   - *Group related words and create category headings. Visually represent the relationship between the categories and the key concept on a semantic map. Once students have practiced creating whole-class semantic maps, they can work individually, in pairs, or in small groups to categorize words and identify relationships related to a key concept.*

3. Extend the activity.

- *Students can use semantic maps as a previewing activity prior to reading, to review important vocabulary and key ideas, or as a starting point for writing an essay or research paper.*

---

## SYSTEMATIC MORPHOLOGY INSTRUCTION*

### *Grade Levels*

Third grade and up

### *Purpose*

Students will use knowledge of affixes and base words to understand the meaning of complex words.

### *Materials*

- Word cards with words that contain one or two target prefixes or suffixes (e.g., *hyper-, anti-*)

| | | |
|---|---|---|
| hyperactive | hypervigilant | hypersensitive |
| antioxidant | antidote | antifreeze |

### *Lesson Routine*

1. Introduce the prefixes and their meanings. For example, *hyper-* means "over" or "above" and *anti-* means "against."
   a. Introduce and show the first word card. For example, "*Hyperactive* means overactive." Direct students to say and practice reading the word.
   b. Identify the prefix and discuss how it changes the meaning of the base word.
   c. Continue with each word.
2. Guided practice with words.
   a. With the words face up, ask students to find a word that means _____ (e.g., overactive).
   b. Provide additional practice opportunities with words. Apply words in sentences. Model the first sentence. For example, "Zach's parents rushed him to the hospital so the doctor could give him the *antidote* to the poison in a snakebite."
   c. Identify the prefix and base word.
   d. Write what you think the word means: "I think *antidote* means protection against the poison.
   e. Check understanding by rereading the sentence.

## Example

| |
|---|
| 1. During kickball practice, Andrew complained that his ister was being <u>hypersensitive</u>; whenever he teased her about the game, she cried. |

**Prefix:** _____  **Base:** _____

**I think** _____  **means** _____

**CHECK:** Reread the sentence. Does your definition make sense? use context clues.    YES    NO

2. In my opinion, Mom's review of the new pizza restaurant was <u>hypercritical</u>. She complained about the size of the pepperoni, the mushy crust, the crowded atmosphere, and the loud rock music!

**Prefix:** _____  **Base:** _____

**I think** _____  **means** _____

**CHECK:** Reread the sentence. Does your definition make sense? use context clues.    YES    NO

3. If you live in a cold climate, such as New York or Michigan, you need to add <u>antifreeze</u> to your car every winter; otherwise, your car may not start in the morning.

**Prefix:** _____  **Base:** _____

**I think** _____  **means** _____

**CHECK:** Reread the sentence. Does your definition make sense? use context clues.    YES    NO

## ESSENTIAL WORDS ROUTINE*

### Grade Levels

Third grade and up

### Purpose

Students will understand vocabulary words and how they are used.

### Materials

- One "Essential Words" document per word selected to preteach from a text, using the template below.

| **Word**<br>Definition |
|---|
| **Visual representation of the word** |
| **Related words** |

| | |
|---|---|
| **Example sentence using the word** | |
| **Example** | |
| **Nonexample** | |
| **Turn-and-talk prompt** | |

### *Lesson Routine*

1. Select words to teach and prepare "Essential Words" documents.
2. Display each "Essential Word" document and teach each word's meaning.
3. Read the example usage and discuss.
4. Review the examples and nonexamples, discussing why each is an example or nonexample.
5. Engage students in the turn and talk, allowing about 5 minutes for peer discussion.
6. Debrief after peer discussion.

### *Example*

## DURING-READING LESSON PLANS

### MAIN IDEA SKETCH

#### Grade Levels

All

#### Purpose

Use drawing to help students conceptualize and remember the main idea of what they read. This strategy works well with narrative text.

#### Materials

- Short passages from curriculum materials
- Paper and pencil

#### Lesson Routine

1. Model the strategy.
   - *Read a passage aloud from a short story.*
   - *Think aloud about the main idea of the passage by using the following guides:*
     - What is the most important *who* or *what*?
     - What is the most important thing about the *who* or *what*?
     - Draw a quick sketch of the main idea.
     - Write a main idea statement under the sketch.
   - *If students need additional clarification, repeat with another passage.*
2. Provide guided practice.
   - *Now read another passage aloud while students follow along in their own text.*
   - *Have students draw their own main idea sketch, including a main idea caption.*
   - *Ask students to share drawings and explain their thinking.*
3. Apply the strategy individually or in partners.
   - *As students become more adept at drawing a response, they can work independently or in partners to read a section or chapter, draw the main idea, and then write a main idea caption. The length of the main idea caption will vary depending on the amount of text. For example, the main idea caption for one paragraph of reading should contain about 10 words or less, whereas a chapter in a novel might contain several sentences.*
   - *Debrief with students by sharing drawings and discussing them with the class. Ask students to think about how their drawings influenced their understanding of what they read. Do they think they were able to remember what they read better after they made their drawings? After doing a few main idea sketches, did students find themselves creating more mental images as they read?*

### *Ideas for Providing Additional Support*

1. Students who struggle to come up with the main idea will need extra opportunities to practice the strategy with guided feedback. Be sure students understand and can apply the strategy before they are asked to use it independently during reading.

2. Some students take a long time to draw, limiting the amount of time they have to read. Stress that these are quick sketches (use pen to limit erasures, if necessary) to help students gather ideas and remember what they read. Limit the amount of space for drawings or set a time limit for drawings (e.g., 5 minutes to draw and write main idea caption) to guide students to use this skill efficiently.

3. For students who need more explicit instruction, break the task into steps.

   a. Look at the main idea picture (created by the student or provided by the teacher) and think about how it relates to the reading.

   b. What is the most important *who* or *what*?

   _____

   c. What is the most important thing about the *who* or *what*?

   _____

   d. Write your main idea caption.

   _____

4. If students continue to struggle to identify the main idea after modeling and guided practice, scaffold their strategy use by providing the main idea statement and having them draw a picture of it. Then create the sketch and ask students to write the main idea. Repeat as needed to support students in learning this valuable strategy.

## GET THE GIST*

### *Grade Levels*

Third grade and up

### *Purpose*

Students will identify the main idea of a paragraph, stating it in a "gist" format.

## *Materials*

- Expository reading passage
- Gist cue card (one per student)
- Gist poster, displayed in the classroom
- Gist student log

---

### Get the Gist Cue Card

Step 1: Who or what is this section about?

Step 2: What is the most important information about the "who" or "what"?

Step 3: Write your gist statement by combining information from Steps 1 and 2.

Remember, your gist should
- include only the most important information,
- leave out unnecessary details, and
- be a complete sentence.

---

## *Lesson Routine*

1. Explain Get the Gist.

   "Get the Gist" helps you to determine the most important ideas about what you read. We are going to go through the steps together. First, you identify the most important "who" or "what" in the section. Then, you identify the most important information about the "who" or "what." Finally, you write a short, complete sentence containing that information.

2. Model Get the Gist.

   a. Using the gist poster and cue cards, briefly explain the steps of the strategy.
   b. Display and read a paragraph aloud.
   c. Using a think-aloud technique, model how you identify the "who" or "what" the paragraph is mainly about. Circle the who or what.
   d. Continue thinking aloud and identify the most important information about the "who" or "what."
   e. Write a "gist" statement about the paragraph and discuss how it uses the most important information, leaves out unnecessary details, and is a complete sentence.

3. Guided practice using Get the Gist.

   a. Using another paragraph, read aloud together and walk through the steps, asking students to identify the "who" or "what" the paragraph is about, then identify and underline key information.
   b. Ask students to write their own gist statements.
   c. Ask students to share their gists, discussing as a whole class how the statements meet the criteria for a good gist.

4.  Partner practice with Get the Gist.

   a.  In pairs, have students practice the process with a new paragraph. Ask students to write their gists in the gist log. Use the log frequently to monitor students' progress.

### *Example*

**The Human Brain**

Your brain is a round, wrinkly, and floppy organ made up of cells and tissues. It is the fattiest organ in your body and is floating in fluid to protect it. This organ is the size of your two fists, weighing about 3 pounds. Even though it might not sound very powerful, the brain is a complex organ that consists of many different parts. Each part of the brain has unique functions, but they are connected and work together to perform many voluntary and involuntary actions. The parts work together to be responsible for your thoughts and feelings, as well as things you may not think about as much, such as breathing and your heartbeat.

### *Who or What*

The most important "what" is the human brain because many of the ideas in the paragraph are about the human brain.

### *Most Important Information about the Who or What*

- The brain is a complex organ made up of cells and tissues.
- Each part of the brain has unique functions that work together.

### *Write a Gist*

The brain is a complex organ with many parts that work together.

## IDENTIFYING THE MAIN IDEA

### *Grade Levels*

Third grade and up

### *Purpose*

Identify the main idea using images and text.

### *Materials*

- Find or create a Main Idea chart and student graphic organizer.

| Topic: Who or what is this mostly about? | Main Idea: What is the most important thing about the topic? |
|---|---|
| Key Details: | |

- Nonfiction texts with images that include a straightforward topic and main idea.

- Additional nonfiction texts at students' reading level that are not too long and that have passages conducive to finding the main idea in paragraphs, in parts, or on pages. Texts should have text features to assist in teaching the preview, predicting, and reading steps.

### *Lesson Routine*

#### *Using Images to Generate the Main Idea*

1. Select an image with a straightforward main idea. Initially, using only one of the *who* or *what* questions to simplify the process, ask: "Whom do you think this is mostly about?" or "What do you think this is mostly about?" Specify that only one- or two-word responses are needed. Model the first few times until students grasp the idea. Explain that *the who* or *the what* refer to the *topic* and write the topic on the chart or overhead. If students mention things such as the details from the image, acknowledge and connect to the details, but draw students' attention to identifying *the who* or *the what* from the image.

2. Point out that *the who* or *the what* is not always a singular. Include images that have more than one attribute so that, as an example, *the who* can be a family and *the what* may be horses.

3. Next, ask: "What is the most important thing to know about the topic (the who or what)?" Model how to determine the most important thing by giving examples. Tell students that the most important thing about a topic is called the *main idea*. The teacher writes the main idea on the chart.

4. Last, point out the other aspects in the image that are not as important but still relevant for understanding the topic a little better. These are called *details*.

#### *Guided Practice*

1. In Day One of guided group practice, select additional images, assisting students in identifying each of the elements (topic, main idea, and details). Continue to record these elements in a chart or student graphic organizer.

2. In Day Two of guided group practice, model the process with a passage divided into sections to tell where to start and stop reading. Students complete the main idea graphic organizer as they read to keep track of their ideas.

3. Integrate prereading strategies by drawing attention to features such as headings, key words, labels, and special print. Model the preview reading of text features and stress the importance of making connections and predictions, which will help when the text is read for the first time. Remind students that previewing, connecting to text, predicting what will happen, and making notes will help them learn from the text and remember what they read.

4. Read a short section of text and identify the topic (who or what the text is mostly about). Record the topic in the main idea graphic organizer and tell students to think about the most important thing that the author wants us to know about the topic. Discuss possible important things with students, finally narrowing it down to the most important ideas. Guide the group through this process part by part. Scaffold or reteach a step as needed.

5. In Day Three of guided group practice, display a large graphic organizer drawn, giving each student a student version. Using a text with preplanned start and stop points, model and assist students to practice each of the main idea steps. You may read or students may take turns reading the parts if the reading level as appropriate. The students take turns on different days rereading and discussing their main idea points to summarize what they learned in the book.

6. When students are comfortable identifying a topic and main idea, they can work on their own or with a partner to apply the main idea strategy. Monitor students as they work through their own texts and provide feedback or reteach as needed.

## DOES IT MAKE SENSE?*

### Grade Levels

Second grade and up

### Purpose

Students will self-monitor by determining whether a sentence makes sense and identify clues in the text to support answers.

### Materials

• Prepare several sentences, some that make sense and some that do not.

### Mini-Lesson Routine

1. Tell students that good readers pay close attention to the meaning of what they read. It is important to think about whether what you are reading makes sense. Tell students that they are going to practice determining if a sentence makes sense.

2. Students read four to five statements, circling "yes" if the statement makes sense or "no" if it does not.

3. If a student circles "no," the student underlines the words that provide the clues.

4. Discuss answers and reasoning with students.

## *Example*

Circle "yes" if the sentence makes sense or "no" if it does not make sense. If you circled "no," underline the part of the sentence that doesn't make sense.

1. The heat in the summer makes some activities difficult or dangerous. It is important to cool off and drink plenty of apples.　　YES　NO

2. The students were on the playground for recess. Someone was playing basketball, someone was flying, and someone was on the swing set.　　YES　NO

3. Babies usually sleep in a crib. However, once they get older, they sleep in a bed.　　YES　NO

4. In Texas, it is common to see animals like birds and squirrels. It is rare to see animals like monkeys because you can only see them at the zoo or the circus.　　YES　NO

5. When you are riding a bike, you should always wear a helmet, even if you are just riding for a short time. Wearing a helmet on your elbow protects your head.　　YES　NO

## ACTIVATING BACKGROUND KNOWLEDGE WHILE READING*

### *Grade Levels*

Elementary/intervention

### *Purpose*

Understand that reading brings back memories through a connection to the text and these connections can support comprehension.

### *Materials*

- Large chart titled "Memories and Connections"
- Individual copies of the graphic organizer for students to complete in small groups
- Text from curriculum materials with vivid pictures or illustrations

### *Lesson Routine*

1. Preplan this introductory group lesson with the purpose of helping students to understand that reading brings back memories through a connection to the text. Memories are a part of our background that help us create a connection so that we can better understand things that we read.

2. Display the "Memories and Connections" chart where it is clearly visible and where the teacher and/or students have easy access to write memories or background knowledge as it is relayed.

3. Model for the students how to activate background knowledge while reading.

4. Choose a story and read it aloud as students follow or read along. Stop at the end of a page or part and model how the words bring back memories. The things that we have in our memory help us to understand what we are reading. Give an example of how something read can inspire a personal memory and help the reader understand what a person in the

story might do (or not do) next. This initiates the concept of prediction while reading. Write on the chart, "This helps me remember that _____."

5. Tell the students that memories include such things as:
   a. Something you have done
   b. Something you can do
   c. A place you went
   d. Something else you have read

6. In guided group practice, remind students to think about things they remember while the book is being read to them. Tell students that they will be asked to relate a memory as they reach predetermined places in the book. At different places in the book, give each student the opportunity to relay a memory to make a connection to the text. Ask students if something they know about might help them predict what might happen next in the story. The student completes the sentence, "This helps me remember that _____." Support students to generate a simple complete sentence (not a whole story). Write the sentence on the "Memories and Connections" chart, or on a sentence strip.

## IDENTIFYING TEXT-TO-SELF CONNECTIONS*

### Grade Levels

Elementary/intervention

### Purpose

Make connections to text to support comprehension and recall of ideas.

### Materials

- Make a text-to-self (TS) connection poster or find one from a published resource. The poster should have prompts like the following for students to make connections to the story and their own lives or feelings.
  o This reminds me of . . .
  o I understand how the character feels because . . .
- Sticky notes or small slips of paper
- Relatable texts in which students are likely to be able to make connections

### Lesson Routine

1. Prior to beginning the lesson, mark with sticky notes a couple of places in the book with which you feel a connection.
2. Show students a book cover and say: "Have you ever read a book that reminded you of something you have seen or experienced in life, such as at school or at home?"
3. Model for students how to make a TS connection by reading a book aloud to the students.
   - Introduce the title of the book to students.
   - Read and discuss a couple of pages.

- When you get to a page to make a personal TS connection, stop and explain to students your TS connection with the story. Say: "This reminds me of . . ."
- Put a small sticky note with a "TS" on the page to mark where a TS connection has been made.

### Guided Practice

1. In guided group practice, give students their own small sticky notes. Continue reading and tell students that they can raise their hands when they have their own TS connection.

2. Students briefly share their own TS connections by saying: "This reminds me of . . ." They put their own sticky note on the page where they had a connection. Use the TS poster with sentence frames to provide examples and ideas for students.

3. It can be helpful for the teacher to call on some students who may not think they have a connection to the pictures. The teacher may need to ask a direct question like: "What do you know about _____?" or "How do you feel when _____?"

4. The teacher may need to model this routine with another book on another day.

### Independent Practice

1. In independent practice, once students are comfortable with the routine, they work in groups or pairs as they all read the same book/passage. Students take turns raising their hands and placing sticky notes in their books to share TS connections. The teacher monitors groups of students.

2. When students make errors or forget the procedure, the teacher models the process again, encouraging students to make TS connections in any reading they do in their lives to help them understand the text. Remind students that the purpose of making TS connections is to help them remember and understand ideas they reading.

## MAKING AND CHECKING PREDICTIONS IN A BOOK*

### Grade Levels

All

### Purpose

Learn to predict what will happen next, based on text-to-self connections, and to verify if predictions are accurate after reading.

### Materials

- Prediction-check chart. Make a graphic organizer chart that can be used to make and check predictions in a book or passage. The graphic organizer should have a place to indicate whether the prediction is correct or incorrect.

| Text-to-self connection | I predict that ... | Verify: My prediction was ... |
|---|---|---|
|  |  |  |

- Student version of the prediction-check chart
- Relatable texts in which students are likely to be able to make connections. Use texts that are intriguing or have surprise endings. Identify texts that will be read only by the teacher as well as student-level books for practice.

### *Lesson Routine*

1. Provide texts that will be used to model the process. Make sure that some TS connections may easily be made in either the title or early illustrations of the books or passage.

2. Prepare TS connections in advance that will be used to model and mark the places in the books with sticky notes as a reminder.

3. Model the TS connection by introducing the first text. Write the title of the text on the graphic organizer chart, then read the title and pull out a sticky note. Tell students that the title brings a TS connection to mind. Remind students that connections help us to understand what we read.

   - Write "TS" on the sticky note and place it on the title while verbalizing the connection made. Say: "I remember that happening once. It makes me think that _____ will happen because _____. I could also say I **predict** that _____ will happen because _____."
   - Fill in the graphic organizer where the statement says, "I predict that . . ." The teacher says: "*Predict* is another way of saying *think* or *guess,* but not the kind of guess you just make up. It is a smart guess because you know something about the topic from your TS connection."
   - Early in this process, provide an example of an incorrect prediction and remind students that the process is not about always being right.

4. Continue to read the story and direct students to think not only about the validity of the prediction already written but also about other possible predictions.

5. After reading a section, or completing the text, go back to check predictions. When the prediction is correct, say: "I know the prediction is right because _____." Place a check mark or plus sign or writes "correct" in the verify box to signify that the prediction was correct. For older students, add evidence that supports the prediction.

6. Throughout the process, remind students that questioning predictions improves understanding of the reading. Be sure to also model incorrect predictions by saying something such as: "I know the prediction was wrong because _____." Tell students that it is OK to make an incorrect prediction, since authors sometimes try to surprise readers with the unexpected to keep them interested. Sometimes an event is unexpected because the reader does not have any connection to a topic or the TS connection in someone's life is different from what is in the book. The teacher places an "X" or writes "incorrect" in the verify box to signify that the prediction was not correct this time.

7. Continue reading and asking students to make TS connections and predictions. Ask students to tell why they think something will happen by saying: "I predict that _____ will happen because _____." The teacher goes through the steps of checking the prediction when coming to the appropriate place in the book. Each student should be involved in making TS connections, verbalizing as well as writing the predictions (the teacher may help with the writing as needed), and finally verifying the predictions' accuracy.

8. In guided practice on another day, the teacher selects one of the student-level reading books or a passage that students will read, then guides the group and monitors their work while students fill out their own prediction-check graphic organizers.

9. In independent practice, once the students understand the process, they may work together as partners or individually on a book at their level of reading. The teacher monitors and assists or models again if required.

## IDENTIFYING TEXT-TO-TEXT CONNECTIONS*

### Grade Levels

Elementary/intervention

### Purpose

Learn to predict what will happen next, based on text-to-text connections, and to verify if predictions are accurate after reading.

### Materials

- Text-to-text (TT) connection chart. The chart should have reminders that connections are being made from one text to another or between parts within a book or passage. The chart should include phrases such as the following:
  - "I remember reading _____ in another book. It said _____."
  - "How is this text the same as or different from other things you have read?"
  - "This helps me understand _____."
- Student version of the TT connection chart
- Sticky notes
- Texts in which students are likely to be able to make TT connections.

### Lesson Routine

1. Flag, with sticky notes marked "TT," a couple of places in two texts where you will model connections between the texts.

2. Select additional texts once the connections between texts in different books or passages are understood. Both fiction and nonfiction books or passages may be used for the TT connection instruction.

3. Introduce the chart and give a brief description of what a TT connection is. Tell students that a TT connection is a connection or link to something from the text you are reading to another text you have read before.

4. Choose a text and read it aloud as students follow along or read with you from their own book.

5. Stop at the end of a page or section and model how a short section bring back memories about another book. Say: "I remember reading _____ in another book. It said _____." OR "This text is the same as (or different from) _____ because _____."

6.  Place a sticky note with a "TT" on it on the pages where a TT connection is modeled. Sometimes students will confuse their connections. Explain how a TS connection is different from a TT connection. As a useful tool to support visual learners, the teacher should also have both texts to show students how the two books or passages are connected.

### Guided Practice

1.  In guided practice, stop halfway through the book or passage to give students their own sticky notes on which to write "TT."

2.  Tell students that their job is to read along and raise their hands when they have a TT connection. If the book or passage is too difficult to read on their own, then the teacher reads and students follow along, thinking about TT connections.

3.  Students put their own sticky notes on pages or part of a passage where they have a connection or link to something already read in another text.

4.  Prompt students to put into their own words the TT connection, saying: "I remember reading _____."

### Independent Practice

1.  In independent practice on another day, pick a text that the students can read independently and that has connections with other texts students have read before. Students have their own sticky notes with "TT" on them, and while taking turns reading, students individually stop to talk about their own connections. Students can work in pairs as the teacher monitors progress.

2.  Before students work in pairs, the teacher models what "pair work" looks like so students have a clear expectation of what to do.

3.  To help students stay on track, the teacher can provide a prompt card to remind them what to say: "I remember reading _____." or "This text is the same as _____ because _____."

4.  When needed, the teacher scaffolds or models the process again.

5.  As students read other books after this lesson is introduced, encourage students to make TT connections.

6.  Over time, encourage students to make different types of connections, text-to-text and text-to-self, as they read.

## IDENTIFYING CHARACTERS AND SETTING*

### Grade Levels

Elementary/intervention

### Purpose

Identify characters and setting in narrative text.

### Materials

- Display the definitions of character and setting, using the same wording found in district core-reading materials.
- Use a published graphic organizer or create your own so that students can record characters and setting.
- Use narrative text in which students can easily figure out the characters and the setting.
- Use copies of another narrative text at a reading level appropriate for small group work.

### Lesson Routine

1. Explain that every story has characters and a setting. Define the terms *character* and *setting* and asks students to give examples from books they have read. You can also have students read the definitions aloud.

2. Talk about how characters and setting can change in a story and tell students that their job during reading is to identify the characters and setting in different parts of the book.

3. Model by reading a story aloud. At the beginning, talk about what is going on in the story to help students figure out the setting. If using a graphic organizer, fill out the section for the setting and characters. Continue reading, talking about new characters and whether the setting changes. If there is confusion about the setting, ask students: "Where did most of the book take place?"

4. In guided practice with the group, read a different story or have students take turns reading their own copy of the same book. Review the definitions of *character* and *setting* and, check for understanding, and continue to ask students to state the definitions in their own words.

5. On another day, for independent practice have students read a story at their reading level and complete a graphic organizer identifying the characters and setting.

## IDENTIFYING SEQUENCE OF EVENTS IN STORY STRUCTURE*

### Grade Levels

Elementary/intervention

### Purpose

Build on story structure elements, and to introduce the sequence of events in narrative text.

### Materials

- Display the definitions of character and setting, sequence of events. Use the same wording as the district reading materials.
- Use a published graphic organizer or create your own so that students can record characters, setting, and sequence of events.
- Sticky notes with numbers on them to place on pages where important story events are happening

- Narrative text in which students can easily figure out the characters and the setting, and that has a sequence of events in the story
- Copies of another narrative text at a reading level appropriate for small group work

### Lesson Routine

1.  Explain that some stories have a sequence of events, or an order in which things happen.
2.  Define the word *sequence*. Model with a series of objects or pictures that show a sequence of events for students, such as what a student does before coming to school. Also define the term *event*.
3.  Model how to identify the sequence of events in a short story.
4.  Read the story for the first time. Tell students that you will read the story aloud and identify the characters and settings while they think about important events that happen. Without taking a lot of time, the teacher or a student writes down the character and setting on the graphic organizer.
5.  Reread the story, modeling where important events are happening by asking students: "What is happening now?" and then putting a sticky note in the book with a number to define whether the event happened first, second, or third. The teacher or student then writes down the event on the graphic organizer. The teacher may need to only model one or two events.

### Guided Practice

For guided group practice, repeat the same process by first reading the story aloud as students follow along in their own text. Each student has sticky notes to help identify the events in order. Students as a group fill out a story map or graphic organizer of the events. Keep the description of events short to keep up the pace and reduce the amount of writing. You may need to repeat guided practice on another day.

### Independent Practice

In independent practice, students read their own books, have their own numbered sticky notes, and fill out graphic organizers on their own. Remind students to first read through the book once to figure out the characters and setting, while also paying attention to events that happen in the story. At the second reading, students find the events and record them.

## IDENTIFYING PROBLEM AND SOLUTION IN STORY STRUCTURE*

### Grade Levels

Elementary/intervention

### Purpose

Build on story structure elements, and introduce the sequence of events in narrative text.

## Materials

- Display a published graphic organizer or create your own that contains areas for character, setting, events, problem, and solution.
- Student copies of the graphic organizer
- Chart paper with questions: What is the problem? What is the solution?
- A story already used to identify character, setting, and events and that has a clear problem and solution and if available, a previously completed graphic organizer with character, setting, and events
- Additional books whose characters, setting, and events have been previously discussed can be used for group and/or individual practice of problem-and-solution learning.

## Lesson Routine

1. Reintroduce the book and remind students that they have already read the book and so now can probably recall each of the story elements. Review the chart quickly, asking students for information and revealing the elements as they are identified by students to verify accurate recall. Remind students that they remember all of this information because they have filled in one of these organizers before.

2. Tell students that there are two more things that are important to understand and remember many stories: the problem and the solution. In the story that has already been read, the character(s) had a problem. Discuss that a problem is something that goes wrong for the character or that the character is unhappy about and does not know how to fix. Also discuss that a story has a solution, which is how the character's problem is solved, or fixed. Refer to these two words on the previously prepared large chart tablet so that it is evident that the problem comes before the solution.

3. When introducing the problem and solution, point to the graphic organizer and discuss each of the events and what might be wrong. Ask students: "What was the character's problem?" and tell them that sometimes the problem is not easy to figure out by just thinking about it and that rereading parts of the book or rereading the events students have written about may help to find the problem. When students determine the problem, record it on the graphic organizer. Then ask: "What was the solution to the problem?" Ask students *why* they think the character's problem is solved and record the solution to the problem.

### Guided Practice

1. For guided group practice, use another book the class has read. Repeat the process by adding to a previously used graphic organizer with character, setting, and events. Reread the book aloud or have students take turns reading parts. The focus is to add the problem and solution to the graphic organizer.

2. The students provide all of the answers (with the teacher's direction, where needed) for the character(s) and setting. Using the questions as a prompt, ask: "What is the problem?" Let the students think about the problem and give responses, but if this seems difficult or the problem is unclear, continue reading the book a page or a part at a time. Assist by

asking questions about some of the related events to guide students into understanding the problem. Once students understand the problem, write the problem in one sentence on the graphic organizer. Then work through each of the events (remembering to use a sticky note to identify each event) and ask students to think about the events and to identify how the problem could be solved. Then read the last item on the story structure chart: "What is the solution?" and record a simple sentence that tells the solution to the problem.

### Independent Practice

In independent practice, once students are comfortable with the routine, they may work in a group or in pairs with a new book. The objective is for each student to eventually be able to work through this process independently. Provide each group with a student version of the graphic organizer. Groups or partners will practice reading, discussing parts, and filling in the story-structure elements. Listen and assist in the discussions and discovery of the elemental answers where needed. Provide assistance and directions, either rereading parts if something is misunderstood or returning to modeling the process step(s) where needed.

## IDENTIFYING CAUSE AND EFFECT*

### Grade Levels

Elementary/intervention

### Purpose

Identify cause and effect while reading.

### Materials

- Published graphic organizer or create your own that contains areas for cause and effect
- Student copies of the graphic organizer
- Definitions of *cause* and *effect*
- Fiction or nonfiction text from which students can easily determine cause and effect from teacher modeling and questioning
- Additional texts at students' reading level that include straightforward causes and effects

### Lesson Routine

1. Prepare several real-life scenarios.
2. Display a sentence that has a cause and an effect. Model the definition of *cause* (why something happens) and *effect* (the result of something happening).

| Example: A hurricane hit the city, so all the schools were closed. | |
|---|---|
| (Cause) | (Effect) |

3. Display the cause–effect graphic organizer with the *cause* side completed. Read the cause: "Why something happens." Students come up with the effect, or the event that happens.

| Cause: Why something happens | Effect: "What happened? |
|---|---|
| He didn't wash his hands. | |
| She didn't want to be late for school. | |
| A blizzard hit overnight. | |

4. Tell students that in all types of literature, fiction as well as nonfiction, things called *events* happen, and these things happen because of, or due to, a cause. In other words, the cause is why something happened.

5. Next, read a text in which some causes have been written on a cause–effect graphic organizer.

6. Read the text or students can take turns reading, stopping at predetermined places. Read the first cause on the graphic organizer and say: "What happened?" The effect is then written under the "effect" column.

7. The terms *why, how,* or *what* are key words to use when asking the reason for something happening. Go through the text and look at the causes listed, and then complete the "effect" column while thinking aloud.

| Cause | Effect: "What happened? |
|---|---|
| List causes in the book. | While reading, list effects (events that happen). |

## Guided Practice

1. On another day, repeat the process with a text at students' reading level. Each student has a student version of the graphic organizer.

2. Read a section of the text and stop to discuss an event. With the students, identify the cause and effect. Model how to fill out the first cause. When the reason is determined, write it on the "cause" side of the graphic organizer.

3. Ask students what happened after the cause—the effect, or the event that followed. Model how to fill out the first effect, which is then written on the "effect" side of the organizer.

4. Remind students to think of *why, what,* and *how* something happened in response to an event in the text. Continue through the text and others as needed to give students enough practice not only to fill in the graphic organizer but also to ensure that they are asking themselves cause–effect questions and making connections for comprehension. A possible scaffold is providing a graphic organizer with a few causes or effects completed, supporting students identify in the rest.

## Independent Practice

Students practice on their own or with a partner using a blank graphic organizer.

## GENERATING QUESTIONS*

### *Grade Levels*

Third grade and up

### *Purpose*

Students will monitor their comprehension by stopping to ask and answer specific and wide questions throughout reading.

### *Materials*

- Poster
- Student cue card
- Reading passage

_____ **Writing Questions While I Read** _____

While I read, I stop every once in a while to see whether the information makes sense.
I check my understanding by challenging myself to ask a question, just like a teacher does.

| Question Type | Description | Possible Stems | Examples |
|---|---|---|---|
| **Specific Questions** | • Questions can be answered in one word or one sentence.<br>• Answers can be found word-for-word in the text. | • Who<br>• What<br>• When<br>• Where<br>• Why<br>• How | **ELA:** In *Number the Stars*, why did Annemarie's parents burn their newspaper?<br><br>**Science:** What is the largest ocean?<br><br>**Social studies:** How many original colonies were there? |
| **Wide Questions** | • Questions can be answered using information from multiple places in the text.<br>• Questions can be answered by making inferences (combining your prior knowledge with information from the text).<br>• Answers require one or more sentences. | • Who<br>• What<br>• When<br>• Where<br>• Why<br>• How<br>• Describe<br>• Explain<br>• Summarize | **ELA:** Explain how the setting in chapters 7 and 8 contrasts with the city setting of previous chapters.<br><br>**Science:** Describe some of the dangers associated with earthquakes.<br><br>**Social studies:** How was the experience of the Jamestown colonists different from what they expected? |

### *Lesson Routine*

1. Explain question writing.
   a. Tell students that stopping to ask questions along the way gives us an opportunity to check our understanding. It makes us stop and think about whether our reading makes sense. Throughout a passage, we will stop several times to write a question and see if we can answer it.
   b. There are two types of questions we can write: specific questions and wide questions. Review the poster and cue card and discuss each type. Start with specific questions and

practice this for several days, then introduce wide questions, which require students to pull information from multiple places in the text.

2. Model question writing.

  a. Remind students that you will read a chunk of text, then stop to write a specific question, one that can be answered in one word or sentence and the information is explicitly in the text.

  b. Display and read aloud a segment of text.

  c. Using a think-aloud technique, show how you would write a question that can be answered from what you have read.

  d. Demonstrate how you can answer the question from what you have just read.

3. Guide practice with question writing.

  a. Read aloud another segment of text.

  b. Direct students to form questions that can be answered in the text and write them on the board.

  c. Ask students to see if they an answer the questions and find the text that gives the answers.

4. Practice question writing with partners.

  a. In pairs, have students practice the process with a segment of text. Ask students to write their questions and answers.

5. Expand question writing to wide questions.

  a. After students are comfortable with specific questions, repeat the steps of modeling, guided practice, and partner practice with wide questions.

### *Example*

*Questions for Comprehension Monitoring*

Segment of Text: Clouds

*A cloud is made of water drops or ice crystals floating in the sky. There are many kinds of clouds. Clouds are an important part of Earth's weather. The sky can be full of water. But most of the time you can't see the water. The drops of water are too small to see. They have turned into a gas called water vapor. As the water vapor goes higher in the sky, the air gets cooler. The cooler air causes the water droplets to start to stick to things like bits of dust, ice, or sea salt.*

(Adapted from *www.nasa.gov/audience/forstudents/k-4/stories/nasa-knows/what-are-clouds-k4.html*)

| Question | Answer | Text Evidence |
|---|---|---|
| Why are drops of water usually too small to see in the sky? | Drops of water are too small to see because they turned into a gas called water vapor. | Paragraph 2 |

## MAKING INFERENCE WITH SENTENCES*

### Grade Levels

All

### Purpose

To make inferences from short sentences.

### Materials

- Student copies of the sample inference sentence graphic organizer page and blank inference sentence graphic organizers. (Choose the sentences you will use from the lists provided or write ones of your own. Write sentences on sentence strip(s) for each pair or group.)

### Lesson Routine

1. Review what an inference is. Explain to students that an inference is never directly stated in the text. It is "reading between the lines," or using your own reasoning, and arriving at an understanding or conclusion based on clues in the text, combined with your own background knowledge.

2. Model with the sample sentence on the first day: "Everyone stopped when the referee blew the whistle." Write the sentence on the board and pass out the handout titled "Inference Sentence Example Graphic Organizer." Note that when you read even a sentence you have to use your own reasoning to understand. Readers form images in their minds as they read information and have to use their background experience to figure things out. You cannot make up an inference; you have to be able to justify "why" you came to that conclusion. Your inference may be slightly different than another person's based on experience, which is OK. All students read the sentence aloud. Then guide them by asking questions on the sample inference sentence graphic organizer:

   - **Where** do you think this is taking place from your experience? Can you figure this out by using what you know? *Yes, because you know in sports games refs blow a whistle as part of a game. Where do people play sports? Sports field, court, in a gym, etc. (Some students may not know what refs are, so explain it.)*

     *Since you used your background and it is not specially stated (or "right there in the sentence"), it is an inference. Circle "inference."*

   - **When** do you think this is happening? *Is this happening before, during, or after a game? From your experience, refs blow whistles after a player breaks a rule, when the team needs a time-out, or at the end of a game.*

     *Since you formed your own opinion and it is not specially stated (or "right there in the sentence"), it is an inference. Circle "inference."*

   - **Who** do you think they are talking about as "everyone"? *From your background or the evidence about the ref blowing the whistle, you believe it is the players on the sports team.*

     *Since you used your background and it is not specially stated (or "right there in the sentence"), it is an inference. Circle "inference."*

- **What happened?** What happened in this sentence in your own words, *not* just restating the sentence? *The ref blew the whistle and everyone stopped, which is directly stated in the sentence, so it is a fact.*

    *We can see it and find it right there in the sentence, so it is a fact. Circle "fact."*

## Guided Practice

1. All students have the same sentence but split up in pairs or groups to see what each pair or group comes up with. If needed, go over the rules of working in pairs (both work together, contribute ideas, be respectful of each other's ideas, etc.). Remind students that they cannot make up an inference—it comes from combining information from the text with their own background experience to draw a logical conclusion.

2. You may need to guide students through each section, first discussing "Where?" as a group. Then monitor and guide students through the other parts of the graphic organizer—"When?" "Who?" and "What happened?" If all groups are struggling, stop all groups and model the section they need help on, and practice filling out the graphic organizer correctly.

3. When all groups are finished filling out the graphic organizer, groups share what they came up with. Remember that each group may have a different inference based on their own experience, but the inference has to make sense.

## Independent Practice

1. Independent practice may need to be done on a different day, but before students complete this part, review what an inference is and briefly look at the example sheet. Then pair up students or group them. Each group gets their own unique sentence or each group may get the same sentence with less support than before. Groups make inferences on their own. Students in pairs or small groups each have their own graphic organizer to fill out in collaboration with their peers. Monitor and scaffold as needed. When groups are done, the whole class comes together to discuss and compare responses.

2. Students will need to explicitly practice with different sentences for a couple of weeks.

    *Note:* The goal is that students will eventually be able to make inferences independently when they read sentences, paragraphs, and longer sections of text. As students internalize inference making, they will no longer need to go through these systematic steps.

### EXAMPLES OF INFERENCE SENTENCES

1. Joey happily blew out the colorful candles and got many presents.
2. Julia plays her new trumpet for 2 hours every day.
3. I honestly forgot to set my digital alarm clock last night.
4. Sharon grabbed her raincoat and her umbrella.
5. Yesterday we cleaned out our lockers and took everything home.
6. Suddenly, Mark ran into the street without looking.
7. In the distance I could see a big black smoke cloud.
8. The red boat drifted into the middle of the river.
9. A student returned from recess crying.

10. Melissa was the star pitcher, but she had a broken finger.

11. Our family bought tickets and some popcorn.

12. When I woke up, there were branches and leaves all over the yard.

13. Everyone stopped when the referee blew the whistle.

14. I heard a crash while walking through the parking lot.

15. Anne was shivering and forgot to grab her mittens and hat.

16. A dirty man along the side of the road was holding up a sign and a cup.

17. Jesse ran after a retreating bus, waving her briefcase frantically.

18. Jamar was driving on the highway, listening to the radio, when a police officer pulled him over.

19. We could see the angry principal and police running down the hall.

20. They waved their hands frantically, as the plane above circled back around.

21. Billy stood in the shade of the only tree in the street while he waited for his ride.

22. Holding the trophy above his head, Sam grinned from ear to ear as he spotted his parents in the crowd.

23. As the movie ended, Allie put the crumpled tissue from her hand into the trash.

24. The hungry student turned red, began to cough, then held his throat.

25. As they looked around the class, the walls and floors were shaking; things were moving or falling off shelves.

| Inference Sentence Graphic Organizer | | |
|---|---|---|
| *Everyone stopped when the referee blew the whistle.* | | |
| **Where?** <br><br> *Sports field/court* | **(Underline or highlight)** <br><br> Fact <br> <u>Inference</u> <br> Not there | **Evidence/background** <br><br> *I know that in sports games refs blow whistles.* |
| **When?** <br><br> *After a game rule is broken or at end of game* | **(Underline or highlight)** <br><br> Fact <br> Inference <br> Not there | **Evidence/background** <br><br> *I know that when a ref blows a whistle, it's either end of the game or someone has broken a game rule.* |
| **Who?** <br><br> *Sports team* | **(Underline or highlight)** <br><br> Fact <br> <u>Inference</u> <br> Not there | **Evidence/background** <br><br> *I know that sports games have refs and whistles.* |
| **What happened?** <br><br> *Ref blew the whistle, everyone stopped.* | **(Underline or highlight)** <br><br> <u>Fact</u> <br> Inference <br> Not there | **Evidence/background** <br><br> *Directly stated in sentence* |

# MAKING INFERENCES IN SCIENCE*

## Grade Level

Upper elementary and up

## Purpose

Practice making inferences while reading or formatively assess students' inferencing. Results can be used to guide instruction.

## Materials

- "Ancient Animals" text
- Multiple-choice "Inference Activity" and "Answer Key"

## Lesson Routine

Have students read the selection, and then answer the questions that follow using your own reasoning, background knowledge, and inference skills. Create additional practice activities as needed.

### ANCIENT ANIMALS

Dinosaurs are everywhere. You see them in movies, books, museums, and TV documentaries. They show up as stuffed toys or on T-shirts. These prehistoric beasts may be extinct—no longer living—but they're definitely not forgotten!

It's been a long time since dinosaurs roamed and ruled Earth. Scientists say the last ones died about 65 million years ago. We know the dinosaurs are gone, but no one knows exactly why. After all, no one was here to witness what happened! Most scientists believe dinosaurs died out after a gigantic meteorite hit Earth's surface and drastically changed the planet's climate. Birds and mammals that were protected by feathers and fur were better able to adapt to the weather changes than cold-blooded dinosaurs.

Other scientists say dinosaurs aren't extinct, they just look different! These experts believe the prehistoric beasts changed and developed into birds! Still other scientists say that Earth's warmer weather caused more male than female dinosaurs to develop. So, they say, dinosaurs died out because there were no more females to increase the population!

How do scientists know what dinosaurs looked like? There were no cameras millions of years ago, so dinosaurs are the only ones who know . . . and they're not talking! Scientists get clues from dinosaur fossils, and infer the rest.

Bones, footprints, and other remains are evidence of how big dinosaurs were and how they moved. To figure out how they looked with their skin on, scientists look at animals that live today. Because dinosaurs were lizard-like, scientists can infer that dinosaurs looked a lot like modern-day lizards. And since modern lizards are brown, gray, or green, then dinosaurs probably were, too! That's why dinosaur pictures and museum models have the same colors as today's lizard populations.

Scientists are always discovering new things about dinosaurs. In recent years, fossils were found in Antarctica, proving that dinosaurs lived on every continent. Experts also figured out that Stegosaurus had only one spread-out row of plates down its back, not two individual rows. And fossils of the smallest and the largest dinosaurs have been found. What will scientists discover next?

## Inference Activity

1. From the first paragraph, you can infer that
    a. you can see dinosaurs only in museums.
    b. all dinosaurs were very tall.
    c. the author doesn't like dinosaurs.
    d. people of all ages are interested in dinosaurs.

2. Scientists found a rare blue lizard in Colombia, so you can infer that
    a. the scientists were looking for missing people.
    b. some dinosaurs might have been blue.
    c. no dinosaurs had ever lived in Colombia.
    d. the lizards built nests near the top of a volcano.

3. Since scientists are always discovering new things about dinosaurs, you can infer that
    a. they still might not have found the smallest or biggest dinosaurs.
    b. science is no longer interested in looking for fossils.
    c. prehistoric people left written records with descriptions of dinosaurs.
    d. when scientists make inferences, they are always right.

4. What can you infer from the fact that Stegosaurus has just one row of plates?
    a. Stegosaurus wasn't as old as scientists thought.
    b. Old pictures and museum models of Stegosaurus had to be changed.
    c. Someone stole the other row of plates from a museum.
    d. Stegosaurus means "roof lizard."

5. What can you infer about lizard eggs?
    a. Cooler temperatures should produce more female lizards.
    b. Hot weather should produce female lizards.
    c. Cold temperatures will produce more male lizards.
    d. Hot weather will produce more orange lizards.

6. What can you infer about scientists?
    a. They never watch TV.
    b. All scientists study about dinosaurs.
    c. They don't always agree.
    d. They never make mistakes.

## Answer Key

1. From the first paragraph, you can infer that
    a. you can see dinosaurs only in museums.
    b. all dinosaurs were very tall.
    c. the author doesn't like dinosaurs.
    d. *people of all ages are interested in dinosaurs.*

2. Scientists found a rare blue lizard in Colombia, so you can infer that
    a. the scientists were looking for missing people.
    b. *some dinosaurs might have been blue.*
    c. no dinosaurs had ever lived in Colombia.
    d. the lizards built nests near the top of a volcano.

3. Since scientists are always discovering new things about dinosaurs, you can infer that
   a. *they still might not have found the smallest or biggest dinosaurs.*
   b. science is no longer interested in looking for fossils.
   c. prehistoric people left written records with descriptions of dinosaurs.
   d. when scientists make inferences, they are always right.

4. What can you infer from the fact that Stegosaurus has just one row of plates?
   a. Stegosaurus wasn't as old as scientists thought.
   b. *Old pictures and museum models of Stegosaurus had to be changed.*
   c. Someone stole the other row of plates from a museum.
   d. Stegosaurus means "roof lizard."

5. What can you infer about lizard eggs?
   a. *Cooler temperatures should produce more female lizards.*
   b. Hot weather should produce female lizards.
   c. Cold temperatures will produce more male lizards.
   d. Hot weather will produce more orange lizards.

6. What can you infer about scientists?
   a. They never watch TV.
   b. All scientists study about dinosaurs.
   c. *They don't always agree.*
   d. They never make mistakes.

## CLICK AND CLUNK[1]

*Note:* Click and clunk is one of the strategies used in the multicomponent strategy instruction collaborative strategic reading (CSR), described in Chapter 9. "Clunks" are words students do not understand.

### Grade Levels

Third grade and up

### Purpose

Students learn to use fix-up strategies to figure out the meaning of unknown words during reading.

### Materials

- Reading passage
- Cue cards with fix-up strategies

---

[1]Click and Clunk is adapted from Klingner et al. (2001). Copyright © 2001 Sopris West. Adapted by permission.

### Lesson Routine

1. Introduce clunks and fix-up strategies using short examples.
   - Clunks are words or concepts that students do not understand and that impair comprehension of a passage. Model how to use fix-up strategies using a sample sentence and the fix-up strategy cue cards.
   - "A snake's body is very *supple*. It can bend easily.  It can fit in small spaces."

   - Use the clunk cards to determine the meaning of the word *supple*. In this case, clunk card 2, "Reread the sentence before and after the clunk and look for clues," provides the fix-up strategy that helps students figure out the meaning of the clunk word, *supple*.
   - Have students work in pairs to use fix-up strategies to find the meaning of the clunks in the following examples, or create examples that are appropriate to your students' reading levels.
     a. In the summer the birds *molt*, or lose their feathers.

     b. You can find out how to make good food in a *cookbook*.
     c. The *falcon* is a hunting bird.

     d. The falcon has a *hooked beak* and strong *talons*.
     e. The moose has big *antlers*.

2. Apply the fix-up strategies to longer passages. Identify two or three "clunks" in the passage. Read the passage aloud to students (students should follow along with their own passage or on the overhead).
   - Model how to use the fix-up strategies to identify which strategy might help students figure out the meaning of the unknown word or idea. Repeat this process for another clunk.
   - Write down each clunk and a brief definition.
   - Have students work with a partner or small group to practice using the fix-up strategies to find the meaning clunks. One student can be a "clunk" expert and hold the clunk cards. After reading a section of the passage (usually a paragraph or two of a content-area or other expository text, depending on the length and difficulty of the reading passage), students stop to identify clunks.
   - The clunk expert reads the first clunk card, and the student who had the clunk attempts to use it to find the meaning. Students can assist each other with using fix-up strategies. If one student knows the definition of a word, using the fix-up strategies should confirm the definition.

Fix-Up Strategies

| #1<br>Reread the sentence without the clunk and ask what word would make sense in its place. | #2<br>Reread the sentence before and after the clunk and look for clues. |
| --- | --- |
| #3<br>Break the word apart and look for smaller words you know. | #4<br>Look for a prefix or suffix in the word that might help. |

3. Use other resources if the fix-up strategies don't work.

*Sometimes students use the fix-up strategies but still can't figure out the meaning of word. You should create a system for what to do next. Examples include the following:*

- If the fix-up strategies don't work, one student raises their hand and waits for the teacher.
- If the fix-up strategies don't work, put the word/concept on a "challenge chart." The teacher can then address the challenge words or concepts when the group comes back together.
- If the fix-up strategies don't work, continue with the reading assignment and use an accepted classroom resource (dictionary, computer) once you have finished.

4. Review clunks with the class.

- Check the clunks students identify. You may need to provide additional instruction for clunks with which many students seem to be struggling as well as those clunks that are very important for students to know well.

### Ideas for Providing Additional Support

If students are not able to use fix-up strategies to find the meaning of clunks, check the following:

- Be sure that students understand the fix-up strategies and how to use them. You may need to provide additional practice with short examples until students are comfortable with the strategies.

- Sometimes students do not identify clunks because they are not aware of what they *do not* understand. In this case, begin by identifying the clunks. For example, you might say, "While you are reading the next section, look for the clunks *viscosity* and *permeable*. Use the fix-up strategies to find the meaning of the clunks and write down a brief definition on your clunk list."

- Students benefit from working in pairs or small heterogeneous groups to read and use fix-up strategies. If students are having difficulty applying the fix-up strategies, pay attention to how they are grouped so that all group members are engaged and actively participating.

- If students have too many clunks, the fix-up strategies may not help. In this case more explicit preteaching of vocabulary may be necessary. Also, consider using lower-level reading material.

## AFTER-READING LESSON PLANS

### WHAT DO YOU KNOW?

*Grade Levels*

All

*Purpose*

To increase comprehension and memory of key ideas by asking questions about what you read.

*Materials*

- Reading passage at appropriate level
- Index cards
- Prepared "What Do You Know?" materials (dollar amount cards, category headings, timer, score-keeping materials)

*Lesson Routine*

*Note:* This lesson is used with students who are familiar with writing questions about what they read.

1. Students read a passage and then write questions with a partner in specific teacher-selected question categories that will be used during the "What Do You Know?" question game. Questions can be arranged by topic area (e.g., dates, travel information, about the explorers), by question type (e.g., Right There, Think and Search, Author and You) or by other categories related to the topic or skills you are addressing in class.

2. Students use index cards to write questions and their answers in the selected categories.

3. The teacher collects and organizes the questions and puts up the game board. The sample game below (which can be drawn on the board) has questions organized by QAR question type.

| Right There | Think and Search | Author and You |
|-------------|------------------|----------------|
| $10 | $20 | $30 |
| $10 | $20 | $30 |
| $10 | $20 | $30 |
| $10 | $20 | $30 |
| $10 | $20 | $30 |

4. To play the game, students form heterogeneous groups of four or five. A group selects a question type, and the teacher asks the question. The group is given a specified amount of time to confer and agree on the answer. The teacher may call on any of the group members to give the group's answer, so everyone is accountable. If a group does not have the correct answer, another group may attempt the answer. Points are awarded accordingly.

5. Additional hints:

   • Many teachers find it useful to have group work rules to manage students during this activity. For example, if students are noisy or are not working cooperatively, they may have to pay a $10 fine that is deducted from their group's score.

   • Teachers may also elect to add a few of their own questions to be sure that key ideas are reviewed.

   • If one or more of the questions are particularly important or difficult, teachers can label them as bonus questions. When a bonus question is pulled, all groups work on the answer (ensuring that everyone knows the information) and write down an answer. Any group who gets the correct answer receives points for that question.

   • Be creative! This activity is a fun way to (a) encourage students to ask questions as they read and (b) to review and remember information about what has been read.

### Ideas for Providing Additional Support

1. During question asking, students can be required to write questions in specific question types (e.g., three Think and Search questions), allowing students with strong question-asking skills to come up with more challenging questions. Likewise, you can vary the number of questions that students are required to ask, provide question stems, or limit the amount of text used to generate questions.

2. Allow students who struggle with comprehension to preview some of the questions and find the answers in the text prior to the whole-class game. Select 5–10 of the questions with important information for this practice activity.

3. Vary the way students find the answers according to individual needs. For example, students can use the text or be required to know the information and answer the questions from memory. Another variation is for all students in the group to find the answer and write it down prior to coming to a group consensus to give everyone the time to search for the answer before the fastest student blurts out a response.

## SUMMARIZING INFORMATION*

### Grade Levels

Third grade and up

### Purpose

Students use main ideas of short sections of text to generate a summary of a longer passage.

## Materials

- Use curriculum materials to identify texts with straightforward main ideas. You may want to use the same texts used in the previous "Identifying the Main Idea" lesson.
- Create a graphic organizer that includes a list of topics and main ideas from the text, and a blank column for the teacher to model how to combine sentences to summarize information across sections used in the previous main idea lessons.
- Student graphic organizers
  - One prefilled with the same information as the teacher's version for group practice and for putting together sentences
  - Others prefilled with topics, main ideas, and a few sentences combined from books students have not read yet; students will finish putting sentences together

| Topics | Main Ideas | Combine Sentences to Summarize |
|---|---|---|
| Dogs | Dogs live on farms to protect livestock. | Dogs live on farms to help, protect, and herd sheep. |
| Dogs | Dogs live on farms to help farmers herd sheep. | |
| Dogs | Dogs need to be fed by humans in order to survive. | |
| Dogs | Dogs need shelter like a doghouse or live in people's homes. | |

## Lesson Routine

1. Display pairs of sentences that have related topics. Tell students that the sentences each have a similar topic (remind students that this is *the who* or *the what*) but a unique main idea.

2. Say, "We are going to learn to put sentences together as a step in learning how to summarize, or simplify what we learned in a reading." Tell students that this type of summarizing helps them remember what they have learned from reading.

3. Demonstrate with the first couple of sentences how the identical topics are identified and circled. Then, combine the two sentences into one, modeling how the duplication topic word is removed, along with a period, and how the word "and" is used to merge them. The teacher works through several pairs of sentences, asking for student assistance.

4. Draw on curriculum materials for ways to find and mark topics, cross out duplicated information or editing marks, and to merge sentences.

## Guided Practice

1. In Day One of guided group practice, display the graphic-organizer topic and main idea sentences. Students practice the topic-merge process to create one sentence that they write on their own student graphic organizers. Observe, correct, and instruct where needed.

2. In Day Two of guided group practice, teach main idea merging of topics at the sentence level. Since merging main ideas into a few sentences, and using pronouns to replace the topic in a following sentence, is not simple to convey, be prepared to provide plenty of practice, with enough materials for different days.

3. Independent or partner practice follows when students are ready to work individually with much less teacher help.

4. As an extension to this activity, students can write down on notepaper the summary of combined sentences. As with the other activities, model how to write the summary and provide group and independent practice.

## KEY WORD REVIEW

### Grade Levels

All

### Purpose

Review key words to summarize and remember important ideas from text.

### Materials

- Nonfiction text from curriculum materials

### Lesson Routine

1. Say to the students, "One way to review what you've read is to identify the most important words from the text. These 'key words' will help you organize a summary of what you've read. For example, the first key word I chose is *revolution*. The Americans were frustrated with England's rules and treatment. This led them to fight for their freedom. Another important word is *independence*. They were tired of having to follow rules that they did not influence. They wanted to be independent from England."

2. Tell students to read (or review) the next paragraph and choose one to three words that they think are key words and will help them summarize what they read.

3. Continue to record the remaining words that students select.

4. Model how to write a summary using the key words that students identified.

# Glossary

**Alphabetic principle**   The concept that letters represent speech sounds.

**Ambiguities**   Words, phrases, or sentences that are open to more than one interpretation (e.g., *Robber gets 6 months in violin case*).

**Classwide peer tutoring**   Students of different reading abilities are paired together (usually one average or high with one low) to complete a reading task.

**Cloze procedure**   Words or other structures are deleted from a passage by the teacher, with blanks left in their places for students to fill in; also used as an assessment of reading ability by omitting every *n*th word in a reading passage and observing the number of correct insertions provided by the reader.

**Cognitive organizers**   Assist students in remembering and following learning strategy procedures; often employ mnemonic devices that cue students to the steps of a strategy.

**Collaborative strategic reading (CSR)**   A multicomponent strategy approach that teaches students to use comprehension strategies while working collaboratively with their peers in small groups.

**Common Core State Standards (CCSS)** A set of academic standards that outlines what students should know and be able to do in English language arts and math.

**Comprehension**   A person's ability to understand what is being read or discussed.

**Computer-assisted instruction (CAI)** Involves learning through the use of computers and/or other multimedia systems.

**Content literacy** Using general reading and writing skills to access new information in a content-area reading (e.g., summarizing). Content literacy skills are not specific to a particular subject area.

**Context clues**   Clues to word meanings or concepts that are found in preceding or following words or sentences.

**Cooperative learning**   Students of mixed abilities work together in small groups toward a common academic goal.

**Criterion-referenced test**   Test designed to measure how well a person has learned information or skills; often uses a cutoff score to determine mastery.

**Curriculum-based assessment (CBA)** Assessment used to measure students' progress toward instructional goals and objectives; items are taken from the curriculum, evaluations are repeated frequently over time, and results are used to develop instructional plans.

**Curriculum-based measurement (CBM)**   A form of CBA that includes a set of standard, simple, short-duration fluency measures of basic skills in reading as well as in other subject areas.

**Decoding**   Strategy for recognizing words.

**Direct instruction**   Systematic teacher-directed lessons in specific instructional strategies that usually include a statement of the objective, modeling, scaffolded practice, and error correction.

**Disciplinary literacy**   Different from content literacy, reading and writing skills are used to access content-area reading materials and tasks that are specific to a particular subject (e.g., organizing science data to reach consensus about results).

**Elaborative processes**   Going beyond the literal meaning of a text to make inferences and connections.

**Expository text**   Informational or factual text.

**Expressions**   Include idioms (*hang on*), proverbs (*Don't count your chickens before they've hatched*), slang (*decked out*), catchphrases (*24/7*), and slogans.

**Figures of speech**   Words that are not used literally but suggest another meaning (e.g., similes, hyperbole).

**Fluency**   The ability to read accurately and quickly.

**Graphic organizer**   A visual representation of textual information and ideas.

**Hierarchical summary procedure**   Technique used to direct students' attention to the organizational structure of passages by previewing, reading, outlining, studying, and retelling.

**Inferring**   Making sense of what is read by using existing information from texts and background knowledge.

**Informal reading inventory (IRI)**   IRIs are individually administered tests that yield information about a student's reading level as well as word analysis and comprehension skills; a student reads lists of words and passages that are leveled by grade and retells or answers comprehension questions about what they read.

**Integrative processes**   Ability to make connections among sentences by understanding and inferring the relationships among clauses.

**Interactive instructional model**   Relies on semantic feature analysis using relationship maps and charts and also incorporates interactive strategic dialogues.

**Keyword strategies**   A memory strategy that assists students in memorizing words or concepts by associating a key word to the concept or word to be remembered.

**Learning disability (LD)**   A neurological disorder that may result in difficulty with reading, writing, spelling, reasoning, recalling, or organizing information; individuals with LD have average or above-average intelligence.

**Macroprocessing**   Summarizing and organizing key information and relating smaller units of what has been read to the text as a whole.

**Main idea**   The central message or gist of a small portion of text.

**Metacognitive processes**   Thinking about thinking; the reader's conscious awareness or control of cognitive processes such as monitoring understanding while reading.

**Microprocessing**   Ability to comprehend at the sentence level; chunking idea units to know what is important to remember.

**Mnemonic**   A memory strategy that assists students in memorizing words or concepts (e.g., by associating them with a key word, image, or rhyme); also called the key word method.

**Morphology**   The system of word formation patterns that includes roots, prefixes, suffixes, and inflected endings.

**Multicomponent strategy instruction** Improves comprehension by teaching a set of strategies to use before, during, and after reading.

**Multistrategy inference intervention** An inference-focused set of comprehension strategies designed for middle-grade struggling readers.

**Narrative text** Text that tells a story; generally fiction.

**Onomastics** The study of names.

**Paraphrasing** Restating what has been heard or read in your own words; usually more detailed than a summary.

**Phonics** The association of speech sounds with printed letters; phonics instruction involves using letter–sound correspondences to read and spell words.

**Phonological awareness** Ability to discriminate between and manipulate speech sounds (e.g., rhyming).

**Phonology** Discriminating between and producing speech sounds.

**Pragmatics** Using language to communicate effectively by following generally accepted principles of communication.

**Progress monitoring** Systematic assessment of students' academic performance that is used to determine what students have learned and to evaluate the effectiveness of instruction.

**Question–answer relationships (QAR) strategy** A strategy for teaching students how to answer different types of comprehension questions.

**Questioning the author** A strategy to increase comprehension and critical thinking that encourages students to ask questions focusing on the author's intent and choices.

**Reader response theory** A literary theory based on the premise that understanding what one reads is related to an individual's experiences and interpretations of these experiences.

**Reciprocal teaching** An instructional approach that uses prediction, summarization, question generation, and clarification to guide group discussions of what has been read.

**Retelling** Measure of comprehension that asks students to recall and restate the events in a story after they have read it or heard it.

**Scaffolding** Instructional technique in which the teacher first models a learning strategy or task, provides learners with appropriate levels of support, and then gradually shifts responsibility to the students until they can perform the task independently.

**Schema theory** The theory that existing representations of information influence how new ideas are learned and remembered.

**Semantic organizer** A visual representation of information used to facilitate understanding.

**Semantics** Meanings of words, phrases, or sentences.

**Standardized norm-referenced test** Assessment that measures proficiency by comparing an individual's score with age-level and grade-level peers.

**Story grammar** The pattern of elements the reader can expect to find in a narrative text, such as the characters, setting, and plot.

**Story maps** Instructional strategy to increase comprehension by creating a graphic representation of a story that includes story elements and shows how they are connected.

**Story structure** The organizational arrangement of written information; when text follows predictable structures it is easier to understand and remember.

**Storybook reading** Technique that uses read-alouds specifically to build vocabulary.

**Summarizing** Generating multiple main ideas from across the reading and then combining them with important supporting information to form a summary.

**Syntax**   A set of rules that includes correct phrasing and sentence organization.

**TELLS**   Comprehension strategy that guides students to (*T*) study story titles, (*E*) examine and skim pages for clues, (*L*) look for important words, (*L*) look for difficult words, and (*S*) think about the story settings.

**Text preview**   Strategies that are used to activate prior knowledge, make predictions, and engage students before reading.

**Text structure**   The way a text is organized to guide readers in identifying key information.

**Theme**   Subject matter, major concept, or topic of a text.

**Theme scheme**   Technique that provides instruction in different text structure strategies.

**Think-aloud**   Verbalizing aloud what one is thinking while reading or performing a task.

**Transactional strategies instruction**   A comprehensive, high-intensity, long-term approach in which the teacher provides support and guidance to students as they apply comprehension strategies; a goal of instruction is the self-regulated use of strategies.

**Vocabulary knowledge**   Knowing what words mean in the context in which they are used.

**Word analysis**   Using letter–sound relationships or other structural patterns (e.g., prefixes) to decode unknown words.

**Word associations**   Ways to connect words to each other, such as synonyms (*ugly, unattractive*), antonyms (*huge, tiny*), homographs (*desert, desert*), and homophones (*plane, plain*).

**Word consciousness**   Learning about, playing with, and being interested in words and their many and varied uses.

**Word formations**   Forms that include acronyms (USDA), compounds (*backyard*), and affixes (*neo-, -ing*).

# References

Alfassi, M. (1998). Reading for meaning: The efficacy of reciprocal teaching in fostering reading comprehension in high school students in remedial classes. *American Educational Research Journal, 35*, 309–332.

Allen, J. (1999). *Word, words, words: Teaching vocabulary in grades 4–12*. Portland, ME: Stenhouse.

Altemeier, L. E., Abbott, R. D., & Berninger, V. W. (2008). Executive functions for reading and writing in typical literacy development and dyslexia. *Journal of Clinical and Experimental Neuropsychology, 30*(5), 588–606.

Amer, A. A. (1992). The effect of story grammar instruction on EFL students' comprehension of narrative text. *Reading in a Foreign Language, 8*(2), 711–720.

Anderson, R. C., & Nagy, W. E. (1992). The vocabulary conundrum. *American Educator, 16*, 14–18, 44–47.

Anderson, R. C., & Pearson, P. D. (1984). A schema-theoretic view of basic processes in reading comprehension. In P. D. Pearson, R. Barr, M. L. Kamil, & P. Mosenthal (Eds.), *Handbook of reading research* (Vol. 1, pp. 255–292). White Plains, NY: Longman.

Anderson, V. (1992). A teacher development project in transactional strategy instruction for teachers of severely reading-disabled adolescents. *Teaching and Teacher Education, 8*, 391–403.

Applegate, M. D., Quinn, K. B., & Applegate, A. J. (2002). Levels of thinking required by comprehension questions in Informal Reading Inventories. *The Reading Teacher, 56*(2), 174–180.

Applegate, M. D., Quinn, K. B., & Applegate, A. J. (2008). *The Critical Reading Inventory: Assessing students' reading and thinking and readers' passages* (2nd ed.). Upper Saddle River, NJ: Pearson.vv

Ardoin, S. P., & Christ, T. J. (2008). Evaluating curriculum based measurement slope estimates using data from triannual universal screenings. *School Psychology Review, 37*(1), 109–125.

Artiles, A. J., Rueda, R., Salazar, J. J., & Higareda, I. (2005). Within-group diversity in minority disproportionate representation: English language learners in urban school districts. *Exceptional Children, 71*(3), 283–300.

Aud, S., Hussar, W., Kena, G., Bianco, K., Frohlich, L., Kemp, J., et al. (2011). *The condition of education 2011* (NCES 2011-033). Washington, DC: U.S. Government Printing Office.

August, D., Branum-Martin, L., Cardenas-Hagan, E., & Francis, D. J. (2009). The impact of an instructional intervention on the science and language learning of middle grade English language learners. *Journal of Research on Educational Effectiveness, 2*(4), 345–376.

August, D., & Shanahan, T. (Eds.). (2006). *Developing literacy in second-language learners: A report of the National Literacy Panel on Language-Minority Children and Youth.* Mahwah, NJ: Erlbaum.

Bader, A. L., & Pearce, D. L. (2012). *Bader reading and language inventory—Seventh edition.* Upper Saddle River, NJ: Pearson.

Baker, L. (2002). Metacognition in strategy instruction. In C. C. Block & M. Pressley (Eds.), *Comprehension instruction: Research-based best practices* (pp. 77–95). New York: Guilford Press.

Baker, S. (2006, March). *English language learners and reading first: Some preliminary evidence of effectiveness.* Paper presented at the CORE Literacy Leadership summit, San Francisco, CA.

Baker, S., Gersten, R., & Graham, S. (2003). Teaching expressive writing to students with learning disabilities: Research-based applications and examples. *Journal of Learning Disabilities, 36*(2), 109–123.

Baker, S., Gersten, R., & Lee, D. (2002). A synthesis of empirical research on teaching mathematics to low-achieving students. *Elementary School Journal, 103,* 51–73.

Baker, S., Lesaux, N., Jayanthi, M., Dimino, J., Proctor, C. P., Morris, J., et al. (2014). *Teaching academic content and literacy to English learners in elementary and middle school. IES Practice Guide.* NCEE 2014-4012. Washington, DC: What Works Clearinghouse.

Ball, E. W., & Blachman, B. A. (1991). Does phoneme awareness training in kindergarten make a difference in early word recognition and developmental spelling? *Reading Research Quarterly, 26,* 49–66.

Bangert-Drowns, R. L., Kulik, J. A., & Kulik, C. C. (1991). Effects of frequent classroom testing. *Journal of Educational Research, 85*(2), 89–99.

Barker, H. B., & Grassi, E. (2011). Culturally responsive practices for the special education eligibility process. *AccELLerate!: The Quarterly Review of the National Clearinghouse for English Language Acquisition 3*(1), 2–4.

Barnett, W. S., Jung, K., Yarosz, D. J., Thomas, J., Hornbeck, A., Stechuk, R., et al. (2008). Educational effects of the Tools of the Mind curriculum: A randomized trial. *Early Childhood Research Quarterly, 23,* 299–313.

Barth, A. E., & Elleman, A. (2017). Evaluating the impact of a multistrategy inference intervention for middle-grade struggling readers. *Language, Speech, and Hearing Services in Schools, 48*(1), 31–41.

Baumann, J. F. (1984). The effectiveness of a direct instruction paradigm for teaching main idea comprehension. *Reading Research Quarterly, 20,* 93–115.

Baumann, J. F., Edwards, E. C., Boland, E. M., Olejnik, S., & Kame'enui, E. J. (2003). Vocabulary tricks: Effects of instruction in morphology and context on fifth-grade students' ability to derive and infer word meanings. *American Educational Research Journal, 40*(2), 447–494.

Beach, R. (1993). *A teachers' introduction to reader response theories.* Urbana, IL: National Council of Teachers of English.

Beaver, J. (2005). *Developmental reading assessment (DRA)—Second edition.* Lebanon, IN: Pearson Learning.

Beck, I. L. (2013). *Making sense of phonics: The hows and whys* (2nd ed.). New York: Guilford Press.

Beck, I. L., & McKeown, M. G. (1983). A program to enhance vocabulary and comprehension. *The Reading Teacher, 36,* 622–625.

Beck, I. L., & McKeown, M. G. (1998). Comprehension: The sine qua non of reading. In S. Patton & M. Holmes (Eds.), *The keys to literacy* (pp. 40–52). Washington, DC: Council for Basic Education.

Beck, I. L., McKeown, M. G., & Kucan, L. (2013). *Bringing words to life: Robust vocabulary instruction* (2nd ed.). New York: Guilford Press.

Beck, I. L., McKeown, M. G., & Omanson, R. C. (1987). The effects and uses of diverse vocabulary instructional techniques. In M. G. McKeown & M. E. Curtis (Eds.), *The nature of vocabulary acquisition* (pp. 147–163). Hillsdale, NJ: Erlbaum.

Beck, I. L., McKeown, M. G., Sandora, C., Kucan, L., & Worthy, J. (1996). Questioning the author: A yearlong classroom implementation to engage students with text. *Elementary School Journal, 96*(4), 385–414.

Beck, I. L., McKeown, M. G., & Sandora, C. A. (2020). *Robust comprehension instruction with Questioning the Author: 15 years smarter.* New York: Guilford Press.

Bell, R. Q. (1968). A reinterpretation of the direction of effects in studies of socialization. *Psychological Review, 75,* 81–95.

Bergman, J. L. (1992). SAIL: A way to success and independence for low-achieving readers. *The Reading Teacher, 45,* 598–602.

Bergman, J. L., & Schuder, T. (1992/1993). Teaching at-risk students to read strategically, *Educational Leadership, 50,* 19–23.

Berkeley, S., & Larsen, A. (2018). Fostering self-regulation of students with learning disabilities: Insights from 30 years of reading comprehension intervention research. *Learning Disabilities Research & Practice, 33,* 75–86.

Berkeley, S., Marshak, L., Mastropieri, M. A., & Scruggs, T. E. (2011). Improving student comprehension of social studies text: A self-questioning strategy for inclusive middle school classes. *Remedial and Special Education, 32,* 105–113.

Berkeley, S., Mastropieri, M. A., & Scruggs, T. E. (2011). Reading comprehension strategy instruction and attribution retraining for secondary students with learning and other mild disabilities. *Journal of Learning Disabilities, 44*(1), 18–32.

Berkeley, S., Scruggs, T. E., & Mastropieri, M. A. (2010). Reading comprehension instruction for students with learning disabilities, 1995–2006: A meta-analysis. *Remedial and Special Education, 36,* 423–436.

Berry, G., Hall, D., & Gildroy, P. G. (2004). Teaching learning strategies. In K. Lenz, D. Deshler, & B. R. Kissam (Eds.), *Teaching content to all: Evidence-based inclusive practices in middle and secondary schools* (pp. 258–278). Boston: Pearson Education.

Bhattacharjee, Y. (2012, March 18). Why bilinguals are smarter. *The New York Times.* Retrieved from *www.nytimes.com/2012/03/18/opinion/sunday/the-benefits-of-bilingualism.html?_r=0.*

Biancarosa, G., & Snow, C. E. (2004). *Reading next: A vision for action and research in middle and high school literacy.* Washington, DC: Alliance for Excellence in Education.

Blachowicz, C., & Ogle, D. (2001). *Reading comprehension: Strategies for independent learners.* New York: Guilford Press.

Blachowicz, C. L. Z., & Fisher, P. (2004). Keep the "fun" in fundamental: Encouraging word awareness and incidental word learning in the classroom through word play. In J. F. Baumann & E. J. Kame'enui (Eds.), *Vocabulary instruction: Research to practice* (pp. 218–238). New York: Guilford Press.

Blair, C. (2002). School readiness: Integrating cognition and emotion in a neurobiological conceptualization of children's functioning at school entry. *American Psychologist, 57,* 111–127.

Blair, C., & Razza, R. P. (2007). Relating effortful control, executive function, and false belief understanding to emerging math and literacy ability in kindergarten. *Child Development, 78,* 647–663.

Blanton, W. E., Wood, K. D., & Moorman, G. B. (1990). The role of purpose in reading instruction. *The Reading Teacher, 43,* 486–493.

Boardman, A. G., Boelé, A. L., & Klingner, J. K. (2018). Strategy instruction shifts teacher and student interactions during text-based discussions. *Reading Research Quarterly, 53*(2), 175–195.

Boardman, A. G., Vaughn, S., Buckley, P., Reutebuch, C., Roberts, G., & Klingner, J. (2016). Collaborative strategic reading for students with learning disabilities in upper elementary classrooms. *Exceptional Children, 82*(4), 409–427.

Boekaerts, M., & Cascallar, E. (2006). How far have we moved toward the integration of theory and practice in self-regulation? *Educational Psychology Review, 18*(3), 199–210.

Bogaerds-Hazenberg, S. T., Evers-Vermeul, J., & van den Bergh, H. (2021). A meta-analysis on the effects of text structure instruction on reading comprehension in the upper elementary grades. *Reading Research Quarterly, 56*(3), 435–462.

Bohaty, J. J. (2015). *The effects of expository text structure instruction on the reading outcomes of 4th and 5th graders experiencing reading difficulties.* PhD dissertation, University of Nebraska–Lincoln.

Boon, R. T., Paal, M., Hintz, A. M., & Cornelius-Freyre, M. (2015). A review of story mapping instruction for secondary students with LD. *Learning Disabilities: A Contemporary Journal, 13*(2), 117–140.

Booth, J. N., Boyle, J. M., & Kelly, S. W. (2010). Do tasks make a difference? Accounting for heterogeneity of performance of children with reading difficulties on tasks of executive function: Findings from a meta-analysis. *British Journal of Developmental Psychology, 28*(1), 133–176.

Borkowski, J. G., Weyhing, R. S., & Carr, M. (1988). Effects of attributional retraining on strategy-based reading comprehension in learning-disabled students. *Journal of Educational Psychology, 80*(1), 46–53.

Bos, C. S. (1987). *Promoting story comprehension using a story retelling strategy.* Paper presented at the Teachers Applying Whole Language Conference, Tucson, AZ.

Bos, C. S., & Vaughn, S. (2002). *Strategies for teaching students with learning and behavior problems* (5th ed.). Boston: Allyn & Bacon.

Bosnjak, A., Boyle, C., & Chodkiewicz, A. R. (2017). An intervention to retrain attributions using CBT: A pilot study. *The Educational and Developmental Psychologist, 34*(1), 19–30.

Boyle, J. R. (2010). Strategic note-taking for middle-school students with learning disabilities in science classes. *Learning Disability Quarterly, 33*(2), 93–109.

Brand-Gruwal, S., Aarnoutse, C. A. J., & Van Den Bos, K. P. (1997). Improving text comprehension strategies in reading and listening settings. *Learning and Instruction, 8*(1), 63–81.

Bransford, J., Brown, A. L., & Cocking, R. R. (1999). *How people learn: Brain, mind, experience, and school.* Washington, DC: Committee on Developments in the Science of Learning, National Research Council.

Bridges, M. S., & Catts, H. W. (2011). The use of a dynamic screening of phonological awareness to predict risk for reading disabilities in kindergarten children. *Journal of Learning Disabilities, 44*(4), 330–338.

Brown, A. L., & Campione, J. C. (1996). Theory and design of learning environments. In L. Schauble & R. Glaser (Eds.), *Innovations in learning: New environments for education* (pp. 289–325). Mahwah, NJ: Erlbaum.

Brown, A. L., & Day, J. D. (1983). Macrorules for summarizing texts: The development of

expertise. *Journal of Verbal Learning and Verbal Behavior, 22*(1), 1–14.

Brown, R., & Dewitz, P. (2013). *Building comprehension in every classroom: Instruction with literature, informational texts, and basal programs.* New York: Guilford Press.

Brown, A. L., & Palincsar, A. S. (1989). Guided, cooperative learning and individual knowledge acquisition. In L. B. Resnick (Ed.), *Knowing, learning, and instruction: Essays in honor of Robert Glaser* (pp. 393–451). Hillsdale, NJ: Erlbaum.

Brown, L. V., Wiederholt, J. L., & Hammill, D. D. (2008). *The Test of Reading Comprehension—Fourth Edition* (TORC-4). Circle Pines, MN: AGS.

Brown, R. (2008). Transactional approach to reading instruction. *The Reading Teacher, 71*(7), 538–547.

Bryant, D. P., Goodwin, M., Bryant, B. R., & Higgins, K. (2003). Vocabulary instruction for students with learning disabilities: A review of the research. *Learning Disability Quarterly, 26*, 117–128.

Bryant, D. P., Vaughn, S., Linan-Thompson, S., Ugel, N., & Hamff, A. (2000). Reading outcomes for students with and without learning disabilities in general education middle school content area classes. *Learning Disability Quarterly, 23*(3), 24–38.

Burns, M., Hodgson, J., Parker, D. C., & Fremont, K. (2011). Comparison of the effectiveness and efficiency of text previewing and preteaching keywords as small-group reading comprehension strategies with middle-school students. *Literacy Research and Instruction, 50*, 241–252.

Cain, K., & Oakhill, J. (2006). Profiles of children with specific reading comprehension difficulties. *British Journal of Educational Psychology, 76*(4), 683–696.

Cao, Y., & Kim, Y. S. G. (2021). Is retell a valid measure of reading comprehension? *Educational Research Review, 32*, 100375.

Carlo, M. S., August, D., McLaughlin, B., Snow, C. E., Dressler, C., Lippman, D. N., et al. (2004). Closing the gap: Addressing the vocabulary needs of English language learners in bilingual and mainstream classrooms. *Reading Research Quarterly, 39*(2), 188–215.

Carr, M., & Borkowski, J. G. (1989). Attributional training and the generalization of reading strategies with underachieving children. *Learning and Individual Differences, 1*, 327–341.

Cartwright, K. B., Coppage, E. A., Lane, A. B., Singleton, T., Marshall, T. R., & Bentivegna, C. (2017). Cognitive flexibility deficits in children with specific reading comprehension difficulties. *Contemporary Educational Psychology, 50*, 33–44.

Cartwright, K. B., Marshall, T. R., Huemer, C. M., & Payne, J. B. (2019). Executive function in the classroom: Cognitive flexibility supports reading fluency for typical readers and teacher-identified low-achieving readers. *Research in Developmental Disabilities, 88*, 42–52.

Castro, D. C., & Artiles, A. J. (Eds.). (2021). *Language, learning, and disability in the education of young bilingual children*. Bristol, UK: Multilingual Matters.

Catts, H. W., Adlof, S. M., & Weismer, S. E. (2006). Language deficits in poor comprehenders: A case for the simple view of reading. *Journal of Speech, Language, and Hearing Research, 49*(2), 278–293.

Cerdán, R., Gilabert, R., & Vidal-Abarca, E. (2011). Selecting information to answer questions. Strategic individual differences when searching texts. *Learning and Individual Differences, 21*, 201–205.

Cervetti, G. N., & Pearson, P. D. (2018). Reading and understanding science texts. In A. L. Bailey, C. A. Maher, & L. C. Wilkinson (Eds.), *Language, literacy, and learning in the STEM disciplines* (pp. 79–100). New York: Routledge.

Chan, L. S. (1996). Combined strategy and attributional training for seventh grade average and poor readers. *Journal of Research in Reading, 19*(2), 111–127.

Chard, D. J., Vaughn, S., & Tyler, B. J. (2002). A synthesis on effective interventions for building reading fluency with elementary students with learning disabilities. *Journal of Learning Disabilities, 35*, 386–406.

Cho, E., Capin, P., Roberts, G., Roberts, G. J., & Vaughn, S. (2019). Examining sources and mechanisms of reading comprehension difficulties: Comparing English learners and non-English learners within the simple view of reading. *Journal of Educational Psychology, 111*(6), 982.

Cirino, P. T., Romain, M. A., Barth, A. E.,

Tolar, T. D., Fletcher, J. M., & Vaughn, S. (2013). Reading skill components and impairments in middle school struggling readers. *Reading and Writing, 26*(7), 1059–1086.

Collins, M. F. (2010). ELL preschoolers' English vocabulary acquisition from storybook reading. *Early Childhood Research Quarterly, 25*(1), 84–97.

Collins, A. A., & Lindström, E. R. (2021). Making sense of reading comprehension assessments: Guidance for evaluating student performance. *Intervention in School and Clinic, 57*(1), 23–31.

Compton, D. L., Fuchs, L. S., Fuchs, D., Lambert, W., & Hamlett, C. (2012). The cognitive and academic profiles of reading and mathematics learning disabilities. *Journal of Learning Disabilities, 45*(1), 79–95.

Conley, M. W. (2008). Cognitive strategy instruction for adolescents. *Harvard Educational Review, 78*, 84–106.

Cooc, N. (2023). National trends in special education and academic outcomes for English learners with disabilities. *The Journal of Special Education, 57*(2).

Cooter, R. B., Jr., Flynt, E. S., & Cooter, K. S. (2013). *Flynt–Cooter Comprehensive Reading Inventory–2*. Columbus, OH: Merrill Education.

Cornoldi, C., & Oakhill, J. V. (Eds.). (2013). *Reading comprehension difficulties: Processes and intervention*. New York: Routledge.

Cox, R., O'Brien, K., Walsh, M., & West, H. (2015). Working with multilingual learners and vocabulary knowledge for secondary schools: Developing word consciousness. *English in Australia (0155-2147), 50*(1), 77–84.

Coxhead, A. (2000). A new academic word list. *TESOL Quarterly, 34*(2), 213–238. Retrieved from *www.victoria.ac.nz/lals/resources/academicwordlist/most-frequent*.

Crabtree, T., Alber-Morgan, S. R., & Moira, K. (2010). The effects of self-monitoring of story elements on the reading comprehension of high school seniors with learning disabilities. *Education and Treatment of Children, 33*, 187–203.

Cromley, J. G., & Azevedo, R. (2007). Testing and refining the direct and inferential mediation model of reading comprehension.

*Journal of Educational Psychology, 99,* 311–325.

Crosson, A. C., & Lesaux, N. K. (2010). Revisiting assumptions about the relationship of fluent reading to comprehension: Spanish-speakers' text-reading fluency in English. *Reading and Writing: An Interdisciplinary Journal, 23,* 475–494.

Cutting, L. E., Materek, A., Cole, C. A. S., Levine, T. M., & Mahone, E. M. (2009). Effects of fluency, oral language, and executive function on reading comprehension performance. *Annals of Dyslexia, 59*(1), 34–54.

Dale, E. (1965). Vocabulary measurement: Techniques and major findings. *Elementary English, 42,* 82–88.

Dalton, B., Proctor, C. P., Uccelli, P., Mo, E., & Snow, C. (2011). Designing for diversity: The role of reading strategies and interactive vocabulary in a digital reading environment for fifth-grade monolingual English and bilingual students. *Journal of Literacy Research, 43,* 68–99.

De La Paz, S. (2005). Reasoning instruction and writing strategy mastery in culturally and academically diverse middle school classrooms. *Journal of Experimental Psychology, 89,* 203–222.

De La Paz, S., & Felton, M. K. (2010). Reading and writing from multiple source documents in history: Effects of strategy instruction with low to average high school writers. *Journal of Contemporary Educational Psychology, 35,* 174–192.

De La Paz, S., Morales, P., & Winston, P. M. (2007). Source interpretation: Teaching students with and without LD to read and write historically. *Journal of Learning Disabilities, 40,* 134–144.

Dembo, M. H., & Eaton, M. J. (2000). Self-regulation of academic learning in middle-level schools. *Elementary School Journal, 100*(5), 473–490.

Deno, S. L. (1985). Curriculum-based measurement: The emerging alternative. *Exceptional Children, 52,* 219–232.

Deno, S. L. (1992). The nature and development of curriculum-based measurement. *Preventing School Failure, 36,* 5–10.

Denton, C. A. (2012). Response to intervention for reading difficulties in the primary grades: Some answers and lingering questions. *Journal of Learning Disabilities, 45,* 232–243.

Denton, C. A., Enos, M., York, M. J., Francis, D. J., Barnes, M. A., Kulesz, P. A., et al. (2015). Text-processing differences in adolescent adequate and poor comprehenders reading accessible and challenging narrative and informational text. *Reading Research Quarterly, 50*(4), 393–416.

Denton, C. A., Fletcher, J. M., Anthony, J. L., & Francis, D. J. (2006). An evaluation of intensive intervention for students with persistent reading difficulties. *Journal of Learning Disabilities, 39,* 447–466.

Denton, C. A., Hall, C., Cho, E., Cannon, G., Scammacca, N., & Wanzek, J. (2022). A meta-analysis of the effects of foundational skills and multicomponent reading interventions on reading comprehension for primary-grade students. *Learning and Individual Differences, 93,* 102062.

Dewitz, P., & Dewitz, P. K. (2003). They can read the words, but they can't understand: Refining comprehension assessment. *The Reading Teacher, 56*(5), 422–435.

Diamond, A., Barnett, W. S., Thomas, J., & Munro, S. (2007). Preschool program improves cognitive control. *Science, 318,* 1387–1388.

Dixon, L. Q., Zhao, J., Shin, J. Y., Wu, S., Su, J. H., Burgess-Brigham, R., et al. (2012). What we know about second language acquisition: A synthesis from four perspectives. *Review of Educational Research, 82,* 5–60.

Dole, J. A. (1991). Moving from old to new: Research on reading comprehension instruction. *Review of Educational Research, 61,* 239–264.

Donegan, R. E., & Wanzek, J. (2021). Effects of reading interventions implemented for upper elementary struggling readers: A look at recent research. *Reading and Writing, 34*(8), 1943–1977.

Duke, N. K., & Cartwright, K. B. (2021). The science of reading progresses: Communicating advances beyond the simple view of reading. *Reading Research Quarterly, 56,* S25–S44.

Duke, N. K., & Pearson, D. (2002). Effective practices for developing reading comprehension. In A. E. Farstrup & S. J. Samuels (Eds.), *What research has to say about read-*

*ing instruction* (3rd ed., pp. 205–242). Newark, DE: International Reading Association.

Duke, N. K., Ward, A. E., & Pearson, P. D. (2021). The science of reading comprehension instruction. *The Reading Teacher, 74*(6), 663–672.

Durkin, D. (1978–1979). What classroom observations reveal about reading comprehension instruction. *Reading Research Quarterly, 14*, 481–533.

Dzombak, R. (2022, September 22). How Many Ants Are There on Earth? You're Going to Need More Zeros. *The New York Times*. Retrieved from *www.nytimes.com/2022/09/22/science/ants-census-20-quadrillion.html*

Editorial Projects in Education. (2021, February 3). Map: Tracking the common core state standards. *Education Week*. Retrieved June 28, 2022, from *www.edweek.org/teaching-learning/map-tracking-the-common-core-state-standards.*

Edmonds, M. S., Vaughn, S., Wexler, J., Reutebuch, C. K., Cable, A., Tackett, K. K., et al. (2009). Synthesis of reading interventions and effects on reading comprehension outcomes for older struggling readers. *Review of Educational Research, 79*, 262–300.

Einstein, A. (1961). *Relativity: The special and the general theory* (R. W. Lawson, Trans.). New York: Bonanza Books.

Elbaum, B., Vaughn, S., Hughes, M. T., & Moody, S. W. (1999). Grouping practices and reading outcomes for students with disabilities. *Exceptional Children, 65*, 399–415.

Elbro, C., & Buch-Iversen, I. (2013). Activation of background knowledge for inference making: Effects on reading comprehension. *Scientific Studies of Reading, 17*(6), 435–452.

Elleman, A. M., Compton, D. L., Fuchs, D., Fuchs, L. S., & Bouton, B. (2011). Exploring dynamic assessment as a means of identifying children at risk of developing comprehension difficulties. *Journal of Learning Disabilities, 44*(4), 348–357.

Ellery, V., & Rosenboom, J. L. (2011). *Sustaining strategic readers: Techniques for supporting content literacy in grades 6–12.* Newark, DE: International Reading Association.

Ellis, E. S., & Farmer, T. (2005). The clarify-ing routine: Elaborating vocabulary instruction. Retrieved from *www.ldonline.org.*

Englert, C. S. (1990). Unraveling the mysteries of writing through strategy instruction. In T. Scruggs & B. Wong (Eds.), *Intervention research in learning disabilities* (pp. 186–223). New York: Springer-Verlag.

Englert, C. S. (1992). Writing instruction from a sociocultural perspective: The holistic, dialogic, and social enterprise of writing. *Journal of Learning Disabilities, 25*, 153–172.

Ericsson, K. A. (2008). Deliberate practice and acquisition of expert performance: A general overview. *Academic Emergency Medicine, 15*(11), 988–994.

Espin, C. A., Shin, J., & Busch, T. W. (2005). Curriculum-based measurement in the content areas: Vocabulary matching as an indicator of progress in social studies learning. *Journal of Learning Disabilities, 38*(4), 353–363.

Faggella-Luby, M., Graner, P. S., Deshler, D. D., & Drew, S. V. (2012). Building a house on sand: Why disciplinary literacy is not sufficient to replace general strategies for adolescent learners who struggle. *Topics in Language Disorders, 32*, 69–84.

Fang, Z. (2006). The language demands of science reading in middle school. *International Journal of Science Education, 28*, 491–520.

Filderman, M. J., Austin, C. R., Boucher, A. N., O'Donnell, K., & Swanson, E. A. (2022). A meta-analysis of the effects of reading comprehension interventions on the reading comprehension outcomes of struggling readers in third through 12th grades. *Exceptional Children, 88*(2), 163–184.

Fitton, L., McIlraith, A. L., & Wood, C. L. (2018). Shared book reading interventions with English learners: A meta-analysis. *Review of Educational Research, 88*(5), 712–751.

Fitzgerald, J. (1995). English-as-a-second-language learners' cognitive reading processes: A review of research in the United States. *Review of Educational Research, 65*, 145–190.

Flavell, J. H. (1979). Metacognition and cognitive monitoring: A new area of cognitive–developmental inquiry. *American Psychologist, 34*, 906–911.

Flavell, J. H. (1992). *Cognitive development*

(3rd ed.). Upper Saddle River, NJ: Prentice Hall.

Fletcher, J. M., Lyon, G. R., Fuchs, L. S., & Barnes, M. A. (2018). *Learning disabilities: From identification to intervention* (2nd ed.). New York: Guilford Press.

Fogarty, M., Clemens, N., Simmons, D., Anderson, L., Davis, J., Smith, A., et al. (2017). Impact of a technology-mediated reading intervention on adolescents' reading comprehension. *Journal of Research on Educational Effectiveness, 10*(2), 326–353.

Follmer, D. J. (2018). Executive function and reading comprehension: A meta-analytic review. *Educational Psychologist, 53*(1), 42–60.

Foorman, B. R., & Torgesen, J. (2001). Critical elements of classroom and small-group instruction promote reading success in all children. *Learning Disabilities and Practice, 16*(4), 203–212.

Francis, D. J., Kulesz, P. A., & Benoit, J. S. (2018). Extending the simple view of reading to account for variation within readers and across texts: The complete view of reading (CVR i). *Remedial and Special Education, 39*(5), 274–288.

Fritschmann, N., Deshler, D., & Schumaker, J. (2007). The effects of instruction in an inference strategy on the reading comprehension skills of adolescents with disabilities. *Learning Disability Quarterly, 30*, 245–262.

Fuchs, D., Fuchs, L. S., Mathes, P. G., & Simmons, D. C. (1997). Peer assisted learning strategies: Making classrooms more responsive to diversity. *American Educational Research Journal, 34*, 174–206.

Fuchs, L. S., & Deno, S. (1992). Effects of curriculum within curriculum-based measurement. *Exceptional Children, 58*, 232–243.

Fuchs, L. S., & Fuchs, D. (1999). Monitoring student progress toward the development of reading competence: A review of three forms of classroom-based assessment. *School Psychology Review, 28*(4), 659–671.

Fuchs, L. S., & Fuchs, D. (2003). Curriculum-Based Measurement: A best practice guide. *NASP Communique, 32*(2), 33–35.

Fuchs, L. S., Fuchs, D., Prentice, K., Burch, M., Hamlett, C. L., Owen, R., et al. (2003). Explicitly teaching for transfer: Effects on third-grade students' mathematical problem solving. *Journal of Educational Psychology, 95*, 293–304.

Fuchs, L. S., & Vaughn, S. R. (2005). Response to intervention as a framework for the identification of learning disabilities. *Trainers of School Psychologists Forum, 25*(1), 12–19.

Fulk, B., & Mastropieri, M. A. (1990). Training positive attitudes: "I tried hard and did well!" *Intervention in School and Clinic, 26*(2), 79–83.

Gajria, M., Jitendra, A., Sood, S., & Sacks, G. (2007). Improving comprehension of expository text in students with LD: A research synthesis. *Journal of Learning Disabilities, 40*, 210–225.

Gajria, M., & Salvia, J. (1992). The effects of summarization instruction on text comprehension of students with learning disabilities. *Exceptional Children, 58*(6), 508–516.

Garcia, E., & Cuellar, D. (2006). Who are these linguistically and culturally diverse students? *Teachers College Record, 108*(11), 2220–2246.

Garcia, G. E., & Godina, H. (2004). Addressing the literacy needs of adolescent English language learners. In T. J. Jetton & J. A. Dole (Eds.), *Adolescent literacy research and practice* (pp. 304–320). New York: Guilford Press.

Geisel, T. S. (1971). *The Lorax by Dr. Suess.* New York: Random House.

Genesee, F., & Riches, C. (2006). Literacy: Instructional issues. In F. Genesee, K. Lindholm-Leary, W. Saunders, & D. Christian (Eds.), *Educating English language learners: A synthesis of research evidence* (pp. 64–108). New York: Cambridge University Press.

Gersten, R., Chard, D., Jayanthi, M., Baker, S., Morphy, P., & Flojo, J. (2008). *A meta-analysis of mathematics instructional interventions for students with learning disabilities: A technical report.* Portsmouth, NH: Center on Instruction RMC Research Corporation.

Gersten, R., Fuchs, L., Williams, J. P., & Baker, S. (2001). Teaching reading comprehension strategies to students with learning disabilities: A review of research. *Review of Educational Research, 71*, 279–320.

Getsie, R. L., Langer, P., & Glass, G. V. (1985). Meta-analysis of the effects of type and combination of feedback on children's discrimination learning. *Review of Educational Research, 55*(1), 9–22.

Giroir, S., Grimaldo, L. R., Vaughn, S., & Roberts, G. (2015). Interactive read-alouds for English learners in the elementary grades. *The Reading Teacher, 68*(8), 639–648.

Goldenberg, C. (2011). Reading instruction for English language learners. In M. Kamil, P. D. Pearson, E. Moje, & P. Afflerbach (Eds.), *Handbook of reading research* (vol. 4, pp. 684–710). Newark, DE: International Reading Association.

Goldenberg, C. (2013). Unlocking the research on English Language learners: What we know—and don't yet know—about effective instruction. *American Educator, 5,* 139–156.

Good, R. H., & Kaminski, R. A. (2002). *Dynamic indicators of basic early literacy skills* (6th ed.). Eugene, OR: Institute for the Development of Educational Achievement.

Graham, S., & Hebert, M. (2011). Writing-to-read: A meta-analysis of the impact of writing and writing instruction on reading. *Harvard Educational Review, 81,* 710–744.

Graham, S., & Perin, D. (2007). *Writing next: Effective strategies to improve writing of adolescents in middle and high school. A report to Carnegie Corporation of New York.* New York: Carnegie Corporation.

Graves, M. F. (2004). Teaching prefixes: As good as it gets? In J. F. Baumann & E. J. Kame'enui (Eds.), *Vocabulary instruction: Research to practice* (pp. 81–99). New York: Guilford Press.

Graves, M. F. (Ed.). (2009). *Essential readings on vocabulary instruction.* Newark, DE: International Reading Association.

Graves, M. F., Juel, C., & Graves, B. B. (2001). *Teaching reading in the 21st century* (2nd ed.). Boston: Allyn & Bacon.

Gunning, T. G. (2013). *Assessing and correcting reading and writing difficulties* (5th ed.). Upper Saddle River, NJ: Pearson.

Guthrie, J. T., Wigfield, A., & Klauda, S. L. (2012). *Adolescents' engagement in academic literacy* (Report No. 7). Final report to the National Institute on Child Health and Human Development.

Haager, D., & Klingner, J. K. (2005). *Differentiating instruction in inclusive classrooms: The special educators' guide.* Boston: Allyn & Bacon.

Haager, D., & Vaughn, S. (2013). The Common Core State Standards and reading: Interpretations and implications for students with LD in elementary grades. *Learning Disabilities Research and Practice, 28*(1), 5–16.

Hagaman, J. L., Casey, K. J., & Reid, R. (2012). The effects of the paraphrasing strategy and goal setting on the reading comprehension of third grade students at-risk for reading failure. *Remedial and Special Education, 33,* 110–123.

Hagaman, J. L., & Reid, R. (2008). The effects of the paraphrasing strategy on the reading comprehension of middle school students at risk for failure in reading. *Remedial and Special Education, 29,* 222–234.

Hale, A. D., Hawkins, R. O., Sheeley, W., Reynolds, J. R., Jenkins, S., Schmitt, A. J., et al. (2011). A investigation of silent versus aloud reading comprehension of elementary students using maze assessment procedures. *Psychology in the Schools, 48,* 4–13.

Hall, C. S. (2016). Inference instruction for struggling readers: A synthesis of intervention research. *Educational Psychology Review, 28,* 1–22.

Hall, C., & Barnes, M. A. (2017). Inference Instruction to support reading comprehension for elementary students with learning disabilities. *Intervention in School and Clinic, 52*(5), 279–286.

Hall, C., Steinle, P. K., & Vaughn, S. (2019). Reading instruction for English learners with learning disabilities: What do we already know, and what do we still need to learn? *New Directions for Child and Adolescent Development, 2019*(166), 145–189.

Hall, C., Vaughn, S., Barnes, M. A., Stewart, A. A., Austin, C. R., & Roberts, G. (2020). The effects of inference instruction on the reading comprehension of English learners with reading comprehension difficulties. *Remedial and Special Education, 41*(5), 259–270.

Hammill, D., Wiederholt, J. L., & Allen, E. (2006). *The Test of Silent Contextual Reading Fluency.* Austin, TX: Pro-Ed, Inc.

Harcourt Assessment. (2006). *Stanford 10 Reading Test.* Upper Saddle River, NJ: Pearson.

Harmon, J. M. (2000). Assessing and supporting word learning strategies of middle school students. *Journal of Adolescent and Adult Literacy, 43,* 518–527.

Harmon, J. M., Katims, D. S., & Whittington, D. (1999). Helping middle school students learn with social studies texts. *Teaching Exceptional Children, 32,* 70–75.

Hasbrouck, J., & Tindal, G. (2017). *An update to compiled ORF norms* (Technical Report No. 1702). Eugene, OR: Behavioral Research and Teaching, University of Oregon.

Hattie, J., Biggs, J., & Purdie, N. (1996). Effects of learning skills interventions on student learning: A meta-analysis. *Review of Educational Research, 66*(2), 99–136.

Hattie, J., & Clarke, S. (2018). *Visible learning: feedback.* New York: Routledge.

Hattie, J., & Timperley, H. (2007). The power of feedback. *Review of Educational Research, 77,* 81–112.

Hattie, J. A. (1999, June). Influences on student learning. Retrieved from *www.arts .auckland.ac.nz/stafflindex.cfm?P=8650.*

Hawkins, G. S. (1983). *Mindsteps to the cosmos.* New York: HarperCollins.

Hebert, M., Bohaty, J. J., Nelson, J. R., & Brown, J. (2016). The effects of text structure instruction on expository reading comprehension: A meta-analysis. *Journal of Educational Psychology, 108*(5), 609.

Hebert, M., Gillespie, A., & Graham, S. (2013). Comparing effects of different writing activities on reading comprehension: A meta-analysis. *Reading and Writing, 26*(1), 111–138.

Herrera, S., Nielsen, D., Bridges, M., & Catts, H. (2015). Early prediction of reading comprehension within the simple view framework. *Reading & Writing, 28*(9), 1407–1425.

Hickman, P., Pollard-Durodola, S., & Vaughn, S. (2004). Storybook reading: Improving vocabulary and comprehension for English language learners. *The Reading Teacher, 57*(8), 720–730.

Hicks, T., & Steffel, S. (2012). Learning with text in English language arts. In T. L. Jetton & T. Shanahan (Eds.), *Adolescent literacy in the academic disciplines: General principles and practical strategies* (pp. 120–153). New York: Guilford Press.

Hiebert, E. H. (2014). *Knowing what's complex and what's not: Guidelines for teachers in establishing text complexity.* Santa Cruz, CA: TextProject, Inc.

Hinchman, K. A., & O'Brien, D. G. (2019). Disciplinary literacy: From infusion to hybridity. *Journal of Literacy Research, 51*(4), 525–536.

Hirsch, E. D., Jr. (2003). Reading comprehension requires word knowledge—of words and the world: Scientific insights into the fourth grade slump and the nation's stagnant comprehension scores. *American Educator, 27*(1), 10–13.

Hodgkinson, T., & Small, D. (2018). Orienting the map: Where K to 12 teachers stand in relation to text complexity. *Literacy Research and Instruction, 57*(4), 369–386.

Hoffman, J. V. (2017). What if just right is just wrong? The unintended consequences of leveling readers. *The Reading Teacher, 71*(3), 265–273.

Hollenbeck, A. F. (2011). Instructional makeover: Supporting reading comprehension of students with learning disabilities in a discussion-based format. *Intervention in School and Clinic, 46,* 211–220.

Hooper, S. R., Swartz, C. W., Wakely, M. B., & de Kruif, R. E. L. (2006). One intervention—Multiple subtypes revisited: Application of a metacognitive intervention to subtypes of written expression in elementary school students. *Developmental Neuropsychology, 29,* 217–241.

Hoover, H. D., Dunbar, S. B., & Frisbie, D. A. (2001/2003/2007). *Iowa Test of Basic Skills* (ITBS). Rolling Meadows, IL: Riverside Publishing.

Hoover, W. A., & Gough, P. B. (1990). The simple view of reading. *Reading and Writing, 2,* 127–160.

Hughes, E. M., Powell, S. R., & Stevens, E. A. (2016). Supporting clear and concise mathematics language: Instead of that, say this. *Teaching Exceptional Children, 49*(1), 7–17.

Hwang, H., Cabell, S. Q., & Joyner, R. E. (2022). Effects of integrated literacy and content-area instruction on vocabulary and comprehension in the elementary years: A meta-analysis. *Scientific Studies of Reading, 26*(3), 223–249.

Hyland, K., & Tse, P. (2007). Is there an "academic vocabulary"? *TESOL Quarterly, 41,* 235–253.

Idol-Maestas, L. (1985). Getting ready to read: Guided probing for poor comprehenders. *Learning Disability Quarterly, 8,* 243–254.

Individuals with Disabilities Education Act, 20 U.S.C. § 1400, *et. seq.* (2004).

International Literacy Association. (2017). What's hot in literacy: 2017 report. Retrieved from *www.literacyworldwide.org/docs/default-source/resource-documents/whats-hot-2017-report.pdf.*

IRIS Center for Training Enhancements. (2005). *SRSD: Using learning strategies to enhance student learning.* Retrieved from *http://iris.peabody.vanderbilt.edu/srs/chalcycle.htm.*

Irwin, J. W. (1991). *Teaching reading comprehension processes* (2nd ed.). Boston: Allyn & Bacon.

Isikdogan, N., & Kargin, R. (2010). Investigation of the effectiveness of the story-map method on reading comprehension skills among students with mental retardation. *Educational Sciences: Theory into Practice, 10,* 1509–1527.

Jenkins, J. R., Heliotis, J. D., Stein, M. L., & Haynes, M. C. (1987). Improving reading comprehension by using paragraph restatements. *Exceptional Children, 54,* 54–59.

Jiménez, R. T. (1997). The strategic reading abilities and potential of five low-literacy Latina/o readers in middle school. *Reading Research Quarterly, 32*(3), 224–243.

Jiménez, R. T., Garcia, G. E., & Pearson, P. D. (1995). Three children, two languages, and strategic reading: Case studies in bilingual/monolingual reading. *American Educational Research Journal, 32,* 67–97.

Jiménez, R. T., Garcia, G. E., & Pearson, P. D. (1996). The reading strategies of bilingual Latino students who are successful English readers: Opportunities and obstacles. *Reading Research Quarterly, 31,* 90–112.

Jitendra, A. K., Chard, D., Hoppes, M. K., Renouf, K., & Gardill, M. C. (2001). An evaluation of main idea instruction in four commercial reading programs: Implications for students with learning problems. *Reading and Writing Quarterly: Overcoming Learning Difficulties, 17*(1), 53–74.

Jitendra, A. K., Cole, C. L., Hoppes, M. K., & Wilson, B. (1998). Effects of a direct instruction main idea summarization program and self-monitoring on reading comprehension of middle school students with learning disabilities. *Reading and Writing Quarterly: Overcoming Learning Difficulties, 14*(4), 379–396.

Jitendra, A. K., Edwards, L. L., Sacks, G., & Jacobson, L. A. (2004). What research says about vocabulary instruction for students with learning disabilities. *Exceptional Children, 70*(3), 299–322.

Jitendra, A. K., Hoppes, M. K., & Xin, Y. P. (2000). Enhancing main idea comprehension for students with learning problems: The role of a summarization strategy and self-monitoring instruction. *Journal of Special Education, 34*(3), 127–139.

Johns, J. (2008). *Basic reading inventory: Preprimer through grade twelve and early literacy assessments* (10th ed.). Dubuque, IA: Kendall-Hunt.

Johnson, D. D., Johnson, B. V. H., & Schlichting, K. (2004). Logology: Word and language play. In J. F. Baumann & E. J. Kame'enui (Eds.), *Vocabulary instruction: Research to practice* (pp. 179–200). New York: Guilford Press.

Johnson, D. J., & Myklebust, H. R. (1967). *Learning disabilities: Educational principles and practice.* New York: Grune and Stratton.

Johnson, D. W., & Johnson, R. T. (1989). Cooperative learning: What special educators need to know. *The Pointer, 33,* 5–10.

Johnson-Glenberg, M. C. (2000). Training reading comprehension in adequate decoders/poor comprehenders: Verbal versus visual strategies. *Journal of Educational Psychology, 92*(4), 772–782.

Joseph, L. M., & Eveleigh, E. (2011). A review of the effects of self-monitoring on the reading performance of students with disabilities. *Journal of Special Education, 45,* 43–53.

Kagan, S. (1991). *Cooperative learning.* San Diego, CA: Kagan Cooperative Learning.

Kame'enui, E., & Baumann, J. (2012). *Vocabulary instruction: 2nd edition. Research to practice.* New York: Guilford Press.

Kamil, M. L. (2004). Vocabulary and comprehension instruction: Summary and implications of the National Reading Panel Findings. In P. McCardle & V. Chhabra (Eds.), *The voice of evidence in reading research* (pp. 213–234). Baltimore: Brookes Publishing.

Kangas, S. E. (2018). Breaking one law to uphold another: How schools provide services to English learners with disabilities. *TESOL Quarterly, 52*(4), 877–910.

Karlsson, J., van den Broek, P., Helder, A., Hickendorff, M., Koornneef, A., & van Leijenhorst, L. (2018). Profiles of young readers: Evidence from thinking aloud while reading narrative and expository texts. *Learning and Individual Differences, 67,* 105–116.

Kaufman, A., & Kaufman, N. (2004). *Kaufman Test of Educational Achievement—Second Edition* (K-TEA-R/NU). Circle Pines, MN: American Guidance Service.

Keenan, J. M., & Betjemann, R. S. (2006). Comprehending the Gray Oral Reading Test without reading it: Why comprehension tests should not include passage-independent items. *Scientific Studies of Reading, 10,* 363–380.

Keenan, J. M., & Meenan, C. E. (2014). Test differences in diagnosing reading comprehension deficits. *Journal of Learning Disabilities, 47*(2), 125–135.

Kelso, K., Whitworth, A., & Leitão, S. (2022). Higher-level language strategy-based intervention for poor comprehenders: A pilot single case experimental design. *Child Language Teaching and Therapy, 38*(2), 151–165.

Kendeou, P., Papadopoulos, T. C., & Spanoudis, G. (2012). Processing demands of reading comprehension tests in young readers. *Learning and Instruction, 22,* 354–367.

Kennedy, M. J., & Ihle, F. M. (2012). The old man and the sea: Navigating the gulf between special educators and the content area classroom. *Learning Disabilities Research and Practice, 27,* 44–54.

Kent, S., Wanzek, J., Swanson, E. A., & Vaughn, S. (2015). Team-based learning for students with high-incidence disabilities in high school social studies classrooms. *Learning Disabilities Research & Practice, 30*(1), 3–14.

Kieffer, M. J., & Lesaux, N. K. (2008). The role of derivational morphological awareness in the reading comprehension of Spanish-speaking English language learners. *Reading and Writing: An Interdisciplinary Journal, 21,* 783–804.

Kieffer, M. J., & Lesaux, N. K. (2012). Knowledge of words, knowledge about words: Dimensions of vocabulary in first and second language learners in sixth grade. *Reading and Writing, 25,* 347–373.

Kim, A., Vaughn, S., Klingner, J. K., Woodruff, A. L., Klein, C., & Kouzekanani, K. (2006). Improving the reading comprehension of middle school students with disabilities through computer-assisted collaborative strategic reading (CACSR). *Remedial and Special Education, 27,* 235–248.

Kim, A., Vaughn, S., Wanzek, J., & Wei, S. (2004). Graphic organizers and their effect on the reading comprehension of students: A synthesis of research. *Journal of Learning Disabilities, 37,* 105–118.

Kim, H. Y., Hsin, L. B., & Snow, C. E. (2018). Reducing academic inequalities for English language learners: Variation in experimental effects of word generation in high-poverty schools. *International Journal of Bilingual Education and Bilingualism, 24*(7), 1024–1042.

Kim, J. S., Hemphill, L., Troyer, M., Thomson, J. M., Jones, S. M., LaRusso, M. D., & Donovan, S. (2017). Engaging struggling adolescent readers to improve reading skills. *Reading Research Quarterly, 52*(3), 357–382.

Kintsch, W. (1988). The role of knowledge in discourse comprehension: A construction-integration model. *Psychological Review, 95*(2), 163.

Kirk, S. A., & Kirk, W. D. (1971). *Psycholinguistic learning disabilities: Diagnosis and remediation.* Urbana, IL: University of Illinois Press.

Klingner, J. K. (2004). Assessing reading comprehension. *Assessment for Effective Instruction* (formerly *Diagnostique*), 29(4), 59–70.

Klingner, J. K., Artiles, A. J., & Méndez Barletta, L. (2006). English language learners who struggle with reading. Language acquisition or learning disabilities? *Journal of Learning Disabilities, 39,* 108–128.

Klingner, J. K., Boardman, A., Vaughn, S., Buckley, P., Reutebuch, C., & Roberts, G. (2014, April). *Collaborative strategic reading for students with learning disabilities in upper elementary classrooms* Poster presented at the annual conference of the Council for Exceptional Children, Philadelphia, PA.

Klingner, J. K., Buckley, P., Boardman, A., Scornavacco, K., & Eppolito, A. (2012, December 1). *The efficacy of collaborative strategic reading in science and social studies middle school classes in a large urban school district.* Paper presented at the annual conference of the Literacy Research Association, San Diego, CA.

Klingner, J. K., & Eppolito, A. (2014). *How to distinguish between language acquisition and learning disabilities: Questions and answers.* Arlington, VA: Council for Exceptional Children.

Klingner, J. K., Sturges, K., & Harry, B. (2003). Conducting ethnographic classroom observations of literacy instruction. In S. Vaughn & K. Briggs (Eds.), *Reading in the classroom: Systems for observing teaching and learning* (pp. 145–177). Baltimore: Brookes.

Klingner, J. K., Urbach, J., Golos, D., Brownell, M., Menon, S. (2010). Teaching reading in the 21st century: A glimpse at how special education teachers promote reading comprehension. *Learning Disability Quarterly, 33*(2), 59–74.

Klingner, J. K., & Vaughn, S. (1996). Reciprocal teaching of reading comprehension strategies for students with learning disabilities who use English as a second language. *Elementary School Journal, 96,* 275–293.

Klingner, J. K., & Vaughn, S. (1999). Promoting reading comprehension, content learning, and English acquisition through collaborative strategic reading (CSR). *The Reading Teacher, 52,* 738–747.

Klingner, J. K., & Vaughn, S. (2000). The helping behaviors of fifth-graders while using collaborative strategic reading (CSR) during ESL content classes. *TESOL Quarterly, 34,* 69–98.

Klingner, J. K., Vaughn, S., Argüelles, M. E., Hughes, M. T., & Ahwee, S. (2004). Collaborative strategic reading: "Real world" lessons from classroom teachers. *Remedial and Special Education, 25,* 291–302.

Klingner, J. K., Vaughn, S., & Boardman, A. (2007). *Teaching reading comprehension to students with learning disabilities.* New York: Guilford Press.

Klingner, J. K., Vaughn, S., Boardman, A., & Swanson, E. (2012). *Now we get it!: Boosting comprehension with collaborative strategic reading.* New York: Wiley.

Klingner, J. K., Vaughn, S., Dimino, J., Schumm, J. S., & Bryant, D. (2001). *Collaborative strategic reading: Strategies for improving comprehension.* Longmont, CO: Sopris West.

Klingner, J. K., Vaughn, S., & Schumm, J. S. (1998). Collaborative strategic reading during social studies in heterogeneous fourth-grade classrooms. *Elementary School Journal, 99,* 3–21.

Kluger, A. N., & DeNisi, A. (1996). The effects of feedback interventions on performance: A historical review, a meta-analysis, and a preliminary feedback intervention theory. *Psychological Bulletin, 119,* 254–284.

Krouse, J. H., & Krouse, H. J. (1981). Toward a multimodal theory of academic achievement. *Educational Psychologist, 16,* 151–164.

Kucan, L., & Beck, I. L. (1997). Thinking aloud and reading comprehension research: Inquiry, instruction, and social interaction. *Review of Educational Research, 67,* 271–299.

Kuhn, M. R., Schwanenflugel, P. J., & Meisinger, E. B. (2010). Aligning theory and assessment of reading fluency: Automaticity, prosody, and definitions of fluency. *Reading Research Quarterly, 45*(2), 230–251.

Kulik, J. A., & Kulik, C. C. (1988). Timing of feedback and verbal learning. *Review of Educational Research, 58*(1), 79–97.

L'Hommedieu, R., Menges, R. J., & Brinko, K. T. (1990). Methodological explanations for the modest effects of feedback from student ratings. *Journal of Educational Psychology, 82*(2), 232–241.

Lammert, C., DeJulio, S. R., & Heibert, E. H. (2022). "Batting" around Ideas: A design/development study of preservice teachers' knowledge of text difficulty and text complexity. *Reading Psychology,* 1–30.

Lapp, D., Fisher, D., & Johnson, K. (2010). Text mapping plus: Improving comprehension through supported retellings. *Journal of Adolescent Literacy, 53,* 423–426.

LaRusso, M., Kim, H. Y., Selman, R., Uccelli, P., Dawson, T., Jones, S., et al. (2016). Contributions of academic language, perspective taking, and complex reasoning to deep reading comprehension. *Journal of Research on Educational Effectiveness, 9*(2), 201–222.

Lawrence, J. F., & Snow, C. (2011). Oral discourse and reading. In M. Kamil, P. D. Pearson, E. B. Moje, & P. Afflerbach (Eds.), *Handbook of reading research* (Vol. 4, pp. 320–338). New York: Routledge.

Lee, S., Basu, S., Tyler, C. W., & Wei, I. W. (2004). Ciliate populations as bio-indicators at a Deer Island treatment plant. *Advances in Environmental Research, 8*(3–4), 371–378.

Lesaux, N. K., & Kieffer, M. J. (2010). Exploring sources of reading comprehension difficulties among language minority learners and their classmates in early adolescence. *American Educational Research Journal, 47,* 596–632.

Lesaux, N. K., Kieffer, M. J., Faller, S. E., & Kelley, J. (2010). The effectiveness and ease of implementation of an academic vocabulary intervention for linguistically diverse students in urban middle schools. *Reading Research Quarterly, 45,* 198–230.

Leslie, L., & Calwell, J. S. (2010). *Qualitative Reading Inventory* (5th ed.). Upper Saddle River, NJ: Pearson.

Lipson, M. Y., Mosenthal, J. H., & Mekkelsen, J. (1999). The nature of comprehension among grade 2 children: Variability in retellings as a function of development, text, and task. In T. Shanahan & F. Rodriguez-Brown (Eds.), *National Reading Conference yearbook 48* (pp. 104–119). Chicago: National Reading Conference.

Lipson, M. Y., & Wixson, K. K. (2012). *Assessment of reading and writing difficulties: An interactive approach* (5th ed., pp. 104–119). Upper Saddle River, NJ: Pearson.

Locascio, G., Mahone, E. M., Eason, S. H., & Cutting, L. E. (2010). Executive dysfunction among children with reading comprehension deficits. *Journal of Learning Disabilities, 43*(5), 441–454.

Lonigan, C. J., Burgess, S. R., & Schatschneider, C. (2018). Examining the simple view of reading with elementary school children: Still simple after all these years. *Remedial and Special Education, 39*(5), 260–273.

Lou, Y., Abrami, P. C., Spence, J. C., Poulsen, C., Chambers, B., & d'Apollonia, S. (1996). Within-class grouping: A meta-analysis. *Review of Educational Research, 66,* 423–458.

Lugo-Neris, M. J., Jackson, C. W., & Goldstein, H. (2010). Facilitating vocabulary acquisition of young English language learners. *Language, Speech, and Hearing Services in Schools, 41,* 314–327.

Lyon, G. R. (1985). Neuropsychology and learning disabilities. *Neurology and Neurosurgery, 5,* 1–8.

Lysakowski, R. S., & Walberg, H. J. (1982). Instructional effects of cues, participation, and corrective feedback: A quantitative synthesis. *American Educational Research Journal, 19,* 559–578.

MacArthur, C. A., Ferretti, R. P., & Okolo, C. M. (2002). On defending viewpoints: Debates of sixth graders about the desirability of early 20th-century American immigration. *Learning Disabilities Research and Practice, 17,* 160–172.

MacArthur, C. A., Graham, S., Schwartz, S. S., & Schafer, W. (1995). Evaluation of a writing instruction model that integrated a process approach, strategy instruction, and word processing. *Learning Disability Quarterly, 18,* 278–291.

MacGinitie, W. H., MacGinitie, R. K., Maria, K., Dreyer, L. G., & Hughes, K. E. (2000). *Gates–MacGinitie reading tests—Fourth edition.* Itasca, IL: Riverside.

Malone, L. D., & Mastropieri, M. (1992). Reading comprehension instruction: Summarization and self-monitoring training for students with learning disabilities. *Exceptional Children, 58*(3), 270–279.

Mancilla-Martinez, J., & Lesaux, N. K. (2011). The gap between Spanish speakers' word reading and word knowledge: A longitudinal study. *Child Development, 82,* 1544–1560.

Mandler, J. M., & Johnson, N. S. (1977). Remembrance of things parsed: Story structure and recall. *Cognitive Psychology, 9,* 111–151.

Mann, L. (1979). *On the trail of process: A historical perspective on cognitive processes and their training.* New York: Grune & Stratton.

Manzo, A. V. (1968). *Improving reading comprehension through reciprocal questioning.* Unpublished doctoral dissertation, Syracuse University, Syracuse, NY.

Marcotte, A. M., & Hintze, J. M. (2009). Incremental and predictive utility of formative assessment methods of reading comprehension. *Journal of School Psychology, 47,* 315–333.

Markman, E. M. (1985). Comprehension monitoring: Developmental and educational issues. In S. F. Chapman, J. W. Segal, & R. Glaser (Eds.), *Thinking and learning skills: Research and open questions* (pp. 275–291). Mahwah, NJ: Erlbaum.

Marston, D., & Magnusson, D. (1985). Implementing curriculum-based measurement in special and regular education settings. *Exceptional Children, 52,* 266–276.

Marston, D., Deno, S. L., Kim, D., Diment, K., & Rogers, D. (1995). Comparison of reading intervention approaches for students with mild disabilities. *Exceptional Children, 62,* 20–37.

Mason, L. H., Meadan-Kaplansky, H., Hedin, L., & Taft, R. (2013). Self-regulating informational text reading comprehension: Perceptions of low-achieving students. *Exceptionality, 21,* 69–86.

Mastropieri, M. A., & Scruggs, T. E. (1998). Enhancing school success with mnemonic strategies. *Intervention in School and Clinic, 33*(4), 201–208.

McCallum, S., Khron, K. R., Skinner, C. H., Hilton-Prillhart, A., Hopkins, M., Waller, S., et al. (2011). Improving reading comprehension of at-risk high school students: The art of reading program. *Psychology in the Schools, 48*(1), 78–86.

McCormick, S. (1999). *Instructing students who have literacy problems* (3rd ed.). Upper Saddle River, NJ: Merrill.

McCormick, S., & Zutell, J. (2011). *Instructing students who have literacy problems* (7th ed.). Upper Saddle River, NJ: Pearson.

McElvain, C. (2010). Transactional literature circles and the reading comprehension of at-risk English learners in the mainstream classroom. *Journal of Research in Reading, 33*(2), 178–205.

McGuire, Himot, B., Clayton, G., Yoo, M., & Logue, M. E. (2020). Booked on math: Developing math concepts in pre-K classrooms using interactive read-alouds. *Early Childhood Education Journal, 49*(2), 313–323.

McIntosh, R., Vaughn, S., Schumm, J., Haager, D., & Lee, O. (1993). Observations of students with learning disabilities in general education classrooms. *Exceptional Children, 60*(3), 249–261.

McKenna, J. W., Shin, M., & Ciullo, S. (2015). Evaluating reading and mathematics instruction for students with learning disabilities: A synthesis of observation research. *Learning Disability Quarterly, 38*(4), 195–207.

McKeown, M. G., & Beck, I. L. (2004). Transforming knowledge into professional development resources: Six teachers implement a model of teaching for understanding text. *Elementary School Journal, 104,* 391–408.

McKeown, M. G., Beck, I. L., & Blake, R. G. (2009). Rethinking reading comprehension instruction: A comparison of instruction for strategies and content approaches. *Reading Research Quarterly, 44*(3), 218–253.

McKeown, M. G., Beck, I. L., Omanson, R. C., & Pople, M. T. (1985). Some effects of the nature and frequency of vocabulary instruction on the knowledge of use of words. *Reading Research Quarterly, 20*(5), 522–535.

Meadows Center for Preventing Educational Risk. (2020). *10 key vocabulary practices for all schools.* Austin, TX: University of Texas at Austin/Meadows Center for Preventing Educational Risk.

Meadows Center for Preventing Educational Risk. (2021). *10 key policies and practices for explicit instruction.* Austin, TX: University of Texas at Austin/Meadows Center for Preventing Educational Risk. Retrieved from *https://meadowscenter.org/files/resources/10Key_ExplicitInstruction.pdf.*

Metsisto, D. (2005). Reading in the mathematics classroom. In J. M. Kenney, E. Hancewicz, L. Heuer, D. Metsisto, & C. L. Tuttle (Eds.), *Literacy strategies for improving mathematics instruction* (pp. 9–23). Alexandria, VA: ASCD.

Meyer, B. J. F. (1984). Text dimensions and cognitive processing. In H. Mandl, N. Stein, & T. Trabasso (Eds.), *Learning and understanding texts* (pp. 3–47). Hillsdale, NJ: Erlbaum.

Meyer, B. J. F. (2003). Text coherence and readability. *Topics in Language Disorders, 23*(3), 204–224.

Miller, C. A., Darch, C. B., Flores, M. M., Shippen, M. E., & Hinton, V. (2010). Main idea identification with students with mild intellectual disabilities and specific learning disabilities: A comparison of explicit and basal instructional approaches. *Journal of Direct Instruction, 12,* 20–35.

Mitchell, C. (2016, December 7). Majority of English learning students are born in the United States, analysis finds. *Education Week.* Retrieved from *www.edweek.org/teaching-learning/majority-of-english-learner-students-are-born-in-the-united-states-analysis-finds/2016/12.*

Moin, A. K. (1986). *Relative effectiveness of various techniques of calculus instruction:*

*A meta-analysis.* Unpublished doctoral dissertation, Department of Mathematics, University of Syracuse, Syracuse, NY.

Mokhtari, K., & Reichard, C. A. (2002). Assessing students' metacognitive awareness of reading strategies. *Journal of Educational Psychology, 94,* 249–259.

Montelongo, J. A., Hernandez, A. C., Herter, R. J., & Cuello, J. (2011). Using cognates to scaffold context clue strategies for Latino ELs. *The Reading Teacher, 64*(6), 429–434.

Moore, D. W., Readence, J. E., & Rickelman, R. J. (1983). An historical exploration of content area reading. *Reading Research Quarterly, 18,* 419–438.

Morris D. (2023). The case for tutoring struggling readers in the primary grades. *Reading & Writing Quarterly, 39*(2), 104–119.

Morsy, L., Kieffer, M., & Snow, C. E. (2010). *Measure for measure: A critical consumers' guide to reading comprehension assessments for adolescents.* New York: Carnegie Corporation.

Murray, C. S., Stevens, E. A., & Vaughn, S. (2022). Teachers' text use in middle school content-area classrooms. *Reading and Writing, 35*(1), 177–197.

Nagy, W. E., Garcia, G. E., Durgunoglu, A. Y., & Hancin-Bhatt, B. (1993). Spanish-English bilingual students' use of cognates in English reading. *Journal of Literacy Research, 25*(3), 241–260.

National Center for Education Statistics. (2011). *The Nation's Report Card: Reading 2011* (NCES 2012-457). U.S. Department of Education, Institute of Education Sciences. Washington, DC: Institute of Education Sciences.

National Center for Education Statistics. (2022). English learners in public schools. *Condition of Education.* U.S. Department of Education, Institute of Education Sciences. Retrieved from *https://nces.ed.gov/programs/coe/indicator/cgf.*

National Governors Association Center for Best Practices & Council of Chief State School Officers. (2010). *Common Core State Standards.* Washington, DC: Authors.

National Institute of Child Health and Human Development. (2000). Report of the National Reading Panel. Teaching children to read: An evidence-based assessment of the scientific research literature on reading and its implications for reading instruc-tion: Reports of the sub-groups. Available at *www.nichd.nih.gov/pubs/nrp/report.pdf.*

Nelson, J. R., Smith, D. J., & Dodd, J. M. (1992). The effects of teaching a summary skills strategy to students identified as learning disabled on their comprehension of science text. *Education and Treatment of Children, 15*(3), 228–243.

Newcomer, P. (1999). *Standardized reading inventory—Second edition (SRI-2).* Austin, TX: Pro-Ed.

Next Generation Science Standards. (2012). *Appendix A: Conceptual Shifts in the Next Generation Science Standards.* Washington, DC: National Academies Press.

Nocedal, J., & Wright, S. J. (2006). *Numerical optimization* (2nd ed.). New York: Springer.

Northrop, L., & Andrei, E. (2019). More than just word of the day: Vocabulary apps for English learners. *The Reading Teacher, 72*(5), 623–2630.

Norton, M. (1959). *The Borrowers afloat.* New York: Scholastic.

Oczkus, L. D. (2018). *Reciprocal teaching at work: Powerful strategies and lessons for improving reading comprehension.* Alexandria, VA: Association for Supervision and Curriculum Development.

Ogle, D. M. (1986). K-W-L: A teaching model that develops active reading of expository text. *The Reading Teacher, 39,* 564–570.

Ogle, D. M. (1989). The know, want to know, learn strategy. In K. D. Muth (Ed.), *Children's comprehension of text: Research to practice* (pp. 205–233). Newark, DE: International Reading Association.

Okkinga, M., van Steensel, R., van Gelderen, A. J., & Sleegers, P. J. (2018). Effects of reciprocal teaching on reading comprehension of low-achieving adolescents. The importance of specific teacher skills. *Journal of Research in Reading, 41*(1), 20–41.

Ortiz, A. A., & Robertson, P. M. (2018). Preparing teachers to serve English learners with language- and/or literacy-related difficulties and disabilities. *Teacher Education and Special Education, 41*(3), 176–187.

Ortiz, A. A., & Wilkinson, C. Y. (1991). Assessment and intervention model for the bilingual exceptional student (AIM for the BESt). *Teacher Education and Special Education, 14,* 35–42.

Oster, L. (2001). Using the think-aloud for

reading instruction. *The Reading Teacher, 55,* 64–69.

Overton, T. (2011). *Assessing learners with special needs: An applied approach* (7th ed.). Hoboken, NJ: Pearson.

Palincsar, A. S. (1986). The role of dialogue in providing scaffolded instruction. *Educational Psychologist, 21,* 73–98.

Palincsar, A. S., & Brown, A. L. (1984). Reciprocal teaching of comprehension-fostering and comprehension monitoring activities. *Cognition and Instruction, 1*(2), 117–175.

Palincsar, A. S., Brown, A. L., & Martin, S. M. (1987). Peer interaction in reading comprehension instruction. *Educational Psychologist, 22,* 231–253.

Papadopoulos, T. C., Spanoudis, G., Ktisti, C., & Fella, A. (2021). Precocious readers: a cognitive or a linguistic advantage? *European Journal of Psychology of Education, 36,* 63–90.

Paris, A. H., & Paris, S. G. (2003). Assessing narrative comprehension in young children. *Reading Research Quarterly, 38,* 36–76.

Paris, S. G., Wasik, B. A., & Turner, J. C. (1991). The development of strategic readers. In R. Barr, M. L. Kamil, P. B. Mosenthal, & P. D. Pearson (Eds.), *Handbook of reading research* (Vol. 2, pp. 609–640). New York: Longman.

Pearson Assessments. (2004). *Aprenda: La Prueba de Logros en Español, 3rd edition.* Portland, OR: Author.

Pearson, P. D. (2002). Thinking about the reading/writing connection with P. David Pearson. *The Voice, 7,* 6, 9.

Pearson, P. D., Moje, E., & Greenleaf, C. (2010). Literacy and science: Each in the service of the other. *Science, 328,* 459–463.

Perez, B. (1998). *Sociocultural contexts of language and literacy.* Mahwah, NJ: Erlbaum.

Perfetti, C. A. (1985). *Reading ability.* New York: Oxford University Press.

Philippakos, Z. A. T., & Graham, S. (Eds.). (2023). *Writing and reading connections.* New York: Guilford Press.

Philippakos, Z. A. T., & MacArthur, C. A. (2022). Developing critical thinkers, writers, and readers: Reading and writing in the genres. In T. S. Hodges (Ed.), *Handbook of research on writing instruction practices for equitable and effective teaching* (pp. 80–103). Hershey, PA: IGI Global.

Phillips Galloway, E., & Uccelli, P. (2019). Examining developmental relations between core academic language skills and reading comprehension for English learners and their peers. *Journal of Educational Psychology, 111*(1), 15–31.

Pintrich, P. R. (1995). Understanding self-regulated learning. *New Directions for Teaching and Learning, 63,* 3–12.

Powell, S. R., Stevens, E. A., & Hughes, E. M. (2019). Math language in middle school: Be more specific. *TEACHING Exceptional Children, 51*(4), 286–295.

Pratt, S. M., Coleman, J. M., & Dantzler, J. A. (2023). A mixed-methods analysis of fourth-graders' comprehension and their reported strategies for reading science texts. *Literacy Research and Instruction, 62*(1), 16–48.

Pressley, M. (2000a). Comprehension instruction in elementary school: A quarter-century of research progress. In M. M. Taylor, M. F. Graves, & P. Can Den Broek (Eds.), *Reading for meaning: Fostering comprehension in middle grades* (pp. 32–51). New York: Teachers College Press.

Pressley, M. (2000b). What should comprehension instruction be the instruction of? In M. Kamil, P. Mosenthal, P. Pearson, & R. Barr (Eds.), *Handbook of reading research* (Vol. 3, pp. 545–561). Mahwah, NJ: Erlbaum.

Pressley, M. (2006). *Reading instruction that works: The case for balanced teaching* (3rd ed.). New York: Guilford Press.

Pressley, M., & Afflerbach, P. (1995). *Verbal protocols of reading: The nature of constructively responsive reading.* Hillsdale, NJ: Erlbaum.

Pressley, M., El-Dinary, P. B., Gaskins, I., Schuder, T., Bergman, J., Almasi, J., et al. (1992). Beyond direct explanation: Transactional instruction of reading comprehension strategies. *Elementary School Journal, 92*(5), 513–555.

Pressley, M., Schuder, T., SAIL faculty and administration, Bergman, J. L., & El-Dinary, P. B. (1992). A researcher–educator collaborative interview study of transactional comprehension strategies instruction. *Journal of Educational Psychology, 84,* 231–246.

Proctor, C. P., Dalton, D., Uccelli, P., Biancarosa, G., Mo, E., Snow, C. E., et al. (2011). Improving Comprehension Online

(ICON): Effects of deep vocabulary instruction with bilingual and monolingual fifth graders. *Reading and Writing: An Interdisciplinary Journal, 24*(5), 517–544.

Proctor, P. C., Harring, J. R., Silverman, R. D. (2017). Linguistic interdependence between Spanish language and English language and reading: A longitudinal exploration from second through fifth grade. *Bilingual Research Journal, 40*, 372–391.

Proctor, C. P., Silverman, R. D., & Jones, R. L. (2021). Centering language and student voice in multilingual literacy instruction. *The Reading Teacher, 75*(3), 255–267.

Pyle, N., Vasquez, A. C., Lignugaris/Kraft, B., Gillam, S. L., Reutzel, D. R., Olszewski, A., et al. (2017). Effects of expository text structure interventions on comprehension: A meta-analysis. *Reading Research Quarterly, 52*(4), 469–501.

Quezada, Y., Williams, E., & Flores, V. (2006). Inspiration outline of basic stages of reciprocal teaching. Retrieved from *http://condor.admin.ccny.cuny.edu/~yq6048/basic1.jpg.*

Rafdal, B. H., McMaster, K. L., McConnell, S. R., Fuchs, D., & Fuchs, L. S. (2011). The effectiveness of kindergarten peer-assisted learning strategies for students with learning disabilities. *Exceptional Children, 77*, 299–316.

Raphael, T. E. (1986). Teaching question answer relationships, revisited. *The Reading Teacher, 39*, 516–522.

Rapp, D. N., Broek, P. V. D., McMaster, K. L., Kendeou, P., & Espin, C. A. (2007). Higher-order comprehension processes in struggling readers: A perspective for research and intervention. *Scientific Studies of Reading, 11*(4), 289–312.

Rasinski, T. V., Blachowicz, C. L., & Lems, K. (Eds.). (2012). *Fluency instruction: Research-based best practices* (2nd ed.). New York: Guilford Press.

Rathvon, N. (2004). *Early reading assessment: A practitioner's handbook.* New York: Guilford Press.

Readence, J. E., Bean. T. W., & Baldwin, R. S. (2012). *Content area literacy: An integrated approach* (10th ed.). Dubuque, IA: Kendall Hunt.

Reed, D. K., & Vaughn, S. (2012). Retell as an indicator of reading comprehension. *Scientific Studies of Reading, 16*(3), 187–217.

Reid, D. K., Hresko, P. W., & Hammill, D. D.

(2001). *Test of Early Reading Ability—Third edition.* Torrance, CA: WPS.

Riches, C., & Genesee, F. (2006). Literacy: Crosslinguistic and crossmodal issues. In F. Genesee, K. Lindholm-Leary, W. Saunders, & D. Christian (Eds.), *Educating English language learners: A synthesis of empirical findings* (pp. 64–108). New York: Cambridge University Press.

Ridge, A. D., & Skinner, C. H. (2011). Using the TELLS pre-reading procedure to enhance comprehension levels and rates in secondary students. *Psychology in the Schools, 48*, 46–58.

Riedel, B. W. (2007). The relationship between DIBELS, reading comprehension, and vocabulary in urban first-grade students. *Reading Research Quarterly, 42*, 546–567.

Ritchey, K. D., Palombo, K., Silverman, R. D., & Speece, D. L. (2017). Effects of an informational text reading comprehension intervention for fifth-grade students. *Learning Disability Quarterly, 40*(2), 68–80.

Rivera, M. O., & McKeithan, G. K. (2022). Progress monitoring of language acquisition and academic content for English learners. *Learning Disabilities Research & Practice, 37*(3), 216–225.

Roberts, G., Vaughn, S., Wanzek, J., Furman, G., Martinez, L., & Sargent, K. (2023). Promoting adolescents' comprehension of text: A randomized control trial of its effectiveness. *Journal of Educational Psychology, 115*(5), 665–682.

Robertson, J. S. (2000). Is attribution theory a worthwhile classroom intervention for K–12 students with learning difficulties? *Educational Psychology Review, 12*(1), 111–134.

Roehling, J. V., Hebert, M., Nelson, J. R., & Bohaty, J. J. (2017). Text structure strategies for improving expository reading comprehension. *The Reading Teacher, 71*(1), 71–82.

Rogoff, B., & Gardner, W. P. (1984). Adult guidance of cognitive development. In B. Rogoff & J. Lave (Eds.), *Everyday cognition: Its development in social context* (pp. 95–116). Cambridge, MA: Harvard University Press.

Roman, A. A., Kirby, J. R., Parrila, R. K., Wade-Woolley, L., & Deacon, S. H. (2009). Toward a comprehensive view of the skills involved in word reading in grades 4, 6, and

8. *Journal of Experimental Child Psychology, 102*(1), 96–113.

Roman, D., Jones, F., Basaraba, D., & Hironaka, S. (2016). Helping students bridge inferences in science texts using graphic organizers. *Journal of Adolescent & Adult Literacy, 60*(2), 121–130.

Rosenshine, B., & Meister, C. (1994). Reciprocal teaching: A review of the research. *Review of Educational Research, 64*, 479–530.

Rosenshine, B., Meister, C., & Chapman, S. (1996). Teaching students to generate questions: A review of the intervention studies. *Review of Educational Research, 66*(2), 181–221.

Roswell, F. G., Chall, J. S., Curtis, M. E., & Kearns, G. (2005). *Diagnostic assessment of reading, 2nd edition.* Austin, TX: PRO-ED.

Rowe, M. B. (1986). Wait time: Slowing down may be a way of speeding up! *Journal of Teacher Education, 37(1),* 43–50.

Rummel, A., & Feinberg, R. (1988). Cognitive evaluation theory: A meta-analytic review of the literature. *Social Behavior and Personality, 16*(2), 147–164.

Sabatini, J., O'Reilly, T., Weeks, J., & Wang, Z. (2020). Engineering a twenty-first century reading comprehension assessment system utilizing scenario-based assessment techniques. *International Journal of Testing, 20*(1), 1–23.

Santangelo, T., Harris, K. R., & Graham, S. (2007). Self-regulated strategy development: A validated model to support students who struggle with writing. *Learning Disabilities: A Contemporary Journal, 5*(1), 1–20.

Saskatchewan Learning. (2002). *English language arts: A curriculum guide for the elementary level.* Saskatchewan, CA: Author.

Scammacca, N. K., Roberts, G. J., Cho, E., Williams, K. J., Roberts, G., Vaughn, S. R., et al. (2016). A century of progress: Reading interventions for students in grades 4–12, 1914–2014. *Review of Educational Research, 86*(3), 756–800.

Scholastic Inc. (2007). *Scholastic Reading Inventory: Educator's guide.* New York: Scholastic.

Schumaker, J. B., Denton, P. H., & Deshler, D. D. (1984). *The paraphrasing strategy.* Lawrence, KS: University of Kansas.

Schunk, D. H. (2003). Self-efficacy for reading and writing: Influence of modeling, goal setting, and self-evaluation. *Reading and Writing Quarterly, 19*, 159–172.

Schwartz, D. M. (1985). *How much is a million?* New York: HarperCollins Children's Books.

Scott, J. A., & Nagy, W. E. (2004). Developing word consciousness. In J. F. Baumann & E. J. Kame'enui (Eds.), *Vocabulary instruction: Research to practice* (pp. 201–217). New York: Guilford Press.

Scruggs, T. E., Mastropieri, M. A., Berkeley, S., & Marshak, L. (2010). Mnemonic strategies: Evidence-based practice and practice-based evidence. *Intervention in School and Clinic, 46*, 79–86.

Sesma, H. W., Mahone, E. M., Levine, T., Eason, S., & Cutting, L. (2009). The contribution of executive skills to reading comprehension. *Child Neuropsychology, 15*, 232–246.

Shanahan, C. (2012). Learning with text in science. In T. L. Jetton & T. Shanahan (Eds.), *Adolescent literacy in the academic disciplines: General principles and practical strategies* (pp. 154–171). New York: Guilford Press.

Shanahan, T. (2020). What constitutes a science of reading instruction? *Reading Research Quarterly, 55*, S235–S247.

Shanahan, T., Callison, K., Carriere, C., Duke, N. K., Pearson, P. D., Schatschneider, C., et al. (2010). *Improving reading comprehension in kindergarten through 3rd grade: A practice guide* (NCEE 2010-4038). Washington, DC: U.S. Department of Education.

Shanahan, T., & Shanahan, C. (2008). Teaching disciplinary literacy to adolescents: Rethinking content-area literacy. *Harvard Educational Review, 78*, 40–59.

Shanahan, T., & Shanahan, C. (2012). What is disciplinary literacy and why does it matter? *Topics in Language Disorders, 32*, 7–18.

Shanahan, T., & Shanahan, C. (2017). Disciplinary literacy: Just the FAQs. *Educational Leadership, 74*(5), 18–22.

Sharifian, F. (2002). *Conceptual–associative system in Aboriginal English: A study of Aboriginal children attending primary schools in metropolitan Perth.* Perth, Australia: Edith Cowan University. Retrieved from *https://ro.ecu.edu.au/theses/757.*

Shapiro, E. S., Solari, E. S., & Petscher, Y. (2008). Use of a measure of reading comprehension to enhance prediction on the state high stakes assessment. *Learning and Individual Differences, 18,* 316–328.

Shin, J., & McMaster, K. (2019). Relations between CBM (oral reading and maze) and reading comprehension on state achievement tests: A meta-analysis. *Journal of School Psychology, 73,* 131–149.

Siebert, D., & Draper, R. J. (2012). Reconceptualizing literacy and instruction for mathematics classrooms. In T. L. Jetton & T. Shanahan (Eds.), *Adolescent literacy in the academic disciplines: General principles and practical strategies* (pp. 172–198). New York: Guilford Press.

Simmons, D. C., & Kame'enui, E. (1998). *What reading research tells us about children with diverse learning needs: Bases and basics.* Mahwah, NJ: Erlbaum.

Simmons, D. C., Kame'enui, E. J., & Darch, C. B. (1988). The effect of textual proximity on fourth- and fifth-grade LD students' metacognitive awareness and strategic comprehension behavior. *Learning Disability Quarterly, 11*(4), 380–395.

Skiba, R., Casey, A., & Center, B. A. (1985–1986). Nonaversive procedures in the treatment of classroom behavior problems. *Journal of Special Education, 19,* 459–481.

Snow, A. B., Morris, D., & Perney, J. (2018). Evaluating the effectiveness of a state-mandated benchmark reading assessment: mClass Reading 3D (Text Reading and Comprehension). *Reading Psychology, 39*(4), 303–334.

Snow, C. E. (2002a). *Reading for understanding: Toward a research and development program in reading comprehension.* Santa Monica, CA: RAND.

Snow, C. E. (2002b). Second language learners and understanding the brain. In A. M. Galaburda, S. M. Kosslyn, & Y. Christen (Eds.), *The languages of the brain* (pp. 151–165). Cambridge, MA: Harvard University Press.

Snow, C. E., Lawrence, J. F., & White, C. (2009). Generating knowledge of academic language among urban middle school students. *Journal of Research on Educational Effectiveness, 2,* 325–344.

Snow, C. E., & Moje, E. B. (2010). What is adolescent literacy? Why is everyone talking about it now? *Phi Delta Kappan, 91*(6), 66–69.

Snowling, M. J., & Hulme, C. (2011).

Evidence-based interventions for reading and language difficulties: Creating a virtuous circle. *British Journal of Educational Psychology, 81,* 1–23.

Snyder, L., Caccamise, D., & Wise, B. (2005). The assessment of reading comprehension: Considerations and cautions. *Topics in Language Disorders, 25,* 33–50.

Solis, M., Ciullo, S., Vaughn, S., Pyle, N., Hassaram, B., & Leroux, A. (2012). Reading comprehension interventions for middle school students with learning disabilities: A synthesis of 30 years of research. *Journal of Learning Disabilities, 45,* 327–340.

Souvignier, E., & Mokhlesgerami, J. (2006). Using self-regulation as a framework for implementing strategy instruction to foster reading comprehension. *Learning and Instruction, 16,* 57–71.

Spörer, N., Brunstein, J. C., & Kieschke, U. (2009). Improving students' reading comprehension skills: Effects of strategy instruction and reciprocal teaching. *Learning and Instruction, 19*(3), 272–286.

Stagliano, C., & Boon, R. T. (2009). The effects of a story mapping procedure to improve the comprehension skills of expository text passages for elementary students with learning disabilities. *Learning Disabilities: A Contemporary Journal, 7*(2), 35–58.

Stahl, R. J. (1994). *Using "think-time" and "wait-time" skillfully in the classroom.* Bloomington, IN: ERIC Clearinghouse for Social Studies and Social Science Education. Available at *www.atozteacherstuff.com/pages/1884.shtml.*

Stahl, S. A. (2003, Spring). How words are learned incrementally over multiple exposures. *American Educator, 44,* 18–19.

Stahl, S. A., & Stahl, K. A. D. (2004). Word wizards all! Teaching word meanings in preschool and primary education. In J. F. Baumann & E. J. Kame'enui (Eds.), *Vocabulary instruction: Research to practice* (pp. 59–80). New York: Guilford Press.

Stauffer, R. G. (1969). *Teaching reading as a thinking process.* New York: Harper & Row.

Stevens, E. A., & Austin, C. R. (2022). Structured reading comprehension intervention for students with reading difficulties. In L. Spear-Sperling (Ed.), *Structured literacy interventions: teaching students with reading difficulties, Grades K–6* (p. 162). New York: Guilford Press.

Stevens, E. A., Leroux, A. J., Mowbray, M. H., & Lee, G. S. (2023). Evaluating the effects of adding explicit vocabulary instruction to a word-problem schema intervention. *Exceptional Children, 89*(3), 275–293.

Stevens, E. A., Park, S., & Vaughn, S. (2019). A review of summarizing and main idea interventions for struggling readers in grades 3 through 12: 1978–2016. *Remedial and Special Education, 40*(3), 131–149.

Stevens, E. A., Walker, M. A., & Vaughn, S. (2017). The effects of reading fluency interventions on the reading fluency and reading comprehension performance of elementary students with learning disabilities: A synthesis of the research from 2001 to 2014. *Journal of Learning Disabilities, 50*(5), 576–590.

Stockard, J., Wood, T. W., Coughlin, C., & Rasplica Khoury, C. (2018). The effectiveness of direct instruction curricula: A meta-analysis of a half century of research. *Review of Educational Research, 88*(4), 479–507.

Susskind, E. (1979). Encouraging teachers to encourage children's curiosity: A pivotal competence. *Journal of Clinical and Child Psychology, 8*, 101–106.

Swanson, E. A., & Vaughn, S. (2010). An observation study of reading instruction provided to elementary students with learning disabilities in the resource room. *Psychology in the Schools, 47*(5), 481–492.

Swanson, H., Zheng, X., & Jerman, O. (2009). Working memory, short-term memory, and reading disabilities: A selective meta-analysis of the literature. *Journal of Learning Disabilities, 42*(3), 260–287.

Swanson, H. L. (1999). Reading research for students with LD: A meta-analysis of intervention outcomes. *Journal of Learning Disabilities, 32*(6), 504–532.

Swanson, H. L. (2000). What instruction works for students with learning disabilities? Summarizing the results from a meta-analysis of intervention studies. In R. M. Gersten, E. P. Schiller, & S. Vaughn (Eds.), *Contemporary special education research: Syntheses of the knowledge base on critical instructional issues* (pp. 1–30). Mahwah, NJ: Erlbaum.

Swanson, H. L. (2001). Reading intervention research outcomes and students with LD: What are the major instructional ingredi-ents for successful outcomes? *Perspectives, 27*(2), 18–20.

Swanson, H. L., Hoskyn, M., & Lee, C. (1999). *Interventions for students with learning disabilities: A meta-analysis of treatment outcomes.* New York: Guilford Press.

Swanson, H. L., & Howell, M. (2001). Working memory, short-term memory, and speech rate as predictors of children's reading performance at different ages. *Journal of Educational Psychology, 93*, 720–734.

Taboada, A., Bianco, S., & Bowerman, V. (2012). Text-based questioning: A comprehension strategy to building English language learners' content knowledge. *Literacy Research and Instruction, 51*(2), 87–109.

Taboada, A., & Rutherford, V. (2011). Developing reading comprehension and academic vocabulary for English language learners through science content: A formative experiment. *Reading Psychology, 32*(2), 113–157.

Taboada B. A., Buehl, M. M., Kidd, J. K., Sturtevant, E. G., Richey Nuland, L., & Beck, J. (2015). Reading engagement in social studies: Exploring the role of a social studies literacy intervention on reading comprehension, reading self-efficacy, and engagement in middle school students with different language backgrounds. *Reading Psychology, 36*(1), 31–85.

Tenenbaum, G., & Goldring, E. (1989). A meta-analysis of the effect of enhanced instruction: Cues, participation, reinforcement and feedback and correctives on motor skill learning. *Journal of Research and Development in Education, 22*, 53–64.

Texas Education Agency & University of Texas Center for Reading and Language Arts. (2001). *Texas second grade teacher reading academy.* Austin, TX: Author.

Torgesen, J. K. (2000). Individual differences in response to early interventions in reading: The lingering problem of treatment resisters. *Learning Disabilities Research and Practice, 15*, 55–64.

Torgesen, J. K., Alexander, A. W., Wagner, R. K., Rashotte, C. A., Voeller, K. K. S., & Conway, T. (2001). Intensive remedial instruction for children with severe reading disabilities: Immediate and long-term outcomes from two instructional approaches. *Journal of Learning Disabilities, 34*, 33–58.

Toste, J. R., Vaughn, S., Martinez, L. R., & Bustillos-SoRelle, D. A. (2019). Content-area reading comprehension and teachers' use of instructional time: Effects on middle school students' social studies knowledge. *Reading and Writing, 32*(7), 1705–1722.

Traga Philippakos, Z. A., & MacArthur, C. A. (2022). Developing critical thinkers, writers, and readers: Reading and writing in the genres. In T. S. Hodges (Ed.), *Handbook of research on writing instruction practices for equitable and effective teaching* (pp. 80–103). Hershey, PA: IGI Global.

Traga Philippakos, Z. A., Munsell, S., & Robinson, L. B. (2018). Supporting primary students' story writing by including retellings, talk, and drama with strategy instruction. *The Language and Literacy Spectrum, 28*(1), Article 1.

Uchihara, T., Webb, S., & Yanagisawa, A. (2019). The effects of repetition on incidental vocabulary learning: A meta-analysis of correlational studies. *Language Learning, 69*(3), 559–599.

U.S. Department of Education (2010). *Reciprocal teaching, Institute of Education Sciences, National Center for Education Evaluation and Regional Assistance*. Washington, DC: What Works Clearinghouse.

U.S. Department of Education. (April, 2022). OSEP Fast facts: Students with disabilities who are English learners (Els) served under IDEA Part B. Retrieved from *https://sites. ed.gov/idea/osep-fast-facts-students-with-disabilities-english-learners*

Valencia, S. W., Smith, A. T., Reece, A. M., Li, M., Wixson, K. K., & Newman, H. (2010). Oral reading fluency assessment: Issues of construct, criterion, and consequential validity. *Reading Research Quarterly, 45*, 270–291.

van den Broek, P., Beker, K., & Oudega, M. (2015). Inference generation in text comprehension: Automatic and strategic processes in the construction of a mental representation. In E. J. O'Brien, A. E. Cook, & R. F. Lorch, Jr. (Eds.), *Inferences during Reading* (pp. 94–121). New York: Cambridge University Press.

VanSledright, B. (2012). Learning with texts in history: Protocols for reading and practical strategies. In T. L. Jetton & T. Shanahan (Eds.), *Adolescent literacy in the academic disciplines: General principles and practical strategies* (pp. 199–226). New York: Guilford Press.

Vaughn, S., Chard, D., Bryant, D. P., Coleman, M., Tyler, B., Thompson, S., et al. (2000). Fluency and comprehension interventions for third-grade students: Two paths to improved fluency. *RASE: Remedial and Special Education, 21*(6), 325–335.

Vaughn, S., & Edmonds, M. (2006). Reading comprehension for older readers. *Intervention in School and Clinic, 41*(3), 131–137.

Vaughn, S., & Fletcher, J. M. (2021). Identifying and teaching students with significant reading problems. *American Educator, 44*(4), 4.

Vaughn, S., Gersten, R., & Chard, D. J. (2000). The underlying message in LD intervention research: Findings from research syntheses. *Exceptional Children, 67*, 99–114.

Vaughn, S., Gersten, R., Dimino, J., Taylor, M. J., Newman-Gonchar, R., Krowka, S., et al. (2022). *Providing reading interventions for students in grades 4–9* (WWC 2022007). Washington, DC: National Center for Education Evaluation and Regional Assistance (NCEE), Institute of Education Sciences, U.S. Department of Education.

Vaughn, S., Kieffer, M. J., McKeown, M., Reed, D. K., Sanchez, M., St Martin, K., et al. (2022). *Providing reading interventions for students in grades 4–9. Educator's Practice Guide* (WWC 2022007). Washington, DC: U.S. Department of Education.

Vaughn, S., Klingner, J. K., Swanson, E., Boardman, A., Roberts, G., Mohammed, S., et al. (2011). Efficacy of collaborative strategic reading with middle school students. *American Educational Research Journal, 48*, 938–954.

Vaughn, S., Linan-Thompson, S., Kouzekanani, K., Bryant, D. P., Dickson, S., & Blozis, S. A. (2003). Grouping for reading instruction for students with reading difficulties. *Remedial and Special Education, 24*, 301–315.

Vaughn, S., Martinez, L. R., Linan-Thompson, S., Reutebuch, C. K., Carlson, C. D., & Francis, D. J. (2009). Enhancing social studies vocabulary and comprehension for seventh-grade English language learners: Findings from two experimental studies. *Journal of Research on Educational Effectiveness, 2*(4), 297–324.

Vaughn, S., Roberts, G. J., Miciak, J., Taylor, P., & Fletcher, J. M. (2019). Efficacy of a word- and text-based intervention for students with significant reading difficulties. *Journal of Learning Disabilities, 52*(1), 31–44.

Vaughn, S., Roberts., G., Swanson, E. A., Wanzek, J., Fall, A. M., & Stillman-Spisak, S. J. (2015a). Improving middle-school students' knowledge and comprehension in social studies: A replication. *Educational Psychology Review, 27,* 31–50.

Vaughn, S., Roberts, G., Wexler, J., Vaughn, M. G., Fall, A. M., & Schnakenberg, J. B. (2015b). High school students with reading comprehension difficulties: Results of a randomized control trial of a two-year reading intervention. *Journal of Learning Disabilities, 48*(5), 546–558.

Vaughn, S., Solís, M., Miciak, J., Taylor, W. P., & Fletcher, J. M. (2016). Effects from a randomized control trial comparing researcher and school-implemented treatments with fourth graders with significant reading difficulties. *Journal of Research on Educational Effectiveness, 9*(1), 23–44.

Vaughn, S., Swanson, E. A., Roberts, G., Wanzek, J., Stillman-Spisak, S. J., Solis, M., et al. (2013). Improving reading comprehension and social studies knowledge in middle school. *Reading Research Quarterly, 48*(1), 77–93.

Vaughn, S., Wanzek, J., Murray, C. S., & Roberts, G. (2011). *Intensive interventions for students struggling in reading and mathematics: A research to practice belief.* Portsmouth, NH: Center on Instruction at RMC Research Corporation.

Vaughn, S., Wexler, J., Leroux, A., Roberts, G., Denton, C. A., Barth, A. E., et al. (2012). Effects of intensive reading intervention for eighth-grade students with persistently inadequate response to intervention. *Journal of Learning Disabilities, 45*(6), 515–525.

Victoria University of Wellington. (n.d.). *School of Linguistics and Applied Language Studies te Kura Tātari reo.* Academic Word List selection.

Vygotsky, L. S. (1978). *Mind in society.* Cambridge, MA: Harvard University Press.

Wade, E., Boon, R. T., & Spencer, V. G. (2010). Use of Kidspiration software to enhance the reading comprehension of story grammar components for elementary-age students with specific learning disabilities. *Learning Disabilities: A Contemporary Journal, 8*(2), 31–41.

Wade, S. E., Buxton, W. M., & Kelly, M. (1999). Using think-alouds to examine reader-text interest. *Reading Research Quarterly, 34,* 194–216.

Walberg, H. J. (1982). What makes schooling effective? *Contemporary Education Review, 1,* 1–34.

Walsh, J. A., & Sattes, B. D. (2005). *Quality questioning: Research-based practice to engage every learner.* Thousand Oaks, CA: Corwin Press.

Wanzek, J., Petscher, Y., Al Otaiba, S., Rivas, B. K., Jones, F. G., Kent, S. C., et al. (2017). Effects of a yearlong supplemental reading intervention for students with reading difficulties in fourth grade. *Journal of Educational Psychology, 109*(8), 1103–1119.

Wanzek, J., & Vaughn, S. (2007). Research-based implications from extensive early reading interventions. *School Psychology Review, 36,* 541–561.

Wanzek, J., & Vaughn, S. (2008). Response to varying amounts of time in reading intervention for students demonstrating insufficient response to intervention. *Journal of Learning Disabilities, 41,* 126–142.

Wanzek, J., Vaughn, S., Scammacca, N. K., Metz, K., Murray, C. S., Roberts, G., et al. (2013). Extensive reading interventions for students with reading difficulties after grade 3. *Review of Educational Research, 83*(2), 163–195.

Wanzek, J., Wexler, J., Vaughn, S., & Ciullo, S. (2010). Reading interventions for struggling readers in the upper elementary grades: A synthesis of 20 years of research. *Reading and Writing, 23*(8), 889–912.

Was, C. A., & Woltz, D. J. (2007). Re-examining the relationship between working memory and comprehension: The role of available long-term memory. *Journal of Memory and Language, 56,* 86–102.

Westby, C., Moore, C., & Roman, R. (2002). Reinventing the enemy's language: Developing narratives in Native American children. *Linguistics and Education, 13*(2), 235–269.

Westera, J., & Moore, D. W. (1995). Reciprocal teaching of reading comprehension in a New Zealand high school. *Psychology in the Schools, 32*(3), 225–232.

Whaley, J. F. (1981). Story grammars and reading instruction. *The Reading Teacher, 34,* 762–771.

White, T. G., Sowell, J., & Yanagihara, A. (1989). Teaching elementary students to use word-part clues. *The Reading Teacher, 42,* 302–309.

Whitney, P., & Budd, D. (1996). Think-aloud protocols and the study of comprehension. *Discourse Processes, 21,* 341–351.

Wiederholt, J. L., & Blalock, G. (2000). *Gray Silent Reading Tests (GSRT).* Austin, TX: Pro-Ed.

Wiederholt, J. L., & Bryant, B. R. (1992). *Gray Oral Reading Test—Third edition* (GORT-D-4). Austin, TX: Pro-Ed.

Wiederholt, J. L., & Bryant, B. R. (2001). *Gray Oral Reading Test—4th edition* (GORT-4). Austin, TX: Pro-Ed.

Wiederholt, J. L., & Bryant, R. R. (2012). *Gray Oral Reading Tests—Fifth edition (GORT-5).* Austin, TX: Pro-Ed.

Wilkinson, S. S. (1981). The relationship of teacher praise and student achievement: A meta-analysis of selected research. *Dissertation Abstracts International, 41*(9–A), 3998.

Williams, J. P. (1998). Improving the comprehension of disabled readers. *Annals of Dyslexia, 48,* 213–238.

Williams, J. P. (2005). Instruction in reading comprehension for primary-grade students: A focus on text structure. *Journal of Special Education, 39,* 6–18.

Williams, J. P., Kao, J. C., Pao, L. S., Ordynans, J. G., Atkins, J. G., Cheng, R., et al. (2016). Close analysis of texts with structure (CATS): An intervention to teach reading comprehension to at-risk second graders. *Journal of Educational Psychology, 108*(8), 1061–1077.

Williams, K. T. (2001). *Group Reading Assessment and Diagnostic Evaluation* (GRADE). Circle Pines, MN: American Guidance Service.

Wise, J. C., Sevcik, R. A., Morris, R. D., Lovett, M. W., & Wolf, M. (2007). The growth of phonological awareness by children with reading disabilities: A result of semantic knowledge or knowledge of grapheme–phoneme correspondences? *Scientific Studies of Reading, 22,* 151–164.

Wood, E., Pressley, M., & Winne, P. H. (1990). Elaborative interrogation effects on children's learning of factual content. *Journal of Educational Psychology, 82,* 741–748.

Wood, P., Bruner, J., & Ross, G. (1976). The role of tutoring in problem solving. *Journal of Child Psychology and Psychiatry, 17,* 89–100.

Woodcock, R. W. (2011). *Woodcock Reading Mastery Test, third edition.* Circle Pines, MN: American Guidance Service.

Woodcock, R. W., Muñoz-Sandoval, A. F., McGrew, K. S., & Mather, N. (2005). *Woodcock–Muñoz Language Survey III.* Itasca, IL: Riverside.

Woods, L. M., & Moe, A. (2010). *Analytical reading inventory—Ninth edition.* Columbus, OH: Merrill Education.

Wright, T. S. (2019). Reading to learn from the start: The power of interactive read-alouds. *American Educator, 42*(4), 4.

Wright, T. S., & Cervetti, G. N. (2017). A systematic review of the research on vocabulary instruction that impacts text comprehension. *Reading Research Quarterly, 52*(2), 203–226.

Yeany, R. H., & Miller, P. A. (1983). Effects of diagnostic/remedial instruction on science learning: A meta-analysis. *Journal of Research in Science Teaching, 20,* 19–26.

Zimmerman, B. J. (1989). A social cognitive view of self-regulated academic learning. *Journal of Educational Psychology, 81*(3), 329–339.

Zimmerman, B. J., & Bandura, A. (1994). Impact of self-regulatory influences on writing course attainment. *American Educational Research Journal, 31*(4), 845–862.

Zimmerman, B. J., Bonner, S., & Kovach, R. (1996). *Developing self-regulated learners: Beyond achievement to self-efficacy.* Washington, DC: American Psychological Association.

Zimmerman, B. J., & Risemberg, R. (1997). Self-regulatory dimensions of academic learning and motivation. In G. D. Phye (Ed.), *Handbook of academic learning: Construction of knowledge* (pp. 105–125). San Diego, CA: Academic Press.

Zipoli, R. P., & Merritt, D. D. (2022). Structured literacy interventions for oral language comprehension. In L. Spear-Swerling (Ed.), *Structured literacy interventions: Teaching students with reading difficulties, grades K–6* (pp. 136–161). New York: Guilford Press.

# Index

*Note.* *f* or *t* following a page number indicates a figure or a table;
**bold** in a page number indicates a glossary entry.

Academic vocabulary, 50*f*, 50–52, 126–127. *See also* Vocabulary instruction
Accuracy of reading, 148*f*
Acronyms, 63
Active engagement, 147–148, 148*f*
Affixes, 7, 63
After-reading strategies
  English learners (ELs) and, 126
  instruction and, 72–84
  sample lesson plans for, 214–217
  think-alouds and, 37
Alphabetic principle, **219**
Ambiguities, 63, **219**
Analytical Reading Inventory, 9th Edition, 24*t*
Anecdotal records, 35
Antonyms, 63
Aprenda: La Prueba de Logros en Español—3rd Edition, 21*t*
Assessment. *See also* Progress monitoring; individual types of measures
  asking and answering questions and, 77
  challenges of measuring reading comprehension, 16–17, 17*t*
  limitations of, 17–18
  metacognitive processes and, 31, 33–38, 36*f*
  overview, 15–16, 38–40
  types of, 18–31, 19*t*, 21*t*–24*t*, 28*f*
  vocabulary instruction and, 46–49, 64–65
Attentional functioning, 136
Attribution, 139
Attributional feedback, 5

Author and You questions, 77. *See also* Questions
Author's purpose, 167
Automaticity. *See* Fluency

Background knowledge. *See also* World knowledge
  assessment and, 39
  building, 171–172
  collaborative strategic reading (CSR) and, 161–162
  comparing good and poor readers and, 4, 5
  content-area literacy and, 106, 116–117
  English learners (ELs) and, 123–124, 125, 130, 133
  instruction and, 69, 72
  intensifying intervention and, 144
  multistrategy inference intervention and, 167
  sample lesson plan for, 193–194
  selecting appropriate texts and, 97
  text levels and, 173
  vocabulary instruction and, 45–46, 61–63
Bader Reading and Language Inventory, 7th Edition, 24*t*
Basic Reading Inventory, 10th Edition, 24*t*
Batería III Woodcock–Muñoz: Pruebas de Aprovechamiento, 21*t*
Before-reading strategies, 37, 126, 180–186
Bilingual education programs, 124
Bilingual students, 123, 133–134. *See also* English learners (ELs)
Brainstorming, 107
Bridging, 127, 130

Cambridge English Vocabulary list, 51
Catchphrases, 63
Cause–effect relationships, 99, 101, 202–203
Characters in narrative text, 99t, 167, 198–199. See
    also Narrative text
Chunking strategies, 174
Clarifying, 55, 55f, 154, 155f
Classroom assessments, 16. See also Assessment
Classroom environment, 50f, 144f
Classwide peer tutoring, 10t, 151t, **219**
Click and clunk strategy, 159, 160–161, 161f, 162,
    211–213
Close reading, 116–117
Cloze procedure, 17–18, **219**
Clunk strategies, 33, 159, 160–161, 161f, 162, 211–213
Cognates, 127, 130
Cognitive flexibility training, 137, 141
Cognitive organizers, **219**. See also Graphic
    organizer
Cognitive processes, 11–12, 37, 136–141, 138f
Collaborative strategic reading (CSR). See also
    Multicomponent strategy instruction
    compared to reciprocal teaching, 158t
    context clues and, 59
    definition of, **219**
    fix-up strategies and, 55
    overview, 33, 157–164, 158t, 161f
Common Core State Standards (CCSS), 13, 106,
    121, **219**
Compare and contrast, 101
Compare–contrast graphic organizer, 103. See also
    Graphic organizer
Compounds, 63
Comprehension in general
    comparing good and poor readers and, 3–5, 5f
    definition of, **219**
    fluency and, 5–6, 8, 10, 10t
    overview, 1–3, 5f, 14
    vocabulary and, 5–6
    what's involved in, 10–13
    word reading and, 5–7, 8f, 9t
Computer-assisted instruction (CAI), **219**
Concept, 50, 51, 55–58, 55f, 57f, 58f. See also
    Concept map
Concept map. See also Concept
    content-area literacy and, 106
    English learners (ELs) and, 131, 132f
    overview, 72
    vocabulary instruction and, 56–57, 57f
Concept-Oriented Reading Instruction (CORI),
    109–110, 151t
Confirmation guide, 71, 71f
Connections
    building background knowledge and, 171–172
    cognitive processing difficulties and, 138
    content-area literacy and, 106, 110, 115
    English learners (ELs) and, 130
    sample lesson plans for, 194–198

Content-area literacy. See also Disciplinary literacy
    definition of, **219**
    English language arts (ELA), 115–118, 118f
    English learners (ELs) and, 123–124, 130
    instruction and, 66
    math, 118–120, 119f
    overview, 105–106
    sample lesson plan for, 209–211
    science, 109–110, 111f, 112f
    secondary content-area instruction, 171
    social studies, 110, 112–115, 114f
    vocabulary instruction and, 52, 64–65
Context clues, 59–61, 97, **219**
Contextualized vocabulary instruction, 128. See
    also Vocabulary instruction
Control processes, 137
Cooperative learning, 35, 162–163, **219**
Coxhead list, 51, 52
Criterion-referenced test, 19f, 20, 24t, 25, **219**. See
    also Assessment; Informal reading inventory
    (IRI)
Critical literacy skill, 117
C-SPACE mnemonic device, 85
Curriculum-based assessment (CBA), 19f,
    25–29, 28f, **219–220**. See also Assessment;
    Curriculum-based measurement (CBM)
Curriculum-based measurement (CBM), 19f,
    26–29, 28f, 48–49, **220**. See also Assessment;
    Curriculum-based assessment (CBA)

Decoding. See also Word reading
    assessment and, 39
    comprehension and, 2, 6–7, 8f, 9t, 169–171
    definition of, **220**
Definitions, 52–53
Deliberate practice, 147–148, 148f. See also Practice
Demonstration, 156f
Description, 101
Developmental Reading Assessment, 2nd Edition,
    24t
Diagnostic assessment, 15, 16. See also Assessment
Diagnostic Assessment of Reading, 2nd Edition
    (DAR), 21t
Dictionaries, 58–59
Direct instruction. See also Instruction
    definition of, **220**
    formulating the main idea, 81–82
    learning disabilities and, 4–5
    overview, 2, 3
    question–answer relationship (QAR) strategy
        and, 78
    reciprocal teaching and, 156f
    vocabulary instruction and, 50
Disciplinary literacy, 106–108, 115–116, 120–121,
    **220**. See also Content-area literacy
Discussions
    asking and answering questions and, 75–80
    content-area literacy and, 117, 118f

English learners (ELs) and, 130, 133
motivation and, 177
narrative text structure and, 100
reciprocal teaching and, 156f
Duration of intervention, 143. *See also* Intervention
During-reading strategies
English learners (ELs) and, 126
instruction and, 72–84
sample lesson plans for, 187–213
think-alouds and, 37
Dynamic Indicators of Basic Early Literacy Skills (DIBELS), 26

Elaborating readers, 37
Elaborative processes, 12, 155–156, **220**
Embedded instruction, 117–118. *See also* Instruction
English as a second language (ESL), 124. *See also* English learners (ELs)
English language arts (ELA), 115–118, 118f. *See also* Content-area literacy
English language development (ELD), 124
English learners (ELs)
connections between reading and writing, 89
factors that affect comprehension for, 125
instruction and, 69, 125–133, 132f
oral reading fluency and, 27
overview, 122–124, 133–134
retellings and, 29
Ethnographic note taking, 35
Euphemisms, 63
Executive functions, 136, 137–139
Explicit instruction. *See also* Instruction
collaborative strategic reading (CSR) and, 160
comprehension and, 5f
content-area literacy and, 106, 113, 120–121
English learners (ELs) and, 126–127, 133
formulating the main idea, 81
intensifying intervention and, 143–144, 144f
overview, 68
Expository text. *See also* Informational text; Text structure
assessment and, 32f
collaborative strategic reading (CSR) and, 157–164, 158t, 161f, 165f
definition of, **220**
multistrategy inference intervention and, 167
overview, 101–104
retellings and, 30
Expressions, 63, **220**
Extrinsic motivation, 177. *See also* Motivation

Feedback
cognitive processing difficulties and, 140
intensifying intervention and, 145–147, 146t
multistrategy inference intervention and, 166–167
reciprocal teaching and, 155–156
Figures of speech, 63, **220**

Fix-up strategies
collaborative strategic reading (CSR) and, 161f
content-area literacy and, 113, 114f
sample lesson plan for, 211–213
vocabulary instruction and, 54–55
Flexibility, cognitive. *See* Cognitive flexibility training
Fluency
assessment and, 39
comprehension and, 5–6, 8, 10, 10t
curriculum-based measurement and, 27–29, 28f
definition of, **220**
Flynt–Cooter Comprehensive Reading Inventory–2, 24t
Formative assessment, 15, 16. *See also* Assessment
Foundational skills, 17t
Frequency of intervention, 142–143. *See also* Intervention

Gates–MacGinitie Reading Tests, 4th Edition, 21t
Genres, 116
Get the gist strategy. *See also* Main idea
collaborative strategic reading (CSR) and, 159, 162
content-area literacy and, 113
overview, 172–173
sample lesson plan for, 188–190
Gist. *See* Main idea
Global Integrated Scenario-Based Assessment (GISA), 39
Goal setting, 138–139, 147, 177
Goals for reading, 3, 177
Good readers, 3–5, 5f
Graphic novels, 173
Graphic organizer
content-area literacy and, 110, 113
definition of, **220**
English learners (ELs) and, 130
information text structure and, 103–104
intensifying intervention and, 144
Gray Oral Reading Test (GORT), 18, 22t
Gray Silent Reading Test, 22t
Group Reading Assessment and Diagnostic Evaluation, 22t
Guided instruction, 5. *See also* Instruction
Guided practice, 156f
Guiding questions, 103. *See also* Questions

Hierarchical summary procedure, **220**
High-frequency words, 7
High-stakes testing, 16. *See also* Assessment
Homographs, 63
Homophones, 63
Hooks, 72
Hyperbole, 63

Identification strategies, 102
Idioms, 63

Illustrations, 97
Images, mental. *See* Mental images
Independence, 96, 174–176
Independent practice, 147–148, 148*f*, 174–176. *See also* Practice
Independent-level texts, 93. *See also* Text
Individual assessments, 18. *See also* Assessment
Inferences
  asking and answering questions and, 77
  assessment and, 18
  cognitive processing difficulties and, 138
  comparing good and poor readers and, 4
  definition of, **220**
  multistrategy inference intervention and, 164, 166–168
  retellings and, 29
  sample lesson plans for, 206–211
  strategies that enhance cognitive processes and, 137, 138*f*
Informal reading inventory (IRI), 25, **220**. *See also* Criterion-referenced test
Informational text. *See* Expository text; Text structure
Inhibition, 141
Instruction. *See also* Content-area literacy; Direct instruction; Strategy instruction; Vocabulary instruction
  assessment of, 39
  connections between reading and writing, 87, 89
  content-area literacy and, 106
  disciplinary literacy and, 106–108
  English language arts (ELA), 115–118, 118*f*
  English learners (ELs) and, 125–133, 132*f*
  intensifying the delivery of for struggling learners, 141–148, 144*f*, 146*t*, 148*f*
  math, 118–120, 119*f*
  narrative text structure and, 98–99
  overview, 2, 3–5, 5*f*, 66–67, 91
  before reading, 68–72, 71*f*
  during and after reading, 72–84
  science, 109–110, 111*f*, 112*f*
  selecting appropriate texts, 96–98
  self-regulation strategies, 139–140
  social studies, 110, 112–115, 114*f*
  strategies for understanding narrative text, 85–87, 88*f*, 89*f*, 90*f*
  struggling learners and, 136
  students with learning disabilities and, 67–68
  text levels and, 93–96, 95*f*
Instructional-level texts, 93, 96–98. *See also* Text
Integrative processes, 11–12, **220**
Interactive instructional model, **220**
Interactive text preview, 70–71, 71*f*. *See also* Text preview
Interest, 125, 174
Intervention, 98–99, 141–148, 144*f*, 146*t*, 148*f*, 149*f*
Interviews, 19*f*, 34. *See also* Assessment

Intrinsic motivation, 177. *See also* Motivation
Iowa Test of Skills, 22*t*

Kaufman Test of Educational Achievement, 2nd Edition, 22*t*
Keyword strategies
  definition of, **220**
  fluency and, 8
  sample lesson plan for, 217
  selecting key words to teach, 50–52
  vocabulary learning and, 48–49, 50, 51, 53–54
Knowledge-based inferences, 138*f*. *See also* Inferences
K-W-L chart, 70–71

Language conventions, 97
Language play, 63
Large-group discussions, 117, 118*f*. *See also* Discussions
Learning disability (LD). *See also* Reading disabilities
  asking and answering questions and, 76, 79
  assessment and, 15, 16–17, 47–49
  definition of, **220**
  English learners (ELs) and, 124
  formulating the main idea, 81–82
  instruction and, 67–68, 91
  overview, 4–5
  strategies for understanding narrative text and, 85–87
  summarizing and, 83
  vocabulary instruction and, 47–49, 55
Learning logs, 164, 165*f*
Length of intervention, 142–143. *See also* Intervention
Lesson plans
  for before reading, 180–186
  for during reading, 187–213
  for after reading, 214–217
Levels of reading, 18. *See also* Text
Linear string graphic organizer, 103. *See also* Graphic organizer
Listening, 102
Literal readers, 37
Literature. *See* Content-area literacy; English language arts (ELA)

Macroprocessing, 12, **220**
Main idea
  cognitive processing difficulties and, 138
  content-area literacy and, 106, 111*f*, 113
  definition of, **220**
  instruction and, 68, 80–84
  multistrategy inference intervention and, 167
  overview, 81–82
  sample lesson plans for, 187–188, 190–192
  selecting appropriate texts and, 97
Math, 118–120, 119*f*. *See also* Content-area literacy

Matrix graphic organizer, 103. *See also* Graphic organizer

Maze fluency measure, 27–29, 28*f*

Memory, 136, 138, 140–141, 214–215

Mental images. *See* Visualization

Metacognitive Awareness of Reading Strategies Inventory (MARSI), 34

Metacognitive processes
  assessment and, 31, 33–38, 36*f*
  comprehension and, 12
  definition of, **220**
  instruction and, 67
  overview, 73

Metalinguistic awareness, 133. *See also* Morphology; Semantics; Syntax

Metaphors, 63

Microprocessing, 11, **220**

Mnemonic strategies, 50, 53–54, 85, **220**

Modeling
  collaborative strategic reading (CSR) and, 160–161, 161*f*
  fluency and, 8
  learning disabilities and, 5
  narrative text structure and, 99
  self-regulation strategies, 139–140

Modifications, 155–156

Monitoring comprehension
  cognitive processing difficulties and, 138
  comparing good and poor readers and, 4
  decoding and, 9*t*
  instruction and, 67, 68, 73–75
  overview, 9*t*, 141
  sample lesson plan for, 204–205
  vocabulary instruction and, 51, 54–55

Morphology
  assessing vocabulary learning, 47
  definition of, **220**
  English learners (ELs) and, 130, 133
  morphological analysis, 128
  selecting appropriate texts and, 97
  vocabulary instruction and, 59, 59*f*

Motivation
  assessment and, 39
  cognitive processing difficulties and, 139
  English learners (ELs) and, 125
  instruction and, 72
  overview, 177–178
  text levels and, 174

Multicomponent strategy instruction, 68, 132–133, 150–152, 151*f*, 168, **221**. *See also* Collaborative strategic reading (CSR); Multistrategy inference intervention; Reciprocal teaching

Multicomponent vocabulary instruction, 128–129. *See also* Vocabulary instruction

Multilingual resources, 130

Multimedia, 129–130

Multimodal texts, 133

Multistrategy inference intervention, 164, 166–168, **221**. *See also* Inferences; Multicomponent strategy instruction

Multisyllabic words, 7, 9*t*, 174

Narrative intervention strategies, 98–99

Narrative text. *See also* Text structure
  definition of, **221**
  multistrategy inference intervention and, 167
  overview, 98–101, 99*t*
  retellings and, 30
  sample lesson plans for, 198–202
  strategies for understanding, 85–87, 88*f*, 89*f*, 90*f*

Next Generation Science Standards, 121

Norm-referenced tests, 19–20, 19*f*, 21*t*–23*t*. *See also* Assessment

Notes, 4, 113, 114

Observation, 19*f*, 35–36, 36*f*. *See also* Assessment

Online word resources, 58–59

Onomastics, 63, **221**

Oral language skills, 123, 125

Oral reading fluency (ORF), 26–27

Oral retellings. *See* Retellings

Organization of text, 3, 103–104. *See also* Text structure

Orthography, 50*f*

Oxymorons, 63

PACT strategies. *See* Promoting Acceleration of Comprehension and Content through Text (PACT)

Parallel narratives, 99. *See also* Narrative text

Paraphrasing, 59, 82–83, **221**

Paraphrasing readers, 37

Peer partners, 8, 176

Peer tutoring, 35

Peer-Assisted Learning Strategies (PALS Reading), 151*t*

Performance criteria, 148*f*

Phonics, 12–13, **221**

Phonological awareness, 2, **221**

Phonology, 47, 50*f*, **221**

Planning, 141

Plot in narrative text, 99*t*. *See also* Narrative text

Point of view in narrative text, 99*t*. *See also* Narrative text

Poor readers
  accelerating the progress of, 135–136
  comprehension and, 3–5
  instruction and, 67–68
  retellings and, 31
  text structure and, 98

Practice
  English learners (ELs) and, 130, 133
  intensifying intervention and, 147–148, 148*f*
  learning disabilities and, 5
  overview, 174–176

Pragmatics, 47, **221**
Praise, 155–156
Predictions. *See also* Metacognitive processes
    comparing good and poor readers and, 4
    content-area literacy and, 113
    overview, 31, 33
    reciprocal teaching and, 154, 155*f*
    sample lesson plan for, 195–198
Prefixes
    content-area literacy and, 110, 112*f*
    decoding and, 7
    sample lesson plan for, 184–185
    vocabulary instruction and, 59, 59*f*
Preview of text. *See* Text preview
Prior knowledge. *See* Background knowledge
Problem–solution relationships, 99, 101
Progress monitoring. *See also* Assessment
    curriculum-based measurement and, 27–29, 28*f*
    definition of, **221**
    fluency and, 8
    learning disabilities and, 5
    narrative text structure and, 99
    overview, 18
    vocabulary instruction and, 46–47
Promoting Acceleration of Comprehension and
    Content through Text (PACT), 113–114, 151*t*
Prompted think-aloud, 41–43. *See also* Think-
    alouds
Prompts, 155–156
Pronoun referent, 138*f*. *See also* Inferences
Proper nouns, 7, 8, 174
Proverbs, 63
Purpose setting, 69–70

Qualitative Reading Inventory (QRI), 24*t*, 25, 31
Quality English and Science Teaching (QuEST), 129
Question generating. *See* Student-generated
    questions
Question–answer relationship (QAR) strategy,
    76–77, 78, 113, **221**
Questioning-the-author technique, 79–80, **221**
Questionnaires, 19*f*, 34. *See also* Assessment
Questions
    asking and answering, 75–80
    decoding and, 9*t*
    English learners (ELs) and, 132
    information text structure and, 103
    instruction and, 68
    monitoring understanding and, 74–75
    multistrategy inference intervention and, 167
    narrative text structure and, 100
    sample lesson plans and, 204–205

RAP paraphrasing strategy, 82–83. *See also*
    Paraphrasing
Rate of reading, 148*f*
Read-alouds, 61, 99, 177
Reader response theory, 2–3, **221**

Reading, 87, 89
Reading disabilities, 2, 5–6. *See also* Learning
    disability (LD)
Recall, 138. *See also* Memory
Reciprocal teaching, 152–156, 155*f*, 156*f*, 157*f*,
    158*t*, **221**. *See also* Multicomponent strategy
    instruction
Repeated reading, 8, 148*f*
Resources, 10*t*
Retellings, 19*f*, 29–31, 32*f*, 85–86, **221**. *See also*
    Assessment
Right There questions, 77, 78. *See also* Questions
Roots, 110
Round robin reading, 176
Rules, 7

Scaffolding
    collaborative strategic reading (CSR) and, 159
    content-area literacy and, 113
    definition of, **221**
    narrative text structure and, 99
    reciprocal teaching and, 152, 155–156
    text levels and, 174
Scenario-based assessments (SBA), 39. *See also*
    Assessment
Schema theory, 2, **221**
Scholastic Reading Inventory, 24*t*
Science, 109–110, 111*f*, 112*f*, 209–211. *See also*
    Content-area literacy
Science of reading, 12–13
Scrambled stories, 87
Screening, 15–16, 18. *See also* Assessment
Secondary content-area instruction, 171
Selecting text. *See* Text selection
Self-concept, 177
Self-efficacy, 139, 177
Self-monitoring, 138–140, 141. *See also* Monitoring
    comprehension
Self-questioning, 5. *See also* Questions
Self-regulation
    cognitive processing difficulties and, 138–139
    instruction and, 139–140
    intensifying intervention and, 144
    overview, 73
    strategies that enhance, 136, 137–138, 140–141
Self-report measures, 34. *See also* Assessment;
    Questionnaires
Self-talk, 139
Semantic awareness, 130
Semantic organizer, 55, 55*f*, 72, 183–184, **221**
Semantics, 47, 133, **221**
Sentence writing, 50, 53, 206–208
Sequence, 101, 199–202
Setting a purpose, 69–70
Setting in narrative text, 99*t*, 198–199. *See also*
    Narrative text
Shared book reading, 127, 130
Shifting, 141

Signal words, 101, 102
Silent reading, 174–176
Similies, 63
Simple view of reading (SVR), 2, 3
Slang, 63
Slogans, 63
Small-group assessments, 18. *See also* Assessment
Small-group discussions. *See also* Discussions
  content-area literacy and, 117, 118*f*
  intensifying intervention and, 141–142
  multistrategy inference intervention and, 166–167
  reciprocal teaching and, 156*f*
Small-group instruction, 136, 162–163
Small-group reading, 176
Social studies, 110, 112–115, 114*f*. *See also* Content-area literacy
Special education, 108–109, 114, 160
Standardized norm-referenced test, 18, **221**
*Standardized Reading Inventory, 2nd Edition*, 24*t*
Stanford 10 Reading Test, 23*t*
Story grammar, 99, **221**
Story maps, 85, 100–101, **221**
Story planner, 87, 88*f*, 89*f*, 90*f*
Story retelling, 85–86. *See also* Retellings
Story structure, 198–202, **221**. *See also* Narrative text
Storybook reading, 61, **221**
Strategy instruction. *See also* Instruction; Strategy use
  cognitive processing and, 136–141, 138*f*
  comprehension and, 5*f*
  connections between reading and writing, 89
  content-area literacy and, 106, 109–110, 112–114
  disciplinary literacy and, 106–108
  English learners (ELs) and, 130, 131–133, 132*f*
  formulating the main idea, 81–82
  learning disabilities and, 4–5
  overview, 68, 172–173
  before reading, 68–72, 71*f*
  during and after reading strategies, 72–84
  self-regulation strategies, 139–140
Strategy use. *See also* Strategy instruction
  assessment and, 18
  cognitive processing and, 136
  comparing good and poor readers and, 4
  English learners (ELs) and, 125
  instruction and, 67
  think-alouds and, 37–38
Stretch-level texts. *See also* Text
  content-area literacy and, 116
  overview, 94–96, 95*f*, 173–174
  selecting appropriate texts, 96–98
Structure of text. *See* Text structure
Struggling readers. *See* Poor readers
Student-generated questions. *See also* Questions
  English learners (ELs) and, 132
  overview, 77–80, 172–173
  reciprocal teaching and, 154, 155*f*
  sample lesson plan for, 204–205

Students Achieving Independent Learning (SAIL), 151*t*
Suffixes, 7, 110, 184–185
Summarizing
  assessment and, 18
  comparing good and poor readers and, 4, 5
  content-area literacy and, 106
  definition of, **221**
  instruction and, 80–84
  overview, 83–84
  reciprocal teaching and, 154, 155*f*
  sample lesson plan for, 215–217
  vocabulary instruction and, 60
Summative assessment, 15, 16. *See also* Assessment
Support, 5
Sustained silent reading (SSR), 175
Syllables, 7, 174
Synonyms, 63
Syntax, 47, 133, **222**
Systematic instruction, 81, 145, 184–185. *See also* Instruction

Teacher-initiated questions, 75–77, 79–80. *See also* Questions
Teacher-presented text preview, 70. *See also* Text preview
Technology, 129–130
TELLS strategy, 84, **222**
Temporal ordering, 99
Test of Early Reading Ability–3, 23*t*
Test of Reading Comprehension, 4th Edition, 23*t*
Test of Silent Contextual Reading Fluency (TOSCRF), 23*t*
Text. *See also* Text preview; Text selection; Text structure
  assessment and, 17*t*
  complexity of, 97
  English learners (ELs) and, 130, 133
  importance of in comprehension, 92–93
  levels of, 93–96, 95*f*, 173–174, 175. See also Levels of reading
  overview, 104, 173–174
  selecting appropriate texts, 96–98
  text clues, 167
  vocabulary instruction and, 61–63
"Text Mapping Plus," 84
Text preview. *See also* Text
  collaborative strategic reading (CSR) and, 159, 161–162
  definition of, **222**
  disciplinary literacy and, 106–108
  overview, 70–72, 71*f*
  sample lesson plan for, 180–181
Text selection. *See also* Text
  English learners (ELs) and, 130
  independent reading and, 175
  overview, 92, 104, 173–174
  selecting appropriate texts, 96–98
  text levels and, 93–96, 95*f*

Text structure. *See also* Expository text; Narrative text; Text
  comparing good and poor readers and, 3
  definition of, **222**
  overview, 98–104, 99*t*
  selecting appropriate texts and, 97
Text-connecting inferences, 138*f. See also* Inferences
Theme
  definition of, **222**
  identifying, 86–87
  instruction and, 72
  in narrative text, 99*t*
  selecting appropriate texts and, 97
  vocabulary instruction and, 51, 55–58, 55*f*, 57*f*, 58*f*
Theme scheme, 100, **222**
Thesauri, 58–59
Think and Search questions, 77. *See also* Questions
Think-alouds. *See also* Assessment
  definition of, **222**
  informal reading inventory (IRI) and, 25
  metacognitive processes and, 31, 33
  narrative text structure and, 99
  overview, 19*f*, 36–38
  prompted think-aloud, 41–43
  self-regulation strategies, 139–140
Topic web, 103. *See also* Graphic organizer
Topics, 97
Training, 19
Transactional strategies instruction, 151*t*, 157, **222**

Venn diagram, 58, 58*f*, 103. *See also* Graphic organizer
Visualization, 4, 83–84. *See also* Mental images
Visuals in text, 97
Vocabulary instruction. *See also* Instruction; Vocabulary knowledge
  around a theme or concept, 55–58, 55*f*, 57*f*, 58*f*
  assessment and monitoring vocabulary learning and, 46–49, 64–65
  best practices for, 49–64, 50*f*, 55*f*, 57*f*, 58*f*, 59*f*
  concept or semantic maps and, 55–57, 57*f*, 72
  content-area literacy and, 110
  English learners (ELs) and, 125–130
  increasing knowledge of and interest in words and, 63
  intensifying intervention and, 144
  monitoring understanding and, 54–55

  multistrategy inference intervention and, 167
  overview, 44–45, 63
  providing definitions, 52–53
  reading a variety of texts and, 61–63
  role of in reading comprehension, 45–46
  sample lesson plans for, 181–184, 185–187
  selecting appropriate texts and, 97
  selecting key words to teach, 51–52
  sentence writing, 54
  teaching strategies for independent word learning, 58–61, 59*f*
  text levels and, 94–96, 95*f*
  using mnemonic or key word strategies, 53–54
Vocabulary knowledge. *See also* Vocabulary instruction
  assessment and, 39, 46–49
  comprehension and, 5–6, 169–171
  content-area literacy and, 119, 119*f*
  definition of, **222**
Vocabulary maps, 181–183

What Works Clearinghouse (WWC), 7, 8*f*, 9*t*, 10*t*
Whole-class assessments, 18. *See also* Assessment
Whole-class discussions, 75–80, 156*f. See also* Discussions
"Why" questions, 78–79. *See also* Questions
Wide reading, 50*f*
Woodcock Reading Mastery Test, 3rd Edition, 23*t*
Word analysis, 58, 59*f*, **222**
Word associations, 63, **222**
Word banks/word walls, 7
Word consciousness, 44, 50*f*, 63, **222**
Word formations, 63, **222**
Word Generation (WordGen), 129
Word knowing, 46–47, 97, 130
Word learning, 50*f*, 58–61, 59*f*, 127. *See also* Vocabulary instruction
Word manipulations, 63
Word reading, 3, 6–7, 8*f*, 9*t*, 169–171. *See also* Decoding
Working memory, 39, 138, 141. *See also* Memory
World knowledge, 45–46, 61–63, 69. *See also* Background knowledge
Wrap-up strategy, 159, 162
Writing, 87, 89, 115, 130

Younger students, 31

Zone of proximal development, 152, 155, 177